BERLITZ®

P9-AQI-221

MUNICH

1989/1990 Edition

By the staff of Berlitz Guides

A Macmillan Company

Deluxe Guide
1989/1990 Edition

How to use our guide

- All the practical information, hints and tips that you will need before and during the trip start on page 102.
- For general background, see the sections The City and the People, p. 6, and A Brief History, p. 12.
- All the sights to see are listed between pages 28 and 77, with suggestions on daytrips from Munich on pages 78 to 86. Our own choice of sights most highly recommended is pinpointed by the Berlitz traveller symbol.
- Entertainment, nightlife and all other leisure activities are described between pages 86 and 94, while information on restaurants and cuisine is to be found on pages 94 to 101.
- Finally, there is an index at the back of the book, pp. 126–127.

Although we make every effort to ensure the accuracy of all the information in this book, changes occur incessantly. We cannot therefore take responsibility for facts, prices, addresses and circumstances in general that are constantly subject to alteration. Our guides are updated on a regular basis as we reprint, and we are always grateful to readers who let us know of any errors, changes or serious omissions they come across.

Text: Jack Altman
Photography: Eric Jaquier; cover picture, Georg Stärk
Layout: Doris Haldemann
Staff editor: Earleen Brunner
For their help in the preparation of this book, we wish to thank Mechthild Meyer-Schneidewind, Karin Goedecke and Barbara Lerch. We are also very grateful to the German National Tourist Office, the Münchner Verkehrs- und Tarifverbund and Lufthansa German Airlines for their considerable assistance.
4 Cartography: 🐦 Falk-Verlag, Hamburg

Contents

Cover picture: Viktualienmarkt.

The City and the People

To northerners seeking the easy, relaxed life of southern Europe, Munich seems almost Mediterranean. This last main stop before the Alps provides, for many, a first breath of Italy.

By the same token, for southern Europeans heading towards the prosperous efficiency of the cooler north, the Bavarian capital—more Baroque than Gothic, more green than grey—makes the transition less abrupt. A lot of them—Greeks, Yugoslavs, Italians—decide quite simply to stop in Munich and enjoy the best of both worlds. And many Berliners fleeing the rigours of the cold war choose Munich as the best possible antidote.

For Munich's genius has always been its ability to combine the Germanic talent for getting things done with a specifically Bavarian need to do them pleasantly. Business lunches seem to last a little longer. Office hours seem a little shorter. Yet no one who has seen the town's impressive affluence, its dynamic car industry, brilliantly constructed Olympic sports complex and splendid new subway system

would suggest that this somewhat casual attitude was unproductive.

If the people of Munich do differ so much from other Germans, that is because, you'll be told, this isn't Germany, it's Bavaria. As the capital of the fervently Catholic and conservative Free State of Bavaria, Munich epitomizes the independent Bavarian spirit. Good-natured local chauvinism knows no bounds. Whole books are filled with jokes at the expense of stiff-necked Prussians. At the city's renowned Oktoberfest, a beer festival, visitors sing *Warum ist es am Rhein so schön?* (Why is it so lovely on the Rhine?) to the great amusement of the locals who, they say, know without asking why Bavaria's so lovely.

The Oktoberfest is, perhaps, what first strikes the popular imagination in regard to Munich. Indeed, with annual consumption of 4,000,000 litres of beer by 5,000,000 visitors— including well over a million kids—it is a grandiose event appropriate to the oversized image the Bavarians have of their capital. It's also the most

Marienplatz, in front of the Town Hall—great spot for a good beer.

extravagant expression of that untranslatable German feeling of warm fellowship known as *Gemütlichkeit*.

But it would be wrong to think of life in Munich as one long Oktoberfest. Since the post-war division of Berlin, Munich has become the undisputed cultural capital of the Federal Republic of Germany—no mean achievement against the considerable claims of Hamburg, Frankfurt and Cologne. The opera house and concert halls make the town a musical mecca, especially for the performance of works by Mozart, Wagner and Richard Strauss.

Painters also enjoy the favourable artistic climate, particularly in the bohemian district of Schwabing, which exploded on the international scene in the 20th century as a focus for the Blaue Reiter school of Wassily Kandinsky, Paul Klee and Franz Marc. Munich galleries are still among the most innovative, and the classical and modern collections of the Alte and Neue Pinakothek museums are richly endowed and superbly displayed.

Munich has become a centre for industry and publishing, as well as for the much admired New German Cinema and its world-famous directors, Volker Schloendorff, Werner Herzog and the late Rainer Werner Fassbinder.

But we cannot forget the darker side of the city—evoked by Adolf Hitler's early association with Munich and the formation there of the Nazi Party —with all the ugliness that this entailed for the social and architectural identity of Bavaria's capital. Yet it was Munich's cultural atmosphere that originally attracted the future dictator to the city, at a time when he still dreamed of becoming a great painter. The years from 1918 to 1945 were, in the end perhaps, only a stormy political interlude for Munich, and the townspeople seem happy to relinquish the political spotlight to Bonn and Berlin.

Munich is attached to its historical identity. After the destruction of World War II, many German cities decided to break with the past and build in a completely modern style. But the Bavarian capital preferred to painstakingly restore and reconstruct the great churches and palaces of its

8

The kings have left the Residenz to the ordinary people of Munich.

Munich is part and parcel of its sleepy rural hinterland: churches with onion domes and cattle barns.

past. There are plenty of modern skyscrapers, but the heart of the old city is fast recapturing its former Baroque charm. Some have complained that the reconstruction and renovation have been too thorough, too "clean", but, in a couple of decades, the ravages of pollution have given the new-old buildings a patina of age that it previously took centuries to acquire. In fact, the reconstruction has been so complete and so convincing that monuments such as the Siegestor (Victory Gate) have been kept in their bomb-scarred condition as a historic warning.

The inner city is a pedestrian's delight, thanks to a clever town plan that keeps much of the traffic circling rather than crossing the city centre (except through underpasses)—and an

And on clear days, the mountains seem to lie just beyond the southern suburbs. That's when the *Föhn* is blowing, the famous wind that gives some people a headache and others phenomenally clear creative insights. A characteristic Munich ambiguity.

When those mountains reappear on the city's doorstep, they remind the people of the country from which many of them or their parents first came. Every weekend there is a massive exodus to the villages and lakes around the city: east to the Chiemsee, west and south to the Ammersee, Starnberger See and Tegernsee, north to Schleissheim and Freising. Here the citizens of Munich can indulge in hiking, sailing, hunting and fishing—or visiting aunts and uncles for coffee and cakes.

excellent system of public transport. Beyond the city centre, the broad, tree-lined avenues and boulevards planned by Bavaria's last kings open up the town with considerable elegance.

In the Englischer Garten, the city has a veritable jewel among Europe's great parks, immensely enhanced by the ebullient River Isar. The swiftly flowing waters are evidence of the proximity of the Alps from which the river flows.

In the winter, they trek further south into the surrounding mountains for skiing, an integral part of Munich life. Munich is undoubtedly a metropolis and in many ways a sophisticated one, but the city also retains a resolutely rural atmosphere, never losing sight of its origins in the peasant hinterland. Visitors would be wrong not to participate in Munich's happy mixture of town and country.

11

A Brief History

Munich arrived late on the Bavarian scene. In the Middle Ages, at a time when Nuremberg, Augsburg and Regensburg were already thriving cities, the present-day state capital was just a small settlement of a few peasants and some Benedictine monks from Lake Tegern. The site was known quite simply as "ze den Munichen", a dialect form of "zu den Mönchen" (the monks' place). Accordingly, the Munich coat of arms today bears the image of a child in a monk's habit, the "Münchner Kindl".

The settlement of the River Isar first attracted attention in 1156, when Heinrich der Löwe (Henry the Lion), Duke of Saxony and Bavaria and cousin of the German Emperor Frederick Barbarossa, was looking for a place to set up a toll station for the passage of salt, a lucrative product from nearby Salzburg. Until then, tolls had been collected by the powerful bishop of Freising at Oberföhring Bridge, a short distance to the north. Duke Heinrich burned the bridge down and established a new one, together with a market, customs house and mint, at a fork in the Isar.

Bishop Otto of Freising, himself an uncle of Frederick Barbarossa, protested to the emperor, who decided to leave Munich in his cousin Heinrich's hands, while granting one-third of the toll revenues to the diocese of Freising, dues that were paid until 1852. The day of the emperor's decision, June 14, 1158, is recognized as the date of Munich's founding.

The salt trade made Munich prosperous and the settlement grew rapidly into a proper town. In 1180, after Heinrich refused military aid for the emperor's foreign wars, Frederick Barbarossa threatened to raze Munich to the ground. But Uncle Otto pleaded the city's case, for the bishop of Freising was making more money from his share of the salt duty than he ever earned from the Oberföhring monopoly. The city was saved but taken away from Heinrich and handed over to the Wittelsbach family, who ruled Bavaria for the next seven centuries.

The city made a fortune from salt tolls collected by the River Isar.

The Wittelsbachs Take Over

By the end of the 13th century, Munich was the largest town in the Wittelsbach dominions. But the prosperous Munich burghers grew discontented and began to press Duke Ludwig the Stern (1229–94) for a larger piece of the pie. In defence, the duke built himself a fortress, the Alter Hof, parts of which can still be seen just west of the Hofbräuhaus.

Munich entered the international political arena when Duke Ludwig IV (1302–47) was made Holy Roman Emperor in 1328. With his court firmly established in Munich, he enlisted scholars from all over Europe as his advisors in a form of royal academy. Most notable among them were Marsiglio of Padua and William of Occam, philosophers who defended secular power against that of the Pope and thus made themselves useful allies for Ludwig. William told him: "You defend me with your sword and I'll defend you with my pen." The philosopher became famous for a piece of common sense known as "Occam's Razor", which states, roughly, that if you've found a simple explanation for a problem, don't look for a complicated one. Bavarians like that kind of thinking.

Troubled Times

The Black Death brought devastation to Munich in 1348. The city suffered social unrest, abrupt economic decline and the debasement of its currency. In a mass psychotic reaction to the catastrophe, citizens went on a rampage, massacring Jews for alleged ritual murder.

High taxes and general penury resulted in a revolt of burghers against the patricians. In 1385, the people took cloth merchant Hans Impler from his house to the Schrannenplatz (now Marienplatz) and beheaded him. The patricians and their princes demanded draconian financial compensation and the situation deteriorated into open rebellion from 1397 to 1403.

By bringing in heavy military reinforcements, the Wittelsbachs regained the upper hand without making any of the far-reaching civic concessions won by the guilds of other German towns, such as Augsburg, Hamburg and Cologne. To secure their position in these troubled times, the Wittelsbachs built a sturdy Residenz on what was then the north-west corner of town. The massive, fortress-like palace (see p. 43) attests to the kind of protection the despotic monarchy needed.

Reform and Counter-Reform

Dissent eased in the 15th century and trade boomed in salt, wine and cloth. The town also served as a transit point for the rich "Venice goods" of spices and gold. Renewed prosperity made it possible to build the great Frauenkirche, still a town symbol, and the Gothic

civic citadel of the Altes Rathaus.

By the middle of the 16th century, an architectural rivalry grew up between the burghers, who favoured the German Gothic style for their homes, and the Bavarian nobles, who preferred the Renaissance styles of Spain and Italy. The look of Munich in the 1500s is preserved in Jakob Sandtner's city model on display in the Bavarian National Museum (see p. 68). But the original construction was al-

The Wittelsbachs' Residenz was a huge fortress and opulent palace.

most completely replaced by the Baroque and Rococo palaces of the 17th and 18th centuries and the neo-Gothic and neo-Classical buildings of the Industrial Revolution.

The predilection of the Bavarian aristocracy for foreign artists was in many ways a reaction to the subversive implications of German nationalism which had grown out of the Reformation. In 1510, when Martin Luther passed through Munich on his way to Rome, his still relatively orthodox preaching met with sympathy. But, some ten years later, Luther's revolutionary positions aroused the ire of the traditionally conservative Bavarians, and Duke Wilhelm IV put into practice the severe measures advocated by the Jesuits. Rebellious monks and priests were arrested and executed; in 1527, the repression culminated in the drowning or burning of 29 members of Munich's Baptist community who refused to recant.

The religious conflict concealed a competition for political and economic power. The city's bourgeoisie had seen in the Reformation an opportunity to push for social reforms which the aristocracy had adamantly resisted. In the struggles that followed, the burghers were forced to relinquish the salt monopoly to the administration of the state.

With a certain vindictiveness, the nobles flaunted their political triumph with sumptuous festivities at court, such as those to pay homage to Emperor Charles V and his Spanish retinue during their Munich visit of 1530. The climax of pomp and circumstance in grand Renaissance style was achieved with the three-week-long wedding celebrations of Duke Wilhelm V and his bride, Renata of Lorraine, in 1568.

The patricians received spiritual support from the Jesuits, brought to Munich by Duke Wilhelm V to establish a school and to set up a theatre for the performance of morality plays. Some people resented this foreign influence, laying the foundation for the now perennial Bavarian distrust of outsiders.

Good Money After Bad

The extravagant expenditures of the aristocracy left the state coffers empty by the time Maximilian I (1573–1651) came to the throne. Although the Bavarian state was facing bankruptcy, Maximilian (who became Prince Elector in 1623) proceeded to build a magnificent collection of art works.

However painful this may have been for his tax-crippled subjects, we can be thankful to Maximilian for thus having laid the foundations of the Alte Pinakothek.

It was also Maximilian who ordered the splendid decorations that embellish the Residenz. Gustavus Adolphus of Sweden was so impressed with it when he invaded Munich in 1632, during the cruel Thirty Years' War, that he said he would have liked to carry the whole thing back to Stockholm on wheels. Instead, he settled for 42 Munich citizens, who were taken hostage against payment by Bavaria of 300,000 *Thaler* in war reparations. (All but six of them returned three years later.)

In the Thirty Years' War (1618–48), Munich suffered less damage by bombardment than many other German towns. But starvation and disease wrought more havoc than cannon, taking a toll of 7,000 inhabitants, one-third of the city's population. In 1632, Maximilian set up the Mariensäule (Column of the Virgin Mary) to commemorate the town's emergence from suffering.

The Prince Electors frequently involved their people in costly foreign adventures,

rubbing salt into the wounds of Munich's civic poverty. In 1683, Max* II Emanuel decided to help the Austrians beat off the Turks besieging Vienna. He continued on to Belgrade and brought back 296 Turks as sedan-chair bearers and road-builders—Munich's first *Gastarbeiter* (immigrant workers). The Turkish Wars are commemorated in huge paintings that can be seen in Schleissheim Castle. The city's war debt was 20 million guilders.

In the War of the Spanish Succession (1701–14) Max Emanuel fought on the losing side, with the French, and Munich had to bear the burden of Austrian occupation from 1704 to 1714. When the farmers rebelled, the ringleaders were arrested and hung, drawn and quartered on Marienplatz. Their heads were displayed on pikes at Isar Gate.

After the war, the Bavarian aristocracy did not show itself sympathetic to the tribulations of the citizenry. The nobles set about building splendid little palaces, such as the Preysing, Erzbischöfliches (Archbishop's) and Törring-Jetten-

---

* "Max" is an accepted and not disrespectful Bavarian alternative to "Maximilian".

bach Palais (now the General Post Office), strategically situated near the Prince Elector's Residenz.

Peace in an English Garden

The people of Munich grew ever more xenophobic as Hungarian hussars took over the city in 1742. They were dispatched by Empress Maria Theresa in retaliation for the Bavarian Prince Elector's opposition to Austro-Hungarian involvement in Germany.

In this atmosphere of hostility, Maximilian III Joseph (1727–77) should not have been surprised when the Munich bourgeoisie resisted his attempt to establish a court monopoly on manufacturing. With the exception of Nymphenburg porcelain, which still thrives today, all the royal manufactures went bankrupt. A brighter note was struck with the building of the delightful Residenztheater and the performance there by one Wolfgang Amadeus Mozart of his operas *The Abduction from the Seraglio, The Marriage of Figaro* and *The Magic Flute.*

In 1777, the Wittelsbach

Turkish workers provide backbone for Munich's municipal services.

succession fell to Karl Theodor, a member of the Mannheim branch of the family. He didn't want to leave Mannheim, he didn't like Munich and the feeling was mutual. The people were starving. There was no bread, but instead of wheat, Karl Theodor sent in soldiers to hold down the angry populace in those revolutionary times.

Benjamin Thompson, an American with British sympathies who had fled Rumford (later Concord), New Hampshire during his own country's revolution, suggested a solution to Karl Theodor's predicament. With the prince's blessing, Count Rumford—as he was subsequently known—provided schools and work to keep the unruly soldiers off the streets. He set up workshops and soup kitchens for the poor. (The potato-and-barley soup that was dispensed there is served in Munich to this day as *Rumfordsuppe.*)

Then, in 1789, Rumford requisitioned a marshy wilderness on the outskirts of town and detailed the soldiers to drain it for development as a gigantic public park. The result of Rumford's efforts, the Englischer Garten, is a lasting monument to American enterprise and know-how. **19**

New Hopes, Ancient Dreams
While Munich was cultivating its garden, the rest of Europe was in a revolutionary uproar. But the city didn't remain isolated for long. In 1800, it was occupied by the French troops of General Jean Victor Moreau, who set up headquarters in Nymphenburg Palace.

Napoleon himself came to town in 1805 to celebrate the marriage of his wife Josephine's son, Eugène de Beauharnais, to Princess Augusta of Bavaria. The journey to Munich did not inconvenience the emperor too much, as it was on the way to Austerlitz, where he was to fight the Russians and Austrians. Napoleon elevated Max IV Joseph from Prince Elector to King of Bavaria and in exchange took a vast contingent of Bavarians on his Russian campaign of 1812, leaving 30,000 of them to die on the battlefield. Under pressure from the French, Max Joseph emancipated the Protestants of Munich, improved conditions for the Jews and introduced a more moderate Bavarian constitution.

And somehow, amid all the troubles of war and revolution, Munich managed to celebrate once again. Heeding the new spirit of the times, the royal court was wise enough not to exclude the populace from the wedding festivities of Max Joseph's son, Ludwig, to Theresa of Saxony. On October 17, 1810, horse races were organized with great success. They grew into an annual event, the world-famous Oktoberfest.

Munich itself was gradually

expanded to the north and west—into an area named Maxvorstadt—linking the centre to Schwabing. The Graeco-Roman architecture of the Nationaltheater brought to the city the first signs of the classical spirit that was to become the obsession of Ludwig I.

Born in Strasbourg, Ludwig (1786–1868) was determined to break the French stranglehold on German culture and make Munich a spearhead for a new nationalist movement. During the Napoleonic occupation, the civic symbol of the Münchner Kindl had been replaced with an imperial lion. Ludwig brought back the little monk.

Familiar with the architecture of Rome and the Greek monuments of Sicily, he wanted to turn Munich into an "Athens-on-the-Isar". He be-

Sober neo-Classicism replaced the exuberance of the 18th century.

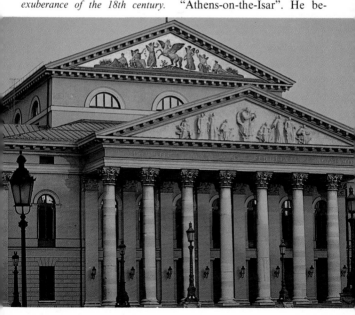

gan by moving Bavaria's university from Landshut to Munich. It was established along Ludwigstrasse in the Schwabing area first developed under his father's rule.

He built majestic Odeonsplatz, with its Siegestor (Gate of Victory). However, the gate was scarred by bombs during World War II and since then it has become a symbol of defeat. But Königsplatz with its Greek Revival architecture was the most complete realization of Ludwig's classical aspirations. Typically, Ludwig laid the foundation stone for the Alte Pinakothek (the gallery designed to house the royal art collections) on April 7, 1826, the anniversary of the painter Raphael's birth.

A prodigious worker, rising before dawn each day to go to his office in the Residenz, the king felt himself entitled to a more than occasional little fling. At least the portraits that hang in the Schönheitengalerie (Gallery of Beautiful Women) at Nymphenburg Palace suggest as much. This reputedly representative collection of his mistresses includes a dancer known as Lola Móntez, with whom he fell head over heels in love when he was 60 and she 28. She was Ludwig's ruin. He made her the Countess von

Landsfeld, to the horror both of his conservative ministers and the radical university students, who saw in Lola the epitome of the king's decadence. In 1848, as revolution was sweeping Europe, the students and angry citizens of Munich forced Ludwig to deport Lola, and he himself abdicated in disgust.

Ludwig's successor, Maximilian II (1811–64), boosted Munich's cultural reputation thanks to his intimacy with illustrious thinkers such as historian Leopold von Ranke and philosopher Friedrich von Schelling.

End of a Dream

The last great king of Bavaria was the romantic Ludwig II (1845–86), famous for his close relationship with Richard Wagner. Under Ludwig's patronage, the composer staged in Munich the premières of his operas *Tristan and Isolde, The Mastersingers of Nuremberg, Rhinegold,* and *Valkyrie.*

In the mundane world of 19th-century industrial expansion, Ludwig II dreamt of making Munich the music capital of the world. He wanted to build a gigantic theatre for his idol Wagner, a place where the composer could develop his concept of *Gesamtkunst-*

werk—a synthesis of music, lyrics and theatre. But the banalities of state finances interfered and Bavarian politicians forced him to relinquish the project to Bayreuth.

Ludwig acted out his fantasies in the crazy fairytale palaces he built outside Munich—a medieval castle at Neuschwanstein, a French château at Linderhof, and a fanciful version of Versailles' Grand Trianon at Herrenchiemsee. But it was at one castle that he didn't build, the

Ludwig II adored French châteaux. At Linderhof he realized a dream.

16th-century Schloss Berg on Lake Starnberg, that his life came to a sad and mysterious end.

By 1886, Ludwig's wild behavior had persuaded the Bavarian government that he was mad, and a special commission declared him as such. The director of an insane asylum accompanied him to Schloss Berg and the two were later found drowned. It was never determined whether murder or suicide was involved.

Uncle Luitpold took over as regent (ruling in place of Ludwig's brother, the insane King Otto). He presided over the grand *fin de siècle* artistic

Trompe-l'œil wall-painting recaptures Munich's war-bombed past.

movement of the Jugendstil. This was followed a generation later by the Blaue Reiter school of Kandinsky, Klee and Marc. Writers such as Thomas Mann, Rilke and Stefan George moved to Schwabing. The artistic ferment also attracted a young painter from Vienna, an embittered fellow named Adolf Hitler.

The Wittelsbach dynasty, like the Habsburg in Vienna and the Hohenzollern in Berlin, ended in the disaster of World War I. Bavarians resented having been dragged into the European conflagration by what they felt was Prussian belligerence, and a new social democratic movement gained support. In November 1918, with the war in its last days, Kurt Eisner, a well-meaning but rather vague intellectual, led a march of workers and peasants from the Theresienwiese. En route, disaffected soldiers took control of their barracks and hoisted the red flag of revolution.

In the Mathäser Bräuhaus—breweries being a favoured spot for political action in Munich—the Bavarian Republic was declared. The people invaded the Residenz and wandered around hooting for echoes in the vast galleries and ballrooms. Ludwig III, the last Wittelsbach king, fled in a car from the palace.

But the new republic of workers, peasants and soldiers, modelled on the soviets of the Russian revolution, came under violent attack from the conservative press and private armies of troops *(Freikorps)* roaming the streets. Playing on Bavarian xenophobia, the right wing attacked Eisner as a Berliner and as a Jew. Just three months after the November revolution, Eisner was shot dead by a young aristocrat hoping to curry favour with an extreme right-wing club.

A group of "coffee-house anarchists" led by writers Ernst Toller and Erich Mühsam took over briefly, but they were quickly replaced by hardline communists. The Bavarian Red Army was then routed in bloody fighting with the Freikorps, and Bavaria as an independent republic was crushed.

In the space of six months, Munich had known in breathtaking succession a monarchy, revolutionary socialism, moderate socialism, anarchy, communism and brutal counterrevolutionary oppression. A tolerant tradition was swept away and the city became a breeding ground for extremist political and paramilitary groups.

Hitler's Munich

Adolf Hitler had first been drawn to Munich by its cultural ambience, but he remained immune to the innovative tendencies of the avantgarde. His own painting was stolidly academic and attracted no attention. He turned to the clamour of German nationalism and a chance photograph of a rally on Odeonsplatz in August 1914 shows Hitler in the crowd, joyfully greeting the declaration of war. **25**

He returned to Munich as a corporal in 1918. It was while working to re-educate soldiers in nationalistic, anti-Marxist ideas at the end of the Bavarian republic that he joined the Deutsche Arbeiter-Partei. By February 1920, he was addressing 2,000 members in the Hofbräuhaus. The association became known as the Nationalsozialistische Deutsche Arbeiter-Partei, or Nazi Party. Its symbol was the swastika. Armed storm troops of the party's Sturm-Abteilung (S.A.) went round Munich breaking up opposition political meetings.

At a January 1923 gathering, Hitler said: "Either the Nazi Party is the German movement of the future, in which case no devil can stop it, or it isn't, in which case it deserves to be destroyed." Both predictions proved true. By November, the party had 55,000 members and 15,000 storm troops—and Hitler felt strong enough to stage his famous Beer Hall Putsch.

It was intended as a first move in the campaign to force the Bavarian state government to cooperate in a Nazi march on Berlin. The putsch ended in a debacle on Odeonsplatz and Hitler was sent to prison, but not before he had turned the whole affair to his advantage.

Hitler made his trial for treason into an indictment of his prosecutors as accomplices of the "November criminals", who, he said, had stabbed Germany in the back in 1918 with their anti-war movement. He became an instant hero.

Beer, Bluff and Bullets
The Beer Hall Putsch, which launched Hitler's national career, was staged in the Bürgerbräukeller. It gave a foretaste of the crazy melodrama, bluff and shameless gall he was later to exhibit on the world scene.

With the Bavarian minister Gustav von Kahr about to speak, Hitler burst into the crowded room, smashed a beer mug to the floor and pushed forward at the head of his storm troops, brandishing a pistol. In the pandemonium, he jumped on a table and fired a shot into the ceiling to get the assembly's undivided attention. "National revolution has broken out!", he yelled. "Farce! South America!" replied a few wags, who were promptly beaten up. The new Hitler style of politics had arrived.

Today the Bürgerbräukeller is quietly being replaced by a cultural centre, but there won't be a plaque to commemorate the putsch.

In prison at nearby Landsberg, Hitler was treated as an honoured guest. He was not required to perform prison work, but held political meetings and wrote *Mein Kampf* instead.

Although Hitler's career took him to Berlin, the Nazis kept their party headquarters in Munich at the Brown House (the colour of their shirts). Brighter spirits such as whimsical comedian Karl Valentin and his great fan, dramatist Bertolt Brecht, also made their home in Munich, but the brown shirts triumphed.

In 1935, Munich was named "Capital of the (Nazi) Movement". It earned its status as the vanguard in June 1938, when the central synagogue was looted, five months before the *Kristallnacht* (Crystal Night) rampage that destroyed the rest of Germany's Jewish houses of prayer.

In September of that year, Munich also became a symbol of the ignominious appeasement of Britain and France. Prime ministers Neville Chamberlain and Edouard Daladier came to the Bavarian capital to negotiate Czechoslovakia's dismemberment with Hitler and Mussolini. The meeting took place in the Führerbau. Later, Chamberlain asked the Führer to sign the piece of paper that the British leader was to wave at his people as a guarantee of "peace in our time".

War and Peace

A gleam of hope in wartime Munich came when two students, Hans and Sophie Scholl, courageously distributed anti-Hitler "White Rose" leaflets. But the brother and sister were betrayed and executed.

World War II brought 71 air raids to the city, killing 6,000 and wounding 16,000. Bombardments, most intense in 1944, heavily damaged the Frauenkirche, St. Peter's and St. Michael's churches and large sections of the Residenz and Alte Pinakothek. The Brown House was destroyed but, ironically, most of Hitler's other buildings were left intact.

Post-war reconstruction has been a triumph of hard work and fiercely loyal attachment to the great traditions of Munich's past. Monuments, palaces and churches have been restored with meticulous care. Traditionally open to the arts and good living in general, Munich rapidly expanded to become West Germany's third largest city (population 1,350,000), welcoming many Berliners and refugees from the former eastern territories. **27**

Emphasizing its reputation for cheerfulness, the "Metropolis with a Heart" played proud host to the 1972 Olympic Games in an atmosphere that began in delightful serenity. But once again, the city came under a shadow as militant Palestinians raided the Olympic Village and killed 12 Israeli athletes.

There is clearly no formula for achieving immunity from world conflicts, but somehow Munich continues to express good will, German-style... sorry, Bavarian-style.

Finding Your Way...
Here are some common terms you may come across in Bavaria:

Allee	boulevard
Bahnhof	railway station
Brücke	bridge
Brunnen	fountain
Burg	castle, fortress
Dom	cathedral
Gasse	alley
Kirche	church
Markt	market
Rathaus	town hall
Platz	square
Schloß*	castle, palace
See	lake
Stift	monastery
Straße	street
Ufer	river bank
Weg	path, way

* read ß as ss.

What to See

Munich has two enormous assets for the visitor. A large majority of museums, monuments, palaces and churches are concentrated in the Innenstadt (inner city), which makes it a great town for walking. And the superb public transport

system of buses, trams, underground *(U-Bahn)* and surface trains *(S-Bahn),* brings all the other sights within easy reach.

Rather than tackle the complicated business of driving your own car around town, find a good parking place and save the car for excursions and the occasional night out. If you walk wherever you can, you'll see more of the town's bustling street life and drop in more easily on the outdoor cafés. You'll be able to indulge in the

Whichever way up you look at it, the Old Town Hall on Marienplatz makes a very colourful backdrop.

serendipity of discovering Munich's unexpected courtyard vistas and hidden alleyways. And you'll happen upon little bars and shops tucked away in odd corners that you would completely miss in a car.

So, apart from the section devoted to excursions, we offer you Munich as a series of walks.

Innenstadt

Munich long ago expanded beyond its confined medieval boundaries, and the old city wall has disappeared. However, the remains of three gates survive to indicate the perimeter of the inner city—Isartor, Karlstor and Sendlinger Tor—together with Odeonsplatz, a rendezvous for salt traders setting off in the 14th century for northern Germany. And, since Munich's earliest beginnings, Marienplatz has been at the heart of it all.

Marienplatz
to Theatinerstrasse

Until the middle of the 19th century, the wheat market was held on **Marienplatz.** The square was the obvious site for the town hall and the place where criminals and other unpopular people were hanged.

Marienplatz was also the focus for the most extravagant wedding Munich has ever seen—that of Duke Wilhelm V to Renata of Lorraine in 1568. Almost inevitably, the square was chosen in 1972 as the central junction for the new U-Bahn and S-Bahn system.

Graced with tubs of flowers and outdoor cafés, Marienplatz today forms part of an attractive pedestrian zone. Here you'll see the **Mariensäule** (Column of the Virgin Mary), erected in 1632 by Maximilian I in gratitude for the town's deliverance from the Swedes during the Thirty Years' War. At the base of the column are a basilisk, dragon, serpent and lion—symbols of plague, hunger, heresy and war—each being vanquished by heroic child-angels. From the top of the monument, the majestic figure of Mary watches over Munich. Holding Jesus in her left arm and a sceptre in her right, she reminds citizens in a secular age of Munich's firmly religious foundation.

The square sports another, more modern monument, the 19th-century Fischbrunnen. Young butchers used to leap into the bronze fountain after completing their apprenticeship, but nowadays the tradition is kept up only by an occasional Fasching (carnival) reveller or happy soccer fan.

At the eastern end of Marienplatz stands the almost too picturesque **Altes Rathaus** (Old Town Hall), a gay example of Munich's efforts to reconstruct, rather than replace, the vestiges of its venerable past. This Gothic-style edifice, with a dove-grey façade, amber-tiled steeple and graceful little spires, captures the spirit of the 15th-century original designed by Jörg von Halsbach (also called Jörg Ganghofer), though it isn't an exact replica. In any case, with the addition over the centuries of a Baroque onion-shaped cupola and then a too-conscientious"regothification", the building destroyed by Al-

There are sweeter rewards to sightseeing than cultural enrichment.

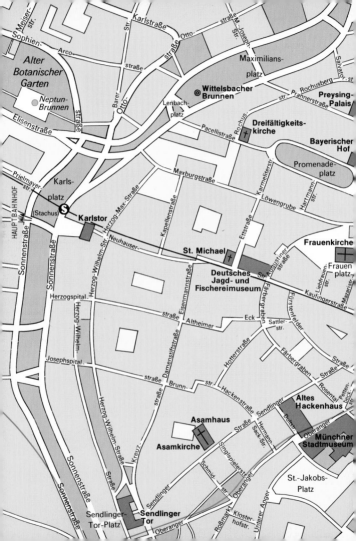

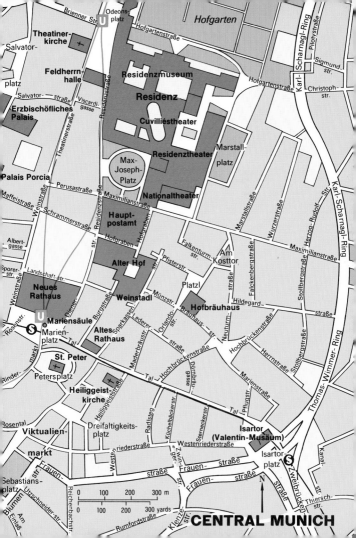

CENTRAL MUNICH

lied bombs was probably further from the original than what you see today. Apart from a banqueting hall on an upper floor, the Altes Rathaus mainly fulfills a decorative function.

The real business of city government takes place at the **Neues Rathaus** (New Town Hall) on the northern side of Marienplatz. This is a classic piece of 19th-century neo-Gothic—proud, self-assertive, its façade elaborately decorated with statues of kings, princes and dukes, saints, allegorical figures and characters from Munich folklore. The tower is around 260 feet high. Its main attraction—apart from the splendid view, if you want to take the lift to the top—is the 43-bell **Glockenspiel** (carillon) which goes wild every day at 11 a.m. Two groups of figures appear, one re-enacting the tournament held during the wedding of Duke Wilhelm V and Renata of Lorraine and the other, underneath, re-creating the cooper's dance *(Schäfflertanz)* that was performed to exorcize the plague of 1517. In the evening (9 p.m.), a nightwatchman with lantern blows his horn and an angel of peace blesses the little Munich monk *(Münchner Kindl)*.

Now go up Weinstrasse (around the corner at the west end of the Neues Rathaus) and left along Sporerstrasse to the **Frauenkirche,** its full title being Domkirche zu Unserer Lieben Frau (Cathedral Church of Our Lady). This building more than any other symbolizes Munich, and its gold-tipped, bulbous domes on twin brick towers dominate the skyline. (An elevator whisks sightseers 350 feet to the top of one of the towers, for an exciting bird's-eye view of town.) The church, an austere, unadorned Gothic structure, was built from 1468 to 1488 by Jörg von Halsbach. The Italian Renaissance domes are an addition of 1524.

The stark interior, reconstructed from the rubble of World War II bombardments, represents a truly heroic work of restoration. The original Gothic windows in the choir, stored in safety during the war, give an idea of the church's former glory. Fine sculptures of the Apostles and Prophets also escaped destruction in 1944 and adorn the choir as before. They were created by Erasmus Grasser in 1502. An admirable altarpiece of 1510 by Friedrich Pacher, the *Baptism of Christ,* hangs in the north chapel. It's flanked by

Jan Polack's panels depicting Jesus on the Mount of Olives and his arrest, crucifixion and burial. Notice, too, the impressive 17th-century funerary monument of Emperor Ludwig the Bavarian, who died in 1347.

Just outside the church, the granite fountain in Frauenplatz strikes a modern note. A waterfall plays and blocks of the stone have been arranged in the shape of an amphitheatre to provide seating. It's the perfect spot for a picnic.

West of the square, Augustinerstrasse leads to Neuhauser Strasse and what was once the church of the Augustinians. The building was transformed into a customs house under Napoleon and then a hunting and fishing museum, the Deutsches Jagd- und Fischereimuseum in 1966. Proclaimed by a wild boar in bronze, the collection will fascinate inveterate hunters and anglers.

Further along pedestrian-zoned Neuhauser Strasse is 16th-century **St. Michael,** an Italian Renaissance church with Baroque overtones, the first of its kind in Germany, largely designed by the Netherlands architect Friedrich Sustris. St. Michael epitomizes the combative spirit of the Counter-Reformation, and it is fitting that the secular defenders of the faith—the Wittelsbach dukes and German emperors—are portrayed on the gabled façade. Above the entrance, third figure from the right, stands the church's patron, Duke Wilhelm V (with a scale model of St. Michael church in his hand). Il Gesù in Rome provided the inspiration for the Baroque interior of St. Michael, which surpasses the former in its masterful lighting.

Karlstor, a city gate dating from the 14th century, links Neuhauser Strasse to busy Karlsplatz, popularly known as the **Stachus** after an innkeeper named Eustachius Föderl. The Stachus conceals a veritable city of underground shops, which extend from the exit of the S-Bahn station. Walk north to Lenbachplatz and the city's loveliest fountain, the neo-Baroque **Wittelsbacher Brunnen** built by Adolf von Hildebrand at the end of the 19th century.

Pacellistrasse, east of Lenbachplatz, takes you past the distinctive faceted Baroque façade of the **Dreifaltigkeitskirche** (Trinity Church). In 1704 a young Munich girl, Anna Maria Lindmayr, dreamed that the city would be in-

vaded and destroyed unless a new church were constructed. Sure enough, the next year, during the War of the Spanish Succession, Austrian soldiers arrived; but work on the Dreifaltigkeitskirche didn't begin until 1711. The town was not destroyed.

Promenadeplatz is noted for the elegance of Palais Montgelas. This neo-Classical building today forms part of the posh Bayerischer Hof hotel, where you might like to refresh yourself with an expensive drink at the bar.

Valentin's Day

Although little known outside Germany, Karl Valentin was regarded by connoisseurs like the dramatist Bert Brecht as a comic genius equal to Charlie Chaplin. While resident in Munich in the early twenties, Brecht went almost every night to watch Valentin's portrayal of the clownish working-class characters of peasant origin peculiar to the city.

Valentin started out in beer halls, but he quickly attracted the attention of Schwabing's artists and intellectuals, who loved his insane, surreal logic. One of his most celebrated sketches involved his efforts to house birds in an aquarium and fish in a bird-cage.

Otherwise, continue north along Kardinal-Faulhaber-Strasse past the Palais Porcia, one of Munich's first Baroque palaces and now a bank, to the **Erzbischöfliches Palais** (Archbishop's Palace) at number 7, a triumph of Rococo harmony with especially fine stucco work. Originally known as Palais Holnstein, it's the only 18th-century palace built by François Cuvilliés (see p. 44) to have survived wholly intact to the present day.

End your walk in the shopping arcades of Theatinerstrasse and stop at a *Konditorei*, a café specializing in pastry and coffee.

Isartorplatz to Platzl

The sturdy **Isartor** in its restored form is the only city gate which retains its original 14th-century dimensions. It was put up in the days when the Bavarian Duke Ludwig IV was Holy Roman Emperor, and a fresco of 1835 on the arch of the gate shows the emperor returning triumphantly from victory over the Habsburgs. The Isartor now serves as a rather overgrown traffic island, but one of the towers houses a

Enjoy the fine Renaissance façade of St. Michael. And a big pretzel.

roof-top café and the Valentin-Museum, devoted to the great cabaret comic of 1920s Munich, Karl Valentin.

From Isartor, walk along Tal, a shopping street that runs to **Heiliggeistkirche** (Church of the Holy Spirit). This 14th-century Gothic structure was extensively altered to the Baroque tastes of the 1720s. The two styles come together most notably in the **Marienaltar**—a beautiful wooden sculpture of 1450, the *Hammerthaler Mut-*

tergottes (Hammerthal Mother of God) from the Lake Tegernsee monastery, set in an opulent gilded Baroque framework. The reconstructed high altar preserves a fine pair of *Adoring Angels* by Johann Georg Greiff, dated 1730.

West of Heiliggeistkirche, with an entrance on Rindermarkt, is **St. Peter.** This is the oldest church in Munich, dating from before the foundation of the city itself in 1158. The original structure gave way to

a building in the Romanesque style, succeeded in time by a Gothic church with a twin-steepled tower. All but the tower was destroyed in the great fire of 1327 and a new Gothic structure went up. This was remodelled along Renaissance lines in the 17th century, and a tower with a single steeple was created. Destroyed in the war, St. Peter has been faithfully reconstructed, down to the asymmetrically placed clocks on the tower. (Follow the crowd to the top for a stunning view of the inner city.)

The crowning piece of the light, bright interior is the **high altar** glorifying Peter and the fathers of the Church. It was restored from the remains of the 18th-century original, inspired by Bernini's altar for St. Peter's in Rome. Egid Quirin Asam (see p. 46) designed the ensemble, which incorporates Erasmus Grasser's *St. Peter*. The gilded wood figures of the Church fathers count among the masterpieces of Egid Asam.

Leading to the altar are splendid Rococo choir stalls. You'll also see Jan Polack's five Late Gothic paintings which once adorned the altar. They show Peter healing the lame, enthroned, at sea, in prison and on the cross. Also from the Late Gothic period is the Schrenk-Altar, a highly prized early 15th-century sandstone relief of the Crucifixion and the Day of Judgment.

Now duck along little Burgstrasse past the Altes Rathaus.

Pious frescoes on private houses are an honoured art in Munich, as exemplified here in Burgstrasse. **39**

Stop at number 5 to admire the **Weinstadl,** one of Munich's few remaining Gothic houses, once the home of the town clerk and now a tavern. Built around 1550, it has a neatly restored, leafy courtyard and staircase tower.

A miracle of inner-city tranquillity pervades the **Alter Hof.** The peaceful, tree-shaded square offers an exquisite panorama of medieval buildings. The reconstructed Burgtor (City Gate) and quaint little Affenturm (Monkey Tower) —incorporated in the west wing—recapture the atmosphere of the Wittelsbachs' first Munich residence as it was in the 15th century. The splendid heraldic painting on the tower came to light in the 1960s.

The Hof was originally built around 1255 on what was then the north-east corner of town, in defence against foreign invaders, as well as the city's own unruly burghers. It was subsequently superseded by the more massive Residenz. The old buildings suffered more from 19th-century urban development than from 20th-century bombs, but the careful reconstruction of the surviving south and west wings afford an idea of their former grandeur.

Turn right on Pfisterstrasse to Platzl (Little Square), the site of a building of no great architectural distinction but nonetheless the most publicized monument in Munich, the **Hofbräuhaus,** a beer hall.

Duke Wilhelm V founded a brewery in the Alter Hof in 1589 to avoid paying the high prices for the imported stuff from Hanover—beer always having been just as much an aristocratic as a plebeian drink in Bavaria. It replaced wine as the staple alcoholic beverage after the Bavarian vineyards were destroyed during the cruel winters of the 13th and 14th centuries, making way for the sturdier hop and barley crops.

The brewery was first set up in the royal bath house, moving to more spacious quarters on Platzl in 1644. The Hofbräuhaus itself was built in 1896, after the brewery had been transferred to the other side of the River Isar. It soon became the most prestigious of Munich's political beer-hall arenas. In fact, in November 1921 Hitler's storm troops first gained notoriety in what became known as the "Schlacht im Hofbräuhaus" (Battle of the Hofbräuhaus). Today, the huge beer hall, with its long tables and oom-pah-pah music, is a magnet for tourists, but locals rarely gather here.

Odeonsplatz to Maximilianstrasse

Odeonsplatz joins the inner city to Schwabing and the university. It's the point at which Ludwig I opened up the crowded heart of town to the more airy "Vorstadt", Schwabing then being no more than a suburb.

This noticeably airy and "liberating" walk begins in the Italian Renaissance-style **Hofgarten** (Court Garden), restored and replanted with the chestnut trees, flower beds and fountains specified in the original 17th-century plan. In the centre stands a 12-sided temple to Diana, topped by a rather sexy bronze statue of Bavaria. The arcades, decorated with frescoes of historic scenes featuring the Wittelsbachs, house art galleries and cafés. There's also a fascinating little **Theatermuseum** on the northern side (Galeriestrasse 4), worthwhile for the display of famous set designs from Munich's rich theatrical past.

Turn and look south-west across the Hofgarten to capture the delightful vista that helps to give Munich its peculiarly Mediterranean flavour—the twin towers and dome of the splendid **Theatinerkirche.** This Italian Baroque church was built from 1663 to 1688 by a relay of two Italian architects, Agostino Barelli and Enrico Zuccalli; the façade was completed later by Cuvilliés.

The joyous impact of its silhouette on the city scene derives in part from the fact that the church was built to celebrate the birth of a baby boy to Princess Henriette Adelaide. This feeling of jubilation animates the rich decoration—ornamental vines, acanthus leaves and rosettes in the most spirited Italian Baroque style —and the splendid grey-and-white stucco embellishments in the cupola. Notice, too, the triumphant pulpit, the high altar (a copy of one destroyed by bombs) and, to the left, the Kajetan altar. This last was dedicated to St. Kajetan, founder of the Theatine Order commemorated in the church's title.

Across the street, facing Odeonsplatz, is the **Feldherrnhalle** (Hall of the Generals), a 19th-century monument to Bavarian military leaders. The building boasts statues of the Belgian-born Count Johann Tilly, a hero in the Thirty Years' War, and Prince Karl-Philipp von Wrede, victorious over the French in 1814. Less gloriously, it was the rendezvous for Nazi storm troops in Hitler's abortive putsch of **41**

1923 and a focus for commemorative marches thereafter. Reinforcing the Italian atmosphere of the area, though with less of a light touch, the building is modelled after the Late Gothic Loggia dei Lanzi in Florence.

Next door, in Residenzstrasse, stands **Preysing-Palais**, the most richly ornamented of Munich's private Rococo palaces. Begun in 1723 by Joseph Effner, only the Residenzstrasse façade survived World War II, but the restoration of the rest has been masterful. Take a look inside at the imposing ceremonial staircase.

At the other end of Residenzstrasse lies another jewel of 18th-century architecture, the **Hauptpostamt** or Main Post Office, formerly the Palais Törring-Jettenbach. You'll never buy a postage stamp in a more beautiful setting. The northern façade was given a face-lift in the 19th century to fit in with the classical demands of the Residenz and Nationaltheater on Maximilianstrasse. But the original Baroque doorway can be seen inside.

The Hofgarten and Theatinerkirche show the city's "Italian" side.

The **Nationaltheater** was completely rebuilt in 1963 as a copy of the original 1818 Greek-temple design by Karl von Fischer. The reconstruction epitomizes Bavarian traditionalism when it comes to cultural monuments.

The spacious **Max-Joseph-Platz** is named after the king whose statue sits in the centre. The fourth Max-Joseph of the Wittelsbach dynasty and the first—thanks to Napoleon—to be king, preferred what he felt would be a more dignified standing pose. But he died before the statue was completed and his son Ludwig I accepted the seated version.

The statue was placed alongside the greatest monument of Max-Joseph's family, the Wittelsbach **Residenz**. In 1385 the citizenry revolted, driving the dukes to construct lodgings safer than the Alter Hof (see p. 40). Over five centuries later, in 1918, another group of rebellious citizens pounded on the Residenz doors in the revolution that resulted in the short-lived Bavarian republic. The Wittelsbachs had to move out again, this time for good.

The German principalities were legion, and many of them rather frivolous, but the Residenz, now a museum, shows just how powerful and im- **43** mensely wealthy the proud Bavarian principality grew to be. To view the exterior, enter from Residenzstrasse and walk through the seven courtyards to Cuvilliéstheater, within the Residenz but not included on museum tours*.

The exquisite **Cuvilliéstheater** or Altes Residenztheater is one of the most enchanting playhouses in the world. Like its architect François de Cuvilliés, a dwarf from the Spanish Netherlands, the theatre is tiny, seating only 450. But in festive intimacy that makes every performance a cosy gala. The four-tiered, horseshoe-shaped auditorium basks in a gilded Rococo décor of Greek nymphs, gods and goddesses— Bacchus, Apollo, Diana— and, with delicious incongruity, an American Indian girl complete with feather headdress, bow, arrows and cactus. The acoustics are correspondingly warm and golden—totally appropriate to the Mozart works played here for the past 200 years.

Cuvilliéstheater was preserved to the present day by a stroke of foresight. In 1943, the stucco ornamentation and sculpture were dismantled bit by bit. Some 30,000 separate pieces were carried away and stored in the vaults of various castles around Munich. Six weeks later the theatre building was gutted by fire bombs. And fifteen years elapsed before the 30,000 pieces were brought out of hiding and put together again.

* For a description of Munich's museums, see pp. 61–72.

Sendlinger Tor to Viktualienmarkt

The walk from Sendlinger Tor takes you through a popular district of the city centre, the busy shopping area of Sendlinger Strasse, and on past the municipal museum to the open-air market beside St. Peter's church. Only two hexago-nal towers remain from the picturesque 14th-century **Sendlinger Tor** (City Gate).

Facing north-east, take the left fork along Sendlinger

Cuvilliés Altes Residenztheater, an exquisite setting for Mozart.

Walking's a joy: from Sendlinger Tor fountains to Viktualienmarkt.

Strasse to **Asamhaus** (number 61) where Egid Quirin Asam, master sculptor and architect of the 18th century, had his home. He was assisted in the decoration of the building by his brother, Cosmas Damian, who specialized in fresco painting. The ornate forenames of the brothers—probably their fathers's revenge for his own mundane Hans Georg—are appropriate to the rich Baroque style favoured by the two.

Stand on the opposite side of Sendlinger Strasse and look at the marvellously intricate façade of the house, dated 1733. Secure in their Catholic faith, the Asams happily mixed pagan and Christian figures in their decorative schemes. Just below the roof to the right (directly above the doorway*) you'll see a representation in stucco of heaven and the monogram of Christ. Below that appears the seated figure of Mary. But to the left is vine-bedecked Olympus, and Apollo with the triumphant gods of Fame and Fortune. Pegasus,

* The original doorway, depicting scenes from the Old and New Testaments, is now displayed in the Bavarian National Museum (see p. 68).

the flying horse, leaps up to them, while, lower down, a riot of nymphs and satyrs dance around the Muses of painting, sculpture and architecture.

The decoration of Asamhaus is marked by enormous diligence and ingenuity. It also confirms the brothers' lighthearted devotion to the good life and the inspiration of their religion.

The ultimate demonstration of this can be seen next door in the Asams' private church of St. Johann Nepomuk, originally linked to Egid Quirin's house by a special entrance. Popularly known as **Asamkirche,** the church was completed

in 1746. It was built at Egid Quirin's own expense and so liberated from the constraints of a patron's demands. The result is a subjective celebration of faith and life.

The variegated marble façade serves as a street-altar for passers-by on busy Sendlinger Strasse. It incorporates unhewn rocks originally intended for a fountain and a statue of Johann Nepomuk, a Bohemian saint popular in 18th-century Bavaria, presides over the porch. Inside, the two-tiered **high altar** carries the eye upwards to a towering Crucifixion dominated by a representation of God the Father, wearing the papal crown. Around this formidable monument all is movement and light, aglow still with the Asams' enthusiasm despite the ravages of wartime destruction.

The imposing four-storey **Altes Hackenhaus** stands on the corner of Hackenstrasse. This rare surviving example of a private dwelling in the classical style has a succession of nine Doric, Ionic and Corinthian pillars running along each façade. The courtyard is especially picturesque. Further along Hackenstrasse, at the corner of Hotterstrasse, you'll find Munich's oldest operating tavern, Gaststätte zur Hundskugel, serving beer since 1440.

Double back across Sendlinger Strasse to St.-Jakobs-Platz and the fascinating **Münchner Stadtmuseum** (Municipal Museum; see p. 69). To the east of the museum lies one of the most colourful places in Munich and a meeting place for anybody with a fine nose—the **Viktualienmarkt**, what Charles Dickens would have called a "vittles market". Since 1807 the city's central food market has stood here. Stroll around the enticing stalls with their myriad cheeses and exotic spices, breads and meats. The cornucopia of vegetables and fruit prove better than anything else that Munich is a crossroads of northern and southern Europe, and a gateway to the East, too.

The cheerful atmosphere of the market makes it the perfect place for annual performances of the Marketwomen's Dance on Shrove Tuesday. It's also the scene of lively celebrations around the flower-bedecked May Pole.

Around Königsplatz

Königsplatz represents a convergence of the noblest and basest aspirations in the last several hundred years of Munich's history. When he was still crown prince, Ludwig I visualized the square as a second Acropolis, a vast open space surrounded by classical temples. There was no particular reason for the choice of this site, no junction of roads, for example. But Ludwig overrode the customary demands of urban planning, and workmen were soon widening stately Brienner Strasse, the street which took the royal family from the Residenz to Nymphenburg Palace.

After inspecting the Greek art on Königsplatz, what do we do next?

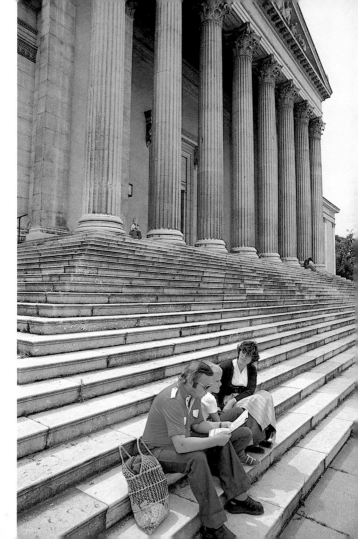

With Leo von Klenze as his architect, Ludwig made the square a grass-covered, tree-lined haven of tranquillity. A hundred years later, Hitler cut down the trees and paved over the grass for the troops and armoured cars of his military parades. (The pompous Nazi Ehrentempel, or Temple of Honour, which stood at the eastern end of the square, was deliberately blown up by Allied military engineers in 1945.) Today Königsplatz is returning to its original serenity, and the greenery is back.

The U-Bahn station brings you out beside the **Propyläen** (Propylaeum), modelled after the entranceway to the Acropolis in Athens. But this splendid monument to Ludwig's sublime imperviousness to functional considerations doesn't lead anywhere, for it closes off Königsplatz rather than providing access to the square. And despite the Doric columns, it's not even properly Greek, since the central "gateway" is flanked by two Egyptian-style pylons or towers. But the friezes that decorate them show the Wittelsbachs' special attachment to things Greek. They depict the Greek war of liberation from the Turks and the Greek people paying homage to Ludwig's son Otto when he was made their king in 1832.

Before visiting the monuments on Königsplatz, continue past the Propyläen to **Lenbachhaus** on Luisenstrasse, an elegant ochre-coloured villa of the 1880s built in the style of Renaissance Florence and reconstructed after World War II. Like Egid Quirin Asam, the wealthy academic painter Franz von Lenbach, a darling of the German aristocracy, built himself a showy palace with the fortune accumulated from his art. Today the villa houses the excellent **Städtische Galerie*** of 19th- and 20th-century art. Coffee is served on the terrace or in the pleasant garden. In the little park opposite, you can play open-air chess on big stone boards.

The **Staatliche Antikensammlungen*** (Classical Art Collections), on the south side of Königsplatz, seems somewhat clumsy in design, with Corinthian columns set on an excessively elevated pedestal. Across the square stands the companion building, the **Glyptothek*** (Sculpture Museum). Designed in 1815 by von Klenze to house Ludwig I's collection of Greek and Roman sculpture, it was the first public museum building planned for that purpose.

Just across Belsberger Strasse, you come to another venerable art institution, the **Alte Pinakothek***. Ludwig commissioned von Klenze to provide a design for a monumental museum in the style of an Italian Renaissance palace. Reconstruction in 1958 preserved the spacious layout of galleries and cabinets on two floors, while imposing the excellent natural and artificial lighting characteristic of Munich museums.

North of nearby Theresienstrasse is the strikingly modern **Neue Pinakothek*** building, opened to the public in 1981. The work of Alexander von Branca, the elegant grey sandstone-and-granite structure replaces the old one destroyed in World War II. Extensive skylights provide superb natural lighting. The architecture breaks with the Alte Pinakothek's classical traditions, but achieves a nice harmony nonetheless.

In case you think it is too facile to relentlessly attack Hitler's legacy in Munich, take a look for yourself at two surviving examples of his architectural contribution to the city: the so-called Führer's Buildings *(Führerbauten)* at the east

end of Königsplatz. It was at Arcisstrasse 12, now a music academy *(Musikhochschule)*, that Hitler received Chamberlain and Daladier, the British and French prime ministers who accepted the infamous Munich agreement of 1938 (see p. 27). Meiserstrasse 10 today houses important archaeological and art-historical institutions, but it was built in 1933 as an administrative centre for the Nazi Party. These grim, bunker-like blocks, designed by Paul Ludwig Troost under the obsessive supervision of Hitler himself, miraculously survived the American bombardments which devastated the Glyptothek and Staatliche Antikensammlungen.

Rather than finish the walk on this sombre note, continue down Meiserstrasse to the **Alter Botanischer Garten.** The town's major botanical garden is now situated at Nymphenburg Palace (see p. 77), but the lawns here still make for a pleasant stroll. Take a seat by the Neptune Fountain and look over the trees at the two cupolas of the Frauenkirche. And remind yourself that the people of Munich found time to lay out this lovely little spot in the middle of the Napoleonic Wars.

* See Museums section, pp. 61–72.

🏃 Schwabing

The Schwabing district belongs to that select group of places around the world—London's Chelsea, Paris's Montparnasse, New York's Greenwich Village —of which it's said, often glibly but nonetheless accurately, that it is not so much a place as a state of mind.

Begin your walk symbolically—Munich loves its symbols —at the **Siegestor** (Victory Gate), which marks the southern boundary of Schwabing. This triumphal arch was designed for Ludwig I as a monument to the Bavarian army. In 1944 it was badly damaged, and in 1958 only partially restored, leaving the scars of war and a new inscription on the south side: *Dem Sieg geweiht, im Krieg zerstört, zum Frieden mahnend* (Dedicated to victory, destroyed in war, exhorting to peace). More than any other part of Munich, Schwabing epitomizes a break with military traditions.

Walk to the entrance of the University and you'll see the little square named Geschwister-Scholl-Platz after the brother and sister who gave their lives in the struggle against Hitler (see p. 27). Across the street stands St. Ludwig, a neo-Romanesque

52

Free for All

During Schwabing's heyday at the turn of the 20th century, when artists, writers and their hangers-on flocked to Munich, townspeople revelled in the creative atmosphere of this bohemian area. Thomas Mann made his home here, as did Frank Wedekind and Bert Brecht, Wassily Kandinsky and Paul Klee. Other illustrious residents included Franz Marc, Rainer Maria Rilke and the symbolist poet Stefan George.

A countess-turned-bohemian, Franziska zu Reventlow, chronicled the neighbourhood's free love, free art, freedom for all and everything; she died penniless from the appropriately romantic illness of tuberculosis. Schwabing was the natural home of the biting satirical weekly *Simplicissimus* and the art magazine *Jugend*, which gave its name to the German version of Art Nouveau—Jugendstil.

A last moment of glory came in 1919 when the "Coffeehouse Anarchists", dramatist Ernst Toller and poet Erich Mühsam, took power after the assassination of prime minister Kurt Eisner. For all of six days—till the communists pushed the poets out—Schwabing ruled Bavaria, proclaiming the republic a "meadow full of flowers".

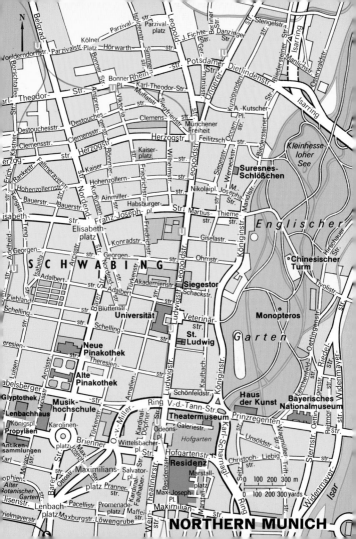

NORTHERN MUNICH

church distinguished mainly for the gigantic fresco of the *Last Judgment* in the choir by Peter Cornelius (1836). At least in terms of size, it's the world's second greatest fresco (60 by 37 feet), after Michelangelo's in the Sistine Chapel.

At night the bohemian spirit of Schwabing animates wide and breezy **Leopoldstrasse,** the street that begins north of Siegestor. The great writers and artists of the past may have disappeared, but the art galleries and cafés are still going strong. Even though the intellectual ferment doesn't bubble as much as before, you sense an underlying excitement as you walk along what local wags call Boulevard Leopold. Having provided a focus for the avant-garde of Jugendstil and the Blaue Reiter, Schwabing now serves as the meeting place for the talents of the new German cinema. You may well catch a glimpse of directors such as Volker Schloen-

dorff and actresses like Hanna Schygulla.

At the major traffic intersection of Münchener Freiheit, cut down Feilitzschstrasse to **Wedekindplatz,** a centre of the theatre, cabaret and café life that in its best moments recaptures the golden past. Continue to nearby Werneckstrasse and **Suresnes-Schlösschen** (Little Château), now the Catholic Academy, designed in 1718 for Prince Elector Max Emanuel. It was built to remind him of the ten happy years he spent in exile west of Paris during the War of the Spanish Succession at the French château of the same name. The Baroque structure went through several neo-Classical remodellings in the 19th century, but some of the original stucco work can still be seen.

Schwabing street theatre draws on the talents of local students.

Olympiapark

Munich's Olympic centre contains some outstanding examples of contemporary architecture. The stadium, sports hall and swimming pools, built for the 1972 Olympic Games, are linked by a spectacular tent-like roof of transparent acrylic which, on a rainy day, resembles a giant spider's web.

The surrounding park, now used for summer theatre and arts festivals, has a man-made lake and artificial, grass-covered hillocks. There's a revolving restaurant and an observation deck half-way up the 950-foot-high Olympic Tower, used for telecommunications.

Just north-east, across the Petuel Ring Autobahn, you can see the curved aluminium skyscraper built as headquarters for the Bavarian Motor Works in 1972. It's known locally as the "four-cylinder". Alongside, in an upturned dome, is the fascinating BMW-Museum (see p. 72).

Englischer Garten Area

From Schwabing, head east to the **Englischer Garten.** Opened in 1793, the park was the brainchild of an American-born adventurer who had fought on the British side during the American Revolution. Benjamin Thompson, better known to Bavarians as Count von Rumford (see p. 19), drew on the ideas of the great English landscape gardeners, Capability Brown and William Chambers. In fact, the Chinesischer Turm (Chinese Tower), the decorative pagoda that serves as a bandstand for a popular beer garden, was directly inspired by Chambers' Cantonese Pagoda in London's Kew Gardens.

Breaking with the French tradition of geometric avenues, elaborately sculptured trees and hedges favoured by the Bavarian aristocracy, Rumford and his German associate Ludwig von Sckell preferred a "natural" grouping of hills, dells and babbling brooks. In keeping with their revolutionary populist ideas, they wanted to create a garden for Munich's poor. Prince Karl Theodor had been under the impression that the Englischer Garten would be no more than an elaborate extension of the Hofgarten, until he saw pigs and cattle grazing where once his lords had hunted for pheasant and stags, and potato patches in place of exotic flowers.

Today the pigs and potatoes have gone, but the natural landscaping is still a joy for picnickers, lovers and all well-meaning loiterers. The Monopteros (love temple) atop a grassy mound south of the

57

A young musician earns her keep as others walk in Englischer Garten.

Chinese Tower attracts the more colourful residents of Schwabing. They bask in a haze of Oriental herbs, admiring the splendid view of the old city.

The gardens stretch 3 miles to the north, making a lovely walk along the swiftly flowing River Isar. Stroll up to the Kleinhesseloher See, a pond that offers some boating for the more energetic. The little Eisbach, a branch of the Isar, rushes helter-skelter under Tivoli Bridge like a veritable mountain rapid, encouraging a particularly breakneck version of wind-surfing. It's a great spectator sport, but if the mere sight of such activity exhausts you, head for the pretty Japanese Tea House (in the southwest corner), donated by Japan in honour of the 1972 Olympic Games.

Just beyond the Tea House, on the southern edge of the garden at Prinzregentenstrasse 1, stands the **Haus der Kunst** (House of Art), a venue for temporary exhibitions and home of the Staatsgalerie moderner Kunst (State Modern Art Gallery; see p. 72). The Haus der Kunst is another building of the Hitler era that Allied bombardments missed. In the bad old days it was known as the Haus der deutschen Kunst (House of German Art), a temple to Hitler's personal vision of a truly German art. The monotonous pile, once again by Paul Ludwig Troost, was quickly endowed with popular nicknames—"Münchner Kunstterminus" (Munich Art Terminal) and "Palazzo Kitschi".

Another museum lies further along Prinzregentenstrasse, the **Bayerisches Nationalmuseum** (Bavarian National Museum; see p. 68). From here, walk across Prinzregentenbrücke **59**

Degenerates Forever!

Hitler's speech inaugurating the Haus der deutschen Kunst in 1937 attacked the "obscenities" of avant-garde art and specifically forbade any painter to use colours that the "normal" eye could not perceive in nature. Two exhibitions were staged to distinguish the good from the bad: one of so-called great German art, the other of officially designated degenerate art.

The trouble was that people preferred the "degenerate" stuff, which attracted a crowd of 2 million, five times as many as the other exhibition. Afterwards, many of these paintings were hidden away. Back in the Haus der Kunst today, they include works by Kandinsky, Mondrian, Kokoschka and Chagall.

spanning the River Isar to the winged **Friedensengel** (Peace Angel). High on her pillar, she surveys Prinzregententerrasse, a pleasant Florentine-style promenade surrounded by gardens. Begun in 1896, the monument celebrates the 25 years of peace that followed the German defeat of the French in 1871. Portraits of the architects of that peace—Bismarck, Kaisers Wilhelm I and II and Generals Moltke and von der Tann—decorate the monument. But the mosaics of *Peace, War, Victory* and the *Blessings of Culture* indicate the rather ambiguous nature of the celebration.

There's nothing ambiguous about the charming **Villa Stuck** (Prinzregentenstrasse 60), built in 1898 for the last of Munich's painter-princes, Franz von Stuck. He amassed a fortune rivalling that of Lenbach by astutely combining the new trends of Jugendstil symbolism with the prevailing salon style for a certain luxury spiced with a dash of decadence. The opulent villa makes the perfect setting for the Jugendstil Museum. All the interior decoration and furniture date from the turn of the century. The house, guarded by Stuck's bold equestrian *Amazone,* is a venue for temporary exhibitions.

To the south lies the phenomenal **Deutsches Museum** (see p. 66) of science and technology. And on the west bank of the Isar, opposite the museum, rises the controversial European Patent Office *(Europäisches Patentamt).* This black steel-and-glass structure has a cool elegance that many find admirable, while others regret the old neighbourhood that had to make way for it.

Museums

The number and diversity of museums and galleries in Munich attest to the city's importance as a cultural centre. For an indication of hours and closing days, see page 116.

Alte Pinakothek

This is one of the world's great art museums, in a class with the Louvre of Paris, the Uffizi of Florence, the Prado of Madrid and New York's Metropolitan.

The gallery (Barer Strasse 27) is the perfect expression of Bavaria's centuries-old dedication to the arts and, more particularly, the resolution of the Wittelsbachs to invest in the great glory of painting. That glory draws not only on the German masters, but also on the highest achievements of the Flemish, the Dutch, the Italians, Spanish and French.

The creation of what is now the Alte Pinakothek began in earnest in the 17th century when Maximilian I installed a Kammergalerie (art gallery) in the Residenz for pictures acquired by his great-grandfather Wilhelm IV, as well as his own growing collection of Dürers and superb German triptychs. Then Max Emanuel

lost his head and bought 105 paintings by Rubens in 1689; it took 80 years to pay for them all. Ludwig I, who struggled 20 years to acquire a Raphael *Madonna* and several other Italian masterworks, commented: "If the money was lost on gambling or horses, people would say that's the way it should be, but you spend it on art and they call it waste."

Here are the highlights of the collection:

One of the outstanding German works is the *Kirchenväter-altar* (Altar of the Church Fathers) painted around 1480 by **Michael Pacher.** This splendid polyptych of Saints Jerome, Augustine, Gregory and Ambrose was brought from the South Tyrol during the French revolution.

On a less monumental scale are two exquisite little paintings of the 15th-century Cologne school by **Stefan Lochner,** *Maria im Rosenhag* (Mary in a Rose Garden) and *Anbetung des Christkindes* (Adoration of the Christ Child).

Pieter Bruegel the Elder produced *Das Schlaraffenland* (Fool's Paradise) in 1567. The artist only half-playfully shows a soldier, a peasant and a scholar sprawled on the ground—at a time when Brueghel wanted **61**

to arouse them to the evils of Spanish military occupation. The gawking *Kopf einer alten Bäuerin* (Head of an Old Peasantwoman) makes no concessions to flattery.

Roger van der Weyden's *Anbetung der Könige* (Adoration of the Magi), a devotional work of 1460, still evokes an attitude of reverence. However, in **Hans Memling's** *Die Sieben Freuden Mariens* (The Seven Joys of Mary), the religious theme is overwhelmed by the setting, a meticulously painted northern landscape.

Albrecht Dürer's *Vier Apostel* (Four Apostles), executed in 1526, is a noble portrayal of John with Peter, and Paul with Mark. The strips of text from Martin Luther's Bible were removed by Maximilian I because he was apparently afraid

Munich's Alte Pinakothek is one of the world's great museums; put aside enough time to visit it.

of criticism by the Jesuits. Another great Dürer is his *Self-portrait* of 1500, imbued with great vanity (note the Christ-like pose), but nonetheless masterful.

His contemporary, **Matthias Grünewald,** is much more down-to-earth, both in the gentle *Hl. Erasmus und Hl. Mauritius im Gespräch vertieft* (Conversation of St. Erasmus and St. Mauritius) and in the at once harsh and moving *Verspottung Christi* (Mocking of Christ). The Wittelsbachs' first great acquisition was **Albrecht Altdorfer's** *Alexanderschlacht* (1529), Alexander's victory over Darius of Persia in 333 B.C. This fervent depiction of the western world's triumph over the Orient was a favourite of Napoleon's and hung in his apartments at St. Cloud.

Peter Paul Rubens is magnificently represented by a vast panoply of his talent. In *Das grosse Jüngste Gericht* (The Great Last Judgment), an enormous work of 1615, a terrible hustle among the damned and the saved takes place on an area of 6 yards by 4. The Jesuits removed the painting from their high altar at Neuburg because they found the nudity offensive. The loving portrait of Rubens' second wife, Hélène Fourment, in her wedding dress (1630) adopts a quieter note.

One of the more intriguing of **Anthony van Dyck's** portraits, *Die Gambenspielerin* (The Viola-da-gamba Player), captures the appeal of a girl who manages to look both haughty and charming.

Of all the self-portraits **Rembrandt** painted, one of the most interesting shows the artist as a young man of 23 in 1629, looking quite surprised, perhaps, by his own talent. The face appears again in *Die Kreuzabnahme* (The Removal of Christ from the Cross), 1633, in the young man next to the ladder. This painting is part of a cycle devoted to the Passion of Christ, another particularly gripping work being *Die Auferstehung* (The Resurrection).

Typical of **Frans Hals'** work is a revealing portrait of an arrogant merchant, *Willem van Heythuysen.*

A representative early work of **Leonardo da Vinci,** *Maria mit dem Kinde* (Mary with Child) was probably painted in 1473, when he was 21. It already possesses much of the serene power of his mature masterpieces.

Munich is also privileged to have one of **Titian's** superb **63** late pictures, the passionately dramatic *Dornenkrönung* (Christ Crowned with Thorns), finished around 1570 when the painter was almost 90. Tintoretto considered this painting to be Titian's legacy, and he bought it for his own collection. Notice another great work by the Venetian on display here, the penetrating portrait of *Kaiser Karl V* (Emperor Charles V).

Raphael, whose cool, classical temperament so impressed Ludwig I, painted the much admired *Madonna Tempi* in 1507. It hangs alongside other distinguished works by the High Renaissance master.

The most coquettish picture in the Italian section, **Tintoretto's** *Vulkan überrascht Venus und Mars* (Vulcan Surprises Venus and Mars), shows Mars hiding under a couch, still wearing his helmet.

A Venetian artist in the circle of **Giorgione** painted the portrait of a young man formerly attributed to the Venetian master and an undeniably fine example of the Giorgione style. There's a similar controversy over three 14th-century panels ascribed to **Giotto**—the earliest pictures in the museum—the best being *Das letzte Abendmahl* (Last Supper). But there's no argument

about the splendid **Tiepolo** *Anbetung der Könige* (Adoration of the Magi), painted in 1753 while the artist was in Bavaria, its rich celebration of red, gold and blue being totally appropriate to Bavaria's Baroque traditions.

If the Spanish room ranks among the most popular in the museum, it may be because of **Murillo's** 17th-century paintings of lively young rascals. They include *Häusliche Toilette* (Domestic Toilet), a grandmother delousing a boy more interested in his dog, *Die kleine Obsthändlerin* (The Little Fruit Vendor) and *Melonen- und Traubenesser* (Melon- and Grape-eaters).

The inspired melancholy of **El Greco** is evident in his *Entkleidung Christi* (Disrobing of Christ) and there's also a superb portrait of a young Spanish noble by **Velázquez.**

A romantic sunrise by **Claude Lorrain** *(Seehafen bei Aufgang der Sonne)*, **Boucher's** *Madame de Pompadour*, and a **Lancret** shepherdess characterize the rosy view of the 18th century that prevailed in France before the revolution. Artistically, the most impressive works are **Poussin's** beautifully stylized *Midas und Bacchus* and *Beweinung Christi* (Lamentation of Christ).

Residenzmuseum

Even with many of the wings still closed off, the Residenz is so huge—112 rooms, halls and galleries, plus the ten rooms of the Schatzkammer (Treasure Chamber)—that the museum is divided into two itineraries, one of which is offered in the morning, another in the afternoon.

Beginning at the main entrance on Max-Joseph-Platz, each tour covers upstairs and downstairs floors. As some of the more important rooms are open all day long, one is usually sufficient for a good overall impression.

Following are some of the rooms you'll visit:

Ahnengalerie (Gallery of the Ancestors). Here you can acquaint yourself with a mere 121 of the Wittelsbachs, beginning with Duke Theodor, who lived around the year 700.

Antiquarium. This monumental 225-foot-long Renaissance library was designed by Friedrich Sustris for Duke Albrecht V in 1558. The room takes its name from the 16th-century busts of ancient Greek and Roman leaders on display.

Porcelain Collections. This prodigious array of French, English and German porcelain includes the delicate work of Meissen from eastern Germany and locally manufactured pieces from Nymphenburg. Japanese and Chinese porcelain and superb lacquer work form part of a separate exhibit.

Grottenhof. Designed by Sustris in 1581, this is perhaps the most elegant courtyard in the Residenz, distinguished by the graceful arcade along the eastern side and by Hubert Gerhard's fine bronze Perseus fountain in the middle. The Grottenwand or Grotto Wall, a fountain set in an alcove, gives the courtyard its name. The statue of Mercury is flanked by Nubian slaves, fish-tailed satyrs, nymphs and parrots, the whole encrusted with thousands of mussel, scallop and winkle shells.

Reiche Zimmer (State Rooms). Together these rooms provide the best example of Rococo décor in Germany. Cuvilliés designed them in 1729, his jewel among jewels being the Grüne Galerie (Green Gallery). But you'll also want to linger in the Spiegelkabinett (Cabinet of Mirrors), Miniaturenkabinett and Chinesisches Kabinett.

Hofkapelle and Reiche Kapelle. The first of these charmingly intimate chapels was originally set aside for common courtiers, the second exclusively for the Wittelsbachs.

Schatzkammer (Treasure Chamber). A separate tour is dedicated to the dynasty's spectacular collection of jewellery, gold, silver, enamelware and crystal, amassed over the course of 1,000 years. One of the earliest Wittelsbach heirlooms is the Arnulfziborium (Arnolph's Ciborium), a communion goblet dated around 890.

Deutsches Museum

Zweibrückenstrasse takes you to the museum (on its own little island in the Isar), where children have all the fun. And since we're all children, none of us should miss the biggest scientific and technological collection in the world. If you faithfully followed the lines guiding you to each and every exhibit, you would cover 12 miles.

But if that sounds too forbidding, relax in the knowledge that you don't, of course, have to see it all, and that displays have been laid out with marvellous attention to the comfort and enjoyment of visitors. The models, experimental machines and audio-visual effects have nearly all been installed in such a way that you yourself can operate them by pushing buttons, turning wheels, and pulling levers. In

a land that has always taken science and technology very seriously, it is reassuring to find a place where the most complex machines are for once presented as monster toys for the delight and enlightenment of little boys and girls.

Setting the tone in the courtyard is "the world's first vertical take-off jet transport plane", the Dornier Do 31 of 1967. This is no model, but the actual aircraft. Now that idea on paper may not move you very much, but the machine itself turns out to be a most endearing thingamajig.

The transport section brings together every kind of boat, from an Indian canoe, Arab dhow and Irish coracle to a splendid black velvet-seated gondola and breathtaking 19th-century German sailing ship, 200 feet long. And each time you see the real thing, not a scale model. Machinery devoted to energy production takes on the beauty of sculpture—windmills, watermills, a wind-turbine of 1900 from Dresden or an exquisite steam-powered fire-engine of 1893 from Nuremberg.

Some kids can't make head or tail of the Deutsches Museum's models.

Train enthusiasts will love the first German "Lokomobil", built in 1862 and still operating with the gentle hiss of a domestic steam iron. And British patriots may note with interest that the Germans are pleased to show a perfect copy of "Puffing Billy", one of the earliest (1813) English locomotives. But the star attraction for youngsters is the model railway and its 670 feet of track, 100-odd curves and vast railway station with a shunting yard of nine parallel tracks.

The cars on display range from Karl Benz's superb "Automobil Nummer 1" of 1886 to an unpainted stainless-steel Porsche sports car made in 1967, immaculate after 155,000 kilometres. They stand alongside the sublimely ridiculous Prunkwagen (State Coach) of Ludwig II. This gilded super-Rococo fairy-tale carriage was designed just eight years before the first car. The technical data note: *Bremsen fehlen*—"No brakes".

Other exhibits deal with printing, nuclear energy, musical instruments and astronomy. There's also a first-rate planetarium, and you can even inspect the old wooden bridge built when Munich was no more than a small, 12th-century settlement (see p. 12). (see p. 12)

67

Other Museums

Tourists too frequently neglect the excellent **Bayerisches Nationalmuseum** (Bavarian National Museum) in Prinzregentenstrasse). Built in 1900, the exterior traces in different architectural styles the artistic evolution of the periods exhibited inside—a Romanesque east wing, Renaissance western façade, Baroque tower and Rococo west wing. The collection provides a truly magnificent survey of German cultural history from the Roman era, through the Middle Ages to the 19th century. It emphasizes both religious and secular arts and craftsmanship.

There are fine Romanesque and Gothic stone carvings, wooden sculptures and paintings from churches and abbeys long since disappeared or transformed. The outstanding pieces include *Inthronisierte Maria* (Enthroned Mary) from Perugia (1200), *Hl. Katerina* (St. Catherine) from Salzburg (1420) and a beautifully ornate polychrome wood *Maria im Rosenhag* (Mary in a Rose Bower) from Straubing (1320), showing Mary as the proudest of mothers and Jesus still a playful little boy.

The highlight for many proves to be the collection of wooden sculptures by Tilman Riemenschneider, Germany's great Late Gothic master, in the **Riemenschneider-Saal.** There are powerful statues of Mary Magdalene, St. Sebastian and the Apostles, carved around 1500.

Among other Late Gothic exhibits is one of the most frightening chiming clocks you're ever likely to come across, from the Heilbronn Monastery. The implications of *tempus fugit* were hammered home by a furious figure of Death riding a frantic-looking lion.

But notice, too, such admirable secular exhibits as the **Augsburger Weberstube,** a room decorated with the original medieval furnishings and carvings of the Augsburg Weavers' Guild. And the **Stadtmodell-Saal,** with Jakob Sandtner's intricate 16th-century scale models of Bavarian ducal cities, Munich taking pride of place beside Ingolstadt and Landshut. Lastly, look for the glorious carved doors illustrating Old and New Testament scenes from Egid Quirin Asam's house on Sendlinger Strasse.

In the east wing of the museum, entered from Lerchenfeldstrasse, is the **Prähistorische Staatssammlung** (Prehistoric Museum), devoted to

Life-like marionettes create a dream-world all their own on the top floor of the Municipal Museum.

Bavarian finds from earliest Celtic times.

The **Münchner Stadtmuseum** (Municipal Museum) in St.-Jakobs-Platz reflects Munich's distinctive personality, and it's well worth spending an hour or two here to get a feel for the town's development since the Middle Ages. The Moriskenraum houses the museum's main attraction: merry wooden carvings of **Morris Dancers** from the Altes Rathaus council chamber. Dated 1480, they are magnificent examples of Erasmus Grasser's Gothic style.

Maps, models and photographs on the first floor illustrate Munich's rich history. On the second floor, a series of 20 rooms has been furnished in various decorative styles from the past. You'll see kitchens, living rooms and bedrooms, examples of sumptuous rooms from the Residenz and cosy bourgeois homes of the 19th century complete with heavy Biedermeier pieces or the more delicate Jugendstil. Highlights include a very inviting 18th-century Weinstube (wine tavern) and a reconstruction of an opulent artist's studio (Makart-Zimmer).

The fashion collection shows the evolution of styles in a town that has long been a centre of German design. A poignant effort has been made to inject a light touch into the display of wartime fashions.

Children (and adults, too) will love the **Puppentheater-Sammlung** (Marionette Theatre Collection) on the third floor, one of the largest of its kind in the world; Bavaria has long been a centre for the production of glove-puppets, shadow plays and mechanical toys.

On the other hand, the ground-floor **Deutsches Brauereimuseum** (German Brewery Museum) caters particularly to adults. This museum-within-a-museum explores the history of Germany's national drink, beginning with the year 3000 B.C. and the sculpture of an Egyptian brewery worker. The exhibition approvingly quotes the first literary allusion to the noble liquid in the *Epic of Gilgamesh*, the tale of a legendary Babylonian hero who apparently said: "Eat bread, you need it to live. Drink beer, it's the local custom." There's also a comprehensive selection of drinking vessels.

Scholars commissioned by

King Ludwig I scouted the classical world for suitable works to display in the **Glyptothek** (Sculpture Museum) on Königsplatz. Some 160 pieces found a spacious home in the massive, Ionic-columned edifice, rebuilt after World War II. The Glyptothek glories in its great treasure, the **sculpture from the gables of the Temple of Aphaia**, found on the Greek island of Aegina. The well-preserved friezes date from 505 B.C. (west gable) and 485 B.C. (east gable). They show warriors with their shields fighting to defend the island's patron goddess, smiling that rather smug ancient Greek smile. Look out, too, for other works of major importance: the *Apollo of Tenea*, a *Medusa*, the goddess of peace *Irene* and the *Barberini Faun* (named after a 17th-century Italian family of classicists).

The valuable displays of the **Antikensammlungen** (Classical Art Collections) include a lovely series of Greek vases and urns and, above all, the highly prized collection of Etruscan gold and silver formed by James Loeb. This German-American benefactor is well known to schoolboys for the famous Loeb's Classical Library of Greek and Latin texts.

The 22-room **Neue Pinakothek** in Barer Strasse emphasizes 19th-century German art, placed in a historical context of English 18th- and 19th-century portraits and landscapes and 19th-century French naturalist and Impressionist works.

A harsh still-life by Goya, *Gerupfte Pute* (Plucked Turkey), hangs here, together with a piercing study of the artist's doctor, *Don José Queralto*. This portrait is believed to be particularly complimen-

This Improvisation *by Kandinsky is on display at Lenbachhaus.*

tary because the subject had cured Goya of a recurring disease.

Look, too, for Turner's superb *Ostende*, Manet's *Frühstück* (Breakfast) and van Gogh's *Vase mit Sonnenblumen* (Vase with Sunflowers). There are also many fine German works: *Riesengebirgslandschaft mit aufsteigendem Nebel* (Sudeten Mountains with Rising Mist) by Caspar David Friedrich delicately expresses the Romantic spirit. You'll be charmed by the wit of Karl Spitzweg, especially his *Armer Poet* (Poor Poet), a caricature of the romantic view of artistic squalor. And to round off your survey, there's the social realism of Max Liebermann and the Jugendstil symbolism of Gustav Klimt, Max Klinger and Franz von Stuck.

The **BMW-Museum** off the Petuel Ring Autobahn provides a fascinating look at the history of the Bavarian Motor Works. You'll see the cars, motorcycles and aircraft engines that made BMW famous: all the classic originals are on display. But officials also had the excellent idea of relating a parallel history of the world events that occurred while these technical innovations were being made. Against a stark background that makes artful use of light-ing to highlight the exhibits, contemporary history unfolds in its political, social and cultural dimensions. There are short video films and vocal testimony is heard from life-sized figures of German chancellors, American presidents, even celebrities like Elvis Presley and Marilyn Monroe. The ultimate comment on the Nazi period comes from a huge statue of Charlie Chaplin in his role as the Great Dictator.

The **Städtische Galerie**, a municipal museum of 19th- and 20th-century art in Lenbachhaus, boasts the largest collection of paintings by Wassily Kandinsky in Germany, plus important canvases by Franz Marc, August Macke and Paul Klee. The four formed the nucleus of Munich's pre-World War I "Blaue Reiter" (Blue Rider) school of painting. The name derives from a blue-and-black horseman drawn by Kandinsky for an almanac in 1912. Horses and the colour blue were also dominant features of Franz Marc's work.

In addition to Picasso, Braque, Dalí and the German Expressionists, the **Staatsgalerie moderner Kunst** collection (in a wing of the Haus der Kunst) includes a distinguished array of contemporary Americans.

GREATER MUNICH

Royal Retreats

Schloss Nymphenburg, now inside the ever-expanding city limits, was the Wittelsbachs' summer refuge from the heat of their Residenz in the city centre. The gleaming palace, with its spacious grounds, ponds, fountains and four enchanting garden pavilions, is a wonderful place to stroll and let your imagination go. Recall the *dolce far niente* of the Wittelsbachs' best days, when they played at nymphs and shepherds and forgot the worries of state. There's no U-Bahn station at the palace, but if you dont-t have a car for the 8-kilometre ride, a No. 17 tram will take you there from the Hauptbahnhof.

The son and heir that Princess Henriette Adelaide presented to her husband in 1662 must have been an extraordinarily welcome gift. He was certainly an absolute boon to the architects of the time, inspiring the building of both the Theatinerkirche and Nymphenburg. The palace began modestly enough as a small summer villa, but it grew over the next century as each succeeding ruler added another wing or his own little pavilion and changed the landscaping of the gardens. Max Emanuel,

the little baby who was the cause of it all, grew up with the ambition of emulating Louis XIV's Versailles. He may not have succeeded completely, but the French armies appreciated his efforts and made Nymphenburg their headquarters in 1800.

The palace is approached by a long canal with avenues on either bank leading to a semi-circle of lawns, the Schlossrondell, site of the building which houses the royal porcelain factory (see SHOPPING, p. 90). The central edifice of the palace proper contains galleries of superb 18th-century stucco work and ceiling frescoes. The majestic two-storey high banqueting hall, known as **Steinerner Saal** (Stone Hall), has lively frescoes by Johann Baptist Zimmermann on the theme *Nymphen huldigen der Göttin Flora* (Nymphs Pay Homage to the Goddess Flora).

The first pavilion to the south holds the famous **Schönheitengalerie** (Gallery of Beautiful Women). Ludwig I commissioned Joseph Stieler to paint the portraits that hang here—a series of women said

Stroll back into another century in Nymphenburg gardens. Ludwig's coach awaits you in the Marstall.

to have been the king's mistresses. Certainly one of them was, a ferocious lady with a belt of snakes around her waist and a whip in her hand, the notorious Lola Móntez. She was born Mary Dolores Eliza Rosanna Gilbert, daughter of an Irish adventurer. But since her mother was reputedly a Spanish countess, she went on stage as Señora Maria de los Dolores Porris y Móntez (see p. 22).

The **Marstallmuseum**—a dazzling collection of state coaches used for coronations, weddings and other royal frolics—has been installed in the south wing, in what was once the royal stables. From the extravagance of Karl Albrecht's 18th-century coronation coaches, the vehicles went on to achieve a state of ornamental delirium under Ludwig II. Note especially his Nymphenschlitten (Nymph sleigh), designed for escapades in the foothills of the Alps.

The **gardens** were originally laid out in a subdued Italian style for Henriette Adelaide, but her son preferred the grandiose French manner. Later, Ludwig von Sckell, landscape artist of the Englischer Garten, was brought in. As a result, the park has lost some of its formality, which makes for a more relaxed stroll. But by the same token, the Baroque and Rococo pavilions seem a little isolated now, like original tenants who stayed on in the house while new owners changed all the furniture around them. Traces of the former classical geometry can be seen in the symmetry of the Schlossrondell and the rectangular Grosses Parterre immediately west of the central edifice. The grounds are decorated with some rather nice marble statues of Greek gods by Dominikus Auliczek and others.

Off to the left lies **Amalienburg,** probably the prettiest little hunting lodge in the country. It was begun in 1734 by the same trio who worked on the State Rooms of the Residenz—architect François de Cuvilliés, sculptor Joachim Dietrich and stucco artist Johann Baptist Zimmermann. Wander through the rooms where the hunting dogs and rifles were kept, the Pheasant Room next to the blue-and-white, Dutch-tiled kitchen, and, above all, the brilliant silver and pastel yellow Rococo **Spiegelsaal** (Hall of Mirrors). This was originally—just imagine—the pavilion's entrance.

Continue west to the **Badenburg** (Bath Pavilion)—fitted

with Delft china fixtures that are an interior decorator's dream—and the Grosser See, a large pond dotted with islands. Overlooking it is a promontory with a little love temple modelled after Rome's Temple of Vesta, goddess of fire.

North of the central canal with its spectacular **cascade** of water is another, smaller pond. On the far side stands the **Pagodenburg,** an octagonal tea pavilion with some exotic black-and-red-lacquered Chinese chambers upstairs.

The fourth of the park's pavilions, the **Magdalenenklause** (Hermitage) was built in 1725 for the private meditations of Max Emanuel. The dominant theme of the paintings and sculptures inside is penitence. Don't be surprised when you see that the building is a crumbling ruin; cracks and flaking plaster were deliberately incorporated in the mock Romanesque and Gothic structure, not to mention the Moorish minaret thrown in for good measure.

The area north of the park has been given over to the **Neuer Botanischer Garten** (New Botanical Gardens), entered from Menzinger Strasse. The Arboretum at the west end of the gardens is cleverly landscaped to resemble different climatic regions of the world with their appropriate flora—pine forest, Arctic tundra, heath and moorland, desert dunes, the steppes and Alpine country alongside an artificial pond.

After the flamboyance of Nymphenburg, continue further west (by car or No. 73 tram from the end of Menziger Strasse) to the refreshing simplicity of **Schloss Blutenburg,** now a convent. It's particularly worth visiting for the **palace chapel,** of a superb Late Gothic type rare in this part of Bavaria. The three altars display splendid paintings by Jan Polack, done in 1491: the *Holy Trinity* (high altar), *Christ Enthroned* (on the left) and the *Annunciation* (to the right). On the walls are fine polychrome wooden sculptures of the Apostles, Mary and a resurrected Christ, dated around 1500.

Finish your tour in nearby Pippinger Strasse with a visit to **Pfarrkirche St. Wolfgang** (St. Wolfgang's Parish Church). Some frescoes attributed to Polack (1479) decorate the admirably serene interior and there are three delicately carved wooden altars from the same period. The church offers perfect meditation at the end of a long day.

Excursions

To take the full measure of Munich, you must visit its hinterland, the beautiful countryside of Bavaria. Go to the lakes, to the little country churches and to Ludwig II's crazy castles. If you don't have a car, take one of the tours organized by the Munich-Upper Bavaria Tourist Office (see p. 123). Each tour we propose can be done easily in one day.

Ludwig's Follies

Ludwig II's castles south of Munich, Neuschwanstein and Linderhof, are best visited separately. Choose one, or, if you're a real fan, do both.

Take the B12 to **Landsberg am Lech** (interesting for its medieval town centre), then B17, the Deutsche Alpenstrasse (German Alpine Road). Stop off at STEINGADEN to visit the beautiful **St. Johann Baptist Church,** which retains much of its 12th-century Romanesque exterior. You'll enjoy the pleasant walk in the old cloister.

It's worth making a detour to the east to visit the magnificent **Wieskirche,** a pilgrimage church of 1754 designed by Dominikus Zimmermann

Neuschwanstein was one of Ludwig II's grander little whims. Kings no longer have dreams like this.

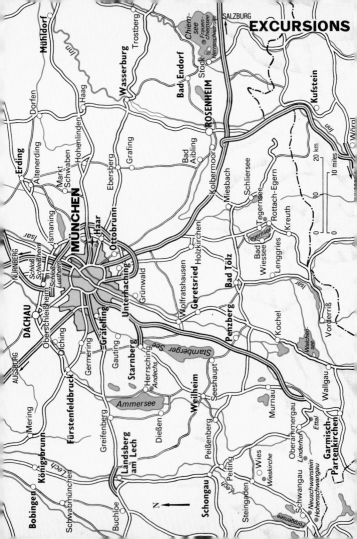

EXCURSIONS

and decorated with a sublime ceiling fresco by his brother Johann Baptist, depicting Christ dispensing divine mercy. In its architecture and decoration, the church is a consummate work, perfect to the last Rococo detail.

Return to the main road for the journey down to the more pagan inspiration of **Neuschwanstein.** After visiting the medieval castle of Wartburg in Thuringia in 1867, Ludwig's imagination was fired with a vision of the Minnesänger—minstrels of the 12th century—and he decided to build a castle that would recapture the aura of that romantic era.

Ludwig replaced a ruined mountain retreat of his father's in the Schwangau with an extraordinary white-turreted castle. Set in the middle of a forest of firs and pines, it overlooks the gorge of Pöllat and Lake Forggen. Visit the great dreamer's throne room and imagine, as did Ludwig, the minstrel contests of another age in the Sängersaal. Wagnerians will recognize the sculptural and painted allusions to *Tannhäuser, The Mastersingers of Nuremburg* and *Tristan and Isolde.*

While Neuschwanstein was under construction, Ludwig kept an eye on progress from the nearby castle of **Hohenschwangau** (just 1 kilometre away), a neo-Gothic building put up by his father, Maximilian II. In fact, Neuschwanstein and Hohenschwangau are known collectively as "die Königsschlösser". Take a look at the music room with its display of Wagner memorabilia (the composer stayed at Hohenschwangau) and Ludwig's bedroom, noted for its star-studded ceiling.

To reach Ludwig's second dream castle, take the Garmisch-Partenkirchen Autobahn from Munich, turning off west to **Ettal.** Set in a gently curving valley is a lovely Benedictine monastery with a fine domed church. Stop to admire Johann Jakob Zeiller's 18th-century fresco of the life of St. Benedict. Then go on to **Oberammergau,** site of the famous ten-yearly Passion Play inaugurated in the plague year of 1633. The town preserves some very attractive 18th-century house façades painted by the so-called *Lüftlmaler* (air painter), Franz Zwinck. The best are Pilatushaus and Geroldhaus.

Linderhof, Ludwig's favourite castle, was the embodiment of his most Baroque fantasies. The palace, inspired by the Grand Trianon of Versailles, is **81**

opulent inside and out. Quite apart from the carefully tailored landscape of pond and park, you could be excused for believing that the whole romantic Alpine backdrop of the Graswangtal had been conjured up from Ludwig's imagination. But the Venus Grotto, carved out of the mountainside with another Wagnerian motif from *Tannhäuser*, is man-made.

The Lakes

Ammersee (35 km. south-west of Munich on B12) is a delightful place for long walks along the lake or up into the wooded hills around it. Make for the Benedictine **Abbey of Andechs** in the hills that overlook Ammersee from the east. The church was put up in the 15th century and was redecorated in the Rococo style by Johann Baptist Zimmermann, then at the peak of his career. The monastery brewery produces first-rate beer.

Starnberger See (south-west of Munich on the Garmisch-Partenkirchen Autobahn) offers quiet, rural scenery and a peaceful rush-fringed shoreline. It was here that Ludwig II drowned in 1886 (see p. 24). He had been held in custody at Schloss Berg, near the resort town of STARNBERG.

Tegernsee (Salzburg Autobahn, Holzkirchen exit) was once a high centre of German culture, dating back to the 8th century. Its monastery was a focus for church intellectuals, who drew on a library that in 1500 was bigger than the Vatican's. With the French revolution came secularization and the removal of the monastery's treasures to Munich. Today the Benedictine Abbey houses a beer hall, and Tegernsee ranks as a high centre of German social life. The élite of Munich society congregate around the lake, partaking of the iodised waters at BAD WIESSEE and dining out in ROTTACH. Join them.

Chiemsee (south-east of Munich on the Salzburg Autobahn) is the largest of the Bavarian lakes and the site of Ludwig II's most ambitious castle. **Herrenchiemsee** stands on an island, the Herreninsel, at the western end of the lake. (You take a boat from the jetty at STOCK.)

Ludwig started his last big castle in 1878 but ran out of money—and time—in 1886.

If you've seen enough monasteries, Andechs is worth it for the beer.

Nevertheless, he made a valiant attempt at recreating the grandeur of Versailles. Certainly the magnificent Spiegelsaal (Hall of Mirrors) can bear comparison with the Galerie des Glaces. It pays homage to the king Ludwig admired most, Louis XIV.

Frauenchiemsee (St. Mary's Monastery Church), together with some charming little fishermen's cottages, occupies another island nearby. The church has some excellent 13th-century frescoes, which only recently came to light. Many would rate Chiemsee as the most romantic of Bavaria's resort lakes.

North of Munich

This excursion takes in the lightest and most sombre aspects of Bavaria's past. You'll probably want to start at the dark end and relax afterwards in the light.

Dachau (17 km. north-west of Munich on B 304) used to be known as a pretty little village, a sleepy place much favoured by painters. People came to see the remains of a 16th-century château and the attractive 18th-century façades on many of its houses. Then, on March 20, 1933, a mere 48 days after Hitler came to power, Dachau was designated as the site of

the first Nazi concentration camp. It was established in a disused gunpowder factory. Today you can still admire the charming town centre, but you should also visit the **Concentration Camp Museum.** Follow the sign (just like one you'll see in a photo of the 1930's on display in the museum), to the "Konzentrationslager".

The museum was built on the camp site by the International Dachau Committee, funded by the Bavarian state government. Discreetly, but uncompromisingly, without unnecessary pathos, exhibitions document the camp's history. You'll see photos, uniforms and the insignia that distinguished the prisoners—black for political dissidents, pink for homosexuals, yellow for Jews, etc. Dachau was not one of the leading centres for extermination—31,951 deaths were recorded between 1933 and 1945

Tegernsee is a smart resort where you can get away from the bustle of the city. Schleissheim's frescoes celebrate the region's renowned hunting.

—but it did serve as a detention camp for major political prisoners and as a research station for the experiments that were carried out in Auschwitz. Some 100,000 inmates were interned here. Apart from the museum itself, you can see the original crematorium and reconstructed prison barracks. Chapels and a synagogue are provided for prayer.

Now continue east to **Schloss Schleissheim** and re-enter the sunny Baroque world of Max Emanuel. The Neues Schloss has a glorious staircase with frescoes by Cosmas Damian Asam. Fine stucco work adorns banqueting halls and galleries like the Barockgalerie, which contains a notable collection of 17th-century Dutch and Flemish paintings.

But the **gardens** are the real triumph, a victory for once of the French style of landscaping. It's a sheer joy to walk around the waterfall, canals and flowerbeds designed by Carbonet and Dominique Girard, a disciple of the French master André Le Nôtre. If you continue east to the other end of the gardens, you come to **Schloss Lustheim,** a hunting lodge, just under a mile away. Admire the superb collection of Meissen porcelain. Then take time out for tea.

What to Do

Entertainment

If there's anything Munich has no problem providing, it's entertainment. There's something for every taste. First and foremost, Munich is a city of **music,** with four major symphony orchestras—the Bavarian State Orchestra, Munich Philharmonic, Bavarian Radio Symphony and Graunke Symphony Orchestra. The main concerts are performed at the Gasteig Kulturzentrum, on the site of the beer hall where Adolf Hitler staged his famous putsch in 1923. A huge complex in the order of New York's Lincoln Center or the Barbican in London, the Gasteig incorporates several concert halls under one roof.

In summer, open-air concerts take place in the Hofgarten, brass bands strike up at the Chinese Tower in the Englischer Garten, winter church concerts are held in the Frauenkirche, St. Michael and St. Peter. For music in a palatial setting, as well as Nymphenburg, there's Blutenburg and the Grosser Saal at Schleissheim.

Opera has been a major Munich attraction for centuries. The town vies with Bayreuth for major performances of Wagner, in addition to its other predilections for Mozart and Richard Strauss. The Italians take second place, but Verdi, Rossini and Donizetti are by no means neglected. The majestic Nationaltheater makes every opera evening seem like a gala. The Bavarian State Orchestra plays under the world's greatest conductors and the summer festival *(Münchner Festspiele)* in July and August attracts the very best international singers

Entertainment for many is first of all Oktoberfest. Get thirsty.

to the city. A Munich Season *(Münchner Saison)* from December to February offers the special joy of Mozart operas in the Cuvilliéstheater. In summer, opera is staged out-of-doors in the Brunnenhof courtyard of the Residenz.

Jazz is much appreciated in Munich, and top American musicians play nightly all over Schwabing. A big summer festival is staged at Olympic Hall.

If your German is up to it, try the first-rate **theatre.** Classical and contemporary plays can be seen at the Residenztheater (Max-Joseph-Platz 1) or the Schauspielhaus (Maximilianstrasse 26). The smaller

theatres of Schwabing specialize in a more avant-garde repertoire, as does the open-air theatre at Olympiapark. For children—and adults—there are two wonderful theatres: the Puppentheater (Glove-puppet Theatre) in the Künstlerhaus on Lenbachplatz, and the Marionettentheater, Blumenstrasse 29a, near Sendlinger Tor, with shows for children in the afternoon and marionette opera for adults in the evening.

For those with an interest in the honourable tradition of **political cabaret,** Schwabing is still the place to go. Most of the troupes have the longevity of butterflies, but the best-established are the Münchner Lach- und Schiessgesellschaft (Ursulastrasse 9) and the Münchner Rationaltheater (Hesseloher Strasse 18).

More conventional **nightclubs** and **discothèques** are to be found in the centre of town and in Schwabing, but **beer halls** still provide the most relaxed night-time entertainment.

And then there is the delightful Hellabrunn **Zoo,** situated south of the city centre on the Isar. Animals are grouped according to their continent of origin—Europe, Africa, Asia, America, Australia and the polar regions. Here you'll see such zoological curiosities as the tarpan, a kind of horse, and the white-tailed gnu. The antics of the chimps "working out" in their own private gym always attract an appreciative audience.

Festivals

The people of Munich always have something to celebrate. Over a hundred days a year are officially devoted to festivals, processions, banquets and street dances commemorating events like the arrival of the first strong beer of the year (*Starkbierzeit*) or the departure—several centuries ago!—of this plague or that occupying army. Any excuse will do.

Fasching (carnival) is almost as mad in Munich as in the Rhineland. It runs from January 7. Some 2,500 balls are held all over town for policemen and doctors, lawyers and butchers, artists and plumbers. There are masked processions and market women at the Viktualienmarkt have their fling at midday on Shrove Tuesday.

Loud, joyous and full of rhythm, Bavarian music keeps you young.

The biggest blow-out of all, of course, is the **Oktoberfest**. Not many people remember that this binge began with the marriage of Crown Prince Ludwig (later Ludwig I) to Princess Theresa in 1810. The wedding was celebrated in October with a horse race and everybody came. They came again the next year, and the year after that, and they're still coming.

The horse race has been dropped and the festivities now take place during the warmer second half of September, but the blushing bride is remembered in the name of the Oktoberfest site—Theresienwiese. Locals, however, refer to it as the "Wies'n", a nickname for the actual festival, too. During the two weeks of Oktoberfest, revellers consume gargantuan quantities of beer, toted around ten litres at a time by hefty beermaids. The brew washes down hundreds of thousands of barbecued chickens, while the operator of a monster roasting spit boasts that he turns out up to 60 whole oxen during the festival. And to work all that off, there's the fun of the fair: roller-coasters, giant ferris-wheel, dodg'em cars. Or to scare it off, Schichtl's age-old horror show.

Shopping

Munich is an elegant town, capital of Germany's fashion industry, so there's no lack of chic boutiques, especially on Theatinerstrasse, Maximilianstrasse and Schwabing's Leopoldstrasse. You'll also find the world's best selection of well-tailored garments (coats, jackets and suits) in **Loden** cloth, a Bavarian speciality. Originally developed for hunters, this waterproof wool fabric in navy, grey or traditional green has kept the people of Munich warm in winter for over a hundred years.

You might even care to try the local Bavarian costume *(Tracht)*. There are smart green-collared grey jackets for men or, for women, gaily coloured dirndl dresses with a full gathered skirt and fitted bodice.

German **leather** and **sportswear** are good buys. And Lederhosen, those slap-happy shorts for Bavarians, may amuse the children.

Nymphenburg **porcelain** is still turned out in traditional Rococo designs. View pieces at the Nymphenburger Schlossrondell factory (see p. 74). Connoisseurs should be on the look-out for old Meissen or modern Rosenthal.

German **cutlery,** kitchen utensils and **electronic gadgets** are of a very high standard and superbly designed. You might also like to consider **linens** with modern or traditional designs, noted for their good old-fashioned quality. The best bet is a sumptuous duck- or goose-down *Federbett*—a good way to save on winter heating bills.

Many people appreciate German **binoculars** and **telescopes.** And, while the competition from Japan is keen, there are still many fine **cameras** on the market, especially at the miniature end of the range.

Germany has always pro-

If you like hats, the whimsical creations of Munich's milliners will almost certainly tickle your fancy.

duced excellent children's **toys** and its industrial prowess is reflected in the intricate building sets and model trains.

The presence of so many great orchestras and musicians in Germany means that the selection of **records** here is probably second only to the United States. The manufacture of **musical instruments,** including the finest grand pianos, violins—even harmonicas —enjoys a venerable reputation.

91

Quite apart from the posh shops in the city centre, you should keep your eyes open for **flea markets.** They pop up all over Schwabing whenever students and artists run out of rent money. But the best are the seasonal ones known as "Auer Dult", which date back to the 14th century. These are held for eight days, three times a year (May, July and October) in the Au district (around Mariahilfplatz south of the Deutsches Museum). You can tell that these markets turn out interesting bargains by the number of city-centre antique dealers on the spot early in the morning. Just beat them to it.

Sports

The city's great boon to sports lovers was the construction of the Olympic facilities in 1972 (see box, p. 56), now open to the public. The Municipal Sports Office (Städtisches Sportamt) can provide information about the daily programme of events and training at the Olympic Stadium's Gesundheitspark (Health Park). Visitors and regulars alike can participate.

Anyone can use the **swimming pool** at the Olympia Schwimmhalle, in addition to eight other indoor and ten open-air pools around town.

The latter all provide lawns for sunbathing. Year-round, **ice-skating** fans congregate at the Olympic ice rink and speed-skating track.

Munich has its share of **tennis** courts, too: the best are at Olympiapark, in the Englischer Garten and, most attractive of all, at Schloss Nymphenburg.

While those who prefer to call themselves "runners" will want to go to the stadium for a work-out, lesser mortals will be more than content **jogging** in the Englischer Garten, especially the 3-mile stretch along the River Isar. **Golf** courses are to be found in outlying Strass-lach and in Thalkirchen on the south-west edge of town.

For people who don't want to exert themselves, delightful **raft trips** (*Flossfahrten*) are organized at weekends. You drift down the Isar from Wolfrats-hausen to Munich, while the beer flows and brass bands play.

Spectator sports are dominated by **soccer,** for one of the

Look hard enough and you'll find the strangest birds at local flea markets. Try sailing on the Starnberger See—or dream about it.

best clubs in Europe, Bayern München, plays at the Olympic Stadium. Rowing and canoeing events are held regularly at Schloss Schleissheim. You can watch horse racing, mostly trotting, near the airport at Riem or Daglfing.

Further out of Munich, you can get down to serious **sailing** or **windsurfing** on the Ammersee, Starnberger See and Tegernsee. The lakes and rivers also offer good **fishing.**

For deer and wild boar **hunting** in the Bavarian forests, apply for a license at the German Hunting Association (Deutscher Jägerverband, Drachenfelsstrasse 3, Bonn). **Hiking** is a major Bavarian pastime, especially as you approach the Alps. Just 97 kilometres from Munich, Garmisch-Partenkirchen, the principal resort, provides guides for **mountain climbing.** There are plenty of peaks to tackle, including the 9,721-foot Zugspitze.

Once you're in the Alps, all the **winter sports** are at your disposal. In addition to skiing (and a very professional ski school), Garmisch has its own Olympic rink for skating and ice hockey. For the more sedate, there's curling; for the less constrained, a bobsleigh run.

Dining Out

Eating and drinking in Bavaria in general, and in Munich in particular, are major occupations. Conviviality reigns supreme, both in the high temples of gastronomy and at the long, communal tables of the Bräuhaus and Gaststätte*.

Meal Times

Lunch *(Mittagessen)* is usually served from 11.30 a.m. to 2 p.m., dinner *(Abendessen)* from 6.30 to 8.30 (to 10.30 or 11 in large establishments). Most Germans like to eat their main meal in the middle of the day. They generally prefer a light supper *(Abendbrot,* or "evening bread") at night, consisting of cold meats and cheeses with the possible addition of a salad.

Where to Eat

With its great prosperity and tradition of good living, Munich has more refined *Restaurants* than might be expected by those who prejudge German cuisine as heavy and unimaginative. Most of them are situated in Maximilianstrasse, Residenzstrasse and Theati-

---

* For a comprehensive guide to dining out in Germany, consult the Berlitz EUROPEAN MENU READER.

nerstrasse, along Schwabing's Leopoldstrasse and in Prinzregentenstrasse at the southern end of the Englischer Garten. Some of the better establishments are combined with high-quality delicatessens.

Munich's growing sophistication is such that elegance, however casual, is more important than the old formality of ties for men or skirts for women. It's a good idea to reserve in advance at the smarter places. Service (15%) is already included in the bill, but no one has ever been known to refuse a little extra.

Niceties of dress and advance reservations are not a problem at the more popular *Gaststätte* or *Bräuhaus,* literally "brewery", but actually a beer hall. These establishments usually serve full meals as well as beer, though not always in every section of the bigger halls. All the great breweries operate their own beer halls in Munich, and beer gardens, too, many of them with brass bands. In the inner city, the beer halls also have an open-air *Bierkeller.* The Englischer Garten's popular beer gardens are to be found at the Chinese Tower, at the Hirschau and beside the Kleinhesseloher See.

Weinstuben (taverns), less numerous in the beer country of Bavaria than in other regions of Germany, serve open wine by the glass—rather than by the carafe or bottle. Taverns also provide meals.

In a separate category is the *Konditorei* (café-cum-pastry shop), the bourgeois fairyland where you can spend a whole afternoon reading newspapers attached to rods. This is just the place to stuff yourself with pastry, ice-cream, coffee, tea and fruit juices, even a good selection of wines. Most provide a limited selection of egg dishes, light snacks and salads.

Local Customs
In a Gaststätte or Bräuhaus, you'll sometimes come across a sign on one of the long tables proclaiming *"Stammtisch".* This means the seats have been reserved for regulars—club, firm or big family. It is otherwise customary for strangers to sit together, usually with a polite query as to whether one of the six or seven empty places is *"frei".* Fellow diners usually wish each other *"Mahlzeit"* or *"Guten Appetit".*

It may come as a surprise that each bread roll *(Semmel)* is charged separately; you're expected to keep a count of how many you've eaten.

But we mustn't forget Munich's myriad ethnic restaurants: French, Italian, Greek and Balkan. The city also has its quota of fast-food chains.

Breakfast *(Frühstück)*
Germans start the day with a meal that is somewhat more substantial than the typical "Continental" breakfast. The distinctive touch is the selection of cold meats—ham, salami and liver sausage (liverwurst)—and cheese served with the bread. Not just one kind of bread, but brown (rye with caraway seeds), rich black (pumpernickel) and white. If you like boiled eggs, try *Eier im Glas,* two four-minute eggs served whole, already shelled, in a glass dish. Gone the problem of whether to crumble or guillotine the top of your eggshell. And with it all comes tea, hot chocolate or coffee that's stronger than the Anglo-American brew, but weaker than the French or Italian.

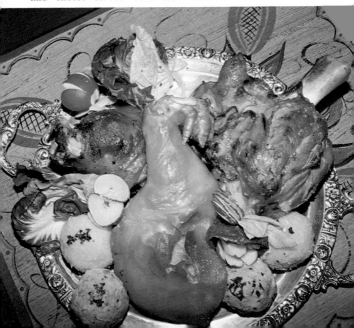

Soups and Starters

Bavarians make excellent *Leberknödlsuppe*, a soup with spicy dumplings of flour, bread crumbs, beef liver, onions, marjoram and garlic. *Kartoffelsuppe* contains potato, celery, leeks and parsnips. Other soups are made with beans *(Bohnensuppe)* or lentils *(Linsensuppe)*, often with pieces of sausage.

If you prefer an hors d'œuvre to a soup, try smoked calf's tongue served with a little horseradish sauce *(Kalbszüngerl)* or pork tongue boiled with juniper berries, bay leaves and peppercorns, accompanied by a small portion of sauerkraut *(Schweinszüngerl im Kraut)*.

Bavarian Specialties

The pig and the calf dominate Bavarian main dishes, often in combination. Pork or veal can either be pot-roasted *(Kalbs-* or *Schweinsbraten)* or grilled on a spit *(Kalbs-* or *Schweinshaxen)* with a marvellous crispy, crackling skin. The ultimate in delicious roasts is *Spanferkel*, suckling pig.

Bavarian food is rich, whether it be suckling pig or chocolate cake.

For a royal change, when in season, sample the excellent game—venison, hare, partridge and pheasant. The venison is usually carefully marinated till tender and served with sweet raisin or red currant sauce or a purée of chestnuts. The best of the local freshwater fish are trout *(Forelle)*, **97**

unbeatable when boiled absolutely fresh *(blau)*, or whitefish *(Renke)*, usually fried.

Accompanying it all is a crisp, green salad or those Bavarian staples, the potato and the cabbage. Choose an old stand-by like sautéed potatoes *(Bratkartoffeln)* or the excellent potato salad *(Kartoffelsalat)*. Cabbage of course means *Sauerkraut*, often beautifully prepared in white wine with juniper berries, caraway seeds and cloves. But there's also the sweet-and-sour red cabbage, *Blaukraut*, done with apples, raisins and white vinegar, or a good green cabbage salad *(Weisskrautsalat)*.

Snacks

Given the importance of beer-drinking in Munich's social life, snacks *(Schmankerl)* are correspondingly important to aid and abet a thirst for beer. Also to keep drinkers "afloat", so to speak. You eat them at any time of day.

Local people favour sausages of all kinds as a snack food. Pork and veal join forces in the *Weisswürste* (white sausages), flavoured with pepper, parsley and onions. The best establishments—and in this case we mean the most observant of traditional standards—never serve *Weisswürste* in the afternoon. They're no longer fresh enough for the discerning palate, i.e. a Bavarian. *Bratwurst*, another sausage staple, is made of pork and grilled or sautéed. The best are the little ones sent down fraternally from Nuremberg. You may also enjoy the spicy *Blutwurst* (blood sausage) or *Leberwurst* (liver sausage or liverwurst).

You should also be on the look-out for a delicious but misleading snack called *Leberkäs*. Literally, this means "liver-cheese", but has neither liver nor cheese in it, being rather a mixture of pork, bacon and beef, spiced with nutmeg, marjoram and onions and eaten hot or cold. Other great snacks include: *Reiberdatschi*, deep-fried potato pancakes; *Obatzta*, a spicy mixture of creamy cheeses with chives, paprika, caraway seeds, salt and pepper; and thin slices of horseradish *(Radi)*.

Failing any of these, stimulate your thirst with the salty pretzels *(Bretzel)*.

Desserts

Apart from a couple of regional variations on apple cake *(Apfelkücherl)*, and plum cake *(Zwetschgendatschi)*, Bavarians are quite happy to join in the national orgy of Konditorei pastries. *Schwarzwälder Kirschtorte*, the cherry cake from the Black Forest and *Apfelstrudel* from Vienna are very welcome treats.

Wines

Bavaria stopped making good wine centuries ago, but Munich restaurants offer an excellent array of Rhine and Mosel wines, mostly white. Here's a guide to the best German vintages:

The most highly reputed Rhine wines are those of the Rheingau, the pick of the crop being *Schloss Johannisberger*, *Hattenheimer*, *Kloster Eberbacher* and *Rüdesheimer*. The next best come from the more southerly vineyards, the famous *Liebfraumilch*, *Niersteiner*, *Domtal* and *Oppenheimer*. Next in quality are the Mittelrhein wines from Bingen, Bacharach, Boppard and Oberwesel.

The Mosel wines, bottled in green glass to distinguish them from the brown Rhine bottles, enjoy a delicate reputation through the fame of the *Bernkasteler*, *Piesporter* and *Zeltinger*.

Germany also produces a very respectable sparkling, champagne-like wine called *Sekt*, from the Rheingau region of Eltville and Hochheim. (The latter provides the English gentleman with his all-purpose name for German white wines, "hock".)

Beer

Bavarians appreciate the old saying that there's good beer and better beer, but there's no bad beer. Not in Bavaria.

Beer *vom Fass* (on tap) can be ordered by the half-litre in restaurants, but elsewhere often only in a one-litre tankard known as the *Masskrug* or simply *"Mass"*. Bottled beer comes in several varieties: *Export*, light and smooth; *Pils*, light and strong; and *Bock*, dark and rich.

Bavarian beer is generally lighter than other German beers, but it has its strong forms, too. If you like it dark with a slightly sweet, malt flavour, order *Dunkles*. This is not served as cold as the more popular light brew, *Helles*, with an inviting mist on the glass.

Other Drinks

If you just want to be refreshed, rather than stimulated, you'll find an unusually wide assortment of fruit juices, the best being *Johannisbeersaft* (red or black currant), *Apfelsaft* (apple) and *Traubensaft* (grape—non-alcoholic).

Keeping It Flowing

Most of the time, there are enough big festivals to keep the beer flowing steadily down the Bavarian gullet. But Munich brewers can't bear slack periods.

In the third and fourth weeks before Easter, the so-called *Starkbierzeit* (Strong-beer Time), they stage beer festivals to promote their *Märzenbier* (March Ale). After Easter comes the *Maibockzeit*, when they push the strong dark stuff. In the summer, everybody's thirsty enough not to need too much prompting.

Then comes the Oktoberfest (see p. 90), the ultimate in beer festivals, when every brewery participates in a colourful parade of horse-drawn wagons. Christmas and Fasching (carnival) tide the poor brewers over till it's time again for *Märzenbier.* In Munich every day's a holiday for beer.

To Help You Order...

Could I/we have a table?	**Ich hätte/Wir hatten gerne einen Tisch.**
Waiter/waitress, please!	**Ober/Fräulein, bitte.**
The check, please.	**Zahlen, bitte.**
I would like...	**Ich möchte gerne...**

beer	**ein Bier**	menu	**die Karte**
bread	**etwas Brot**	milk	**Milch**
butter	**etwas Butter**	mineral water	**Mineralwasser**
cheese	**Käse**	mustard	**etwas Senf**
coffee	**einen Kaffee**	potatoes	**Kartoffeln**
cold cuts	**Aufschnitt**	saccharin	**Süssstoff**
dessert	**eine Nachspeise**	salad	**Salat**
eggs	**Eier**	salt	**Salz**
fish	**Fisch**	soup	**eine Suppe**
fruit	**Obst**	sugar	**Zucker**
hors d'œuvre	**eine Vorspeise**	tea	**einen Tee**
ice-cream	**Eiskrem**	vegetables	**Gemüse**
lemon	**Zitrone**	whipped cream	**Schlagsahne**
meat	**Fleisch**	wine	**Wein**

...and Read the Menu

Apfel	apple	**Lachs**	salmon
Blumenkohl	cauliflower	**Lamm**	lamb
Bohnen	green beans	**Nierchen**	kidneys
Braten	roast beef	**Nudeln**	noodles
Ente	duck	**Pilze**	mushrooms
Erdbeeren	strawberries	**Radi/Kren**	horse-radish
Geselchtes	smoked meat	**Reis**	rice
Gurkensalat	cucumber salad	**Rindfleisch**	beef
Hühnchen	chicken	**Rippchen**	smoked pork chops
Jägerschnitzel	cutlet with mushroom sauce	**Rollmops**	marinated herring
Kalbfleisch	veal	**Schinken**	ham
Klösse	dumplings	**Schweinefleisch**	pork
Kraut	cabbage	**Spargel**	asparagus
Kraftbrühe	bouillon	**Wild**	game
Krautwickerl	stuffed cabbage	**Wurst**	sausage
Kuchen	cake	**Zwiebeln**	onions

BLUEPRINT for a Perfect Trip

How to Get There

Because of the complexity and variability of the many fares, you should ask the advice of an informed travel agent well before departure.

BY AIR

Scheduled flights

Munich airport (see also p. 107) is served by many European and some intercontinental flights. However, the main airport for transatlantic flights is Frankfurt, from where there are daily direct flights to Munich. Average journey time from London to Munich is 1½ hours, from New York 9 hours.

Charter flights and package tours

From the U.K. and Ireland: A variety of combinations is offered for stays of a weekend to six nights or longer. Many tours include accommodation, breakfast, sightseeing tours of the city or nearby towns and free admission to museums and galleries in Munich. Budget packages are available from the Munich tourist office under the "Key to Munich" scheme. Contact any travel agency or the tourist office itself (see pp. 122–23).

From North America: Several packages to Germany and Austria feature Munich. These all-inclusive tours provide transport, hotel accommodation, tranfers, baggage handling, taxes and tips, meals as specified in each itinerary, some or all sightseeing and the services of an English-speaking guide.

BY ROAD

Munich can be reached by motorway (expressway) from nearly anywhere in Europe (Brussels–Munich 815 km./505 miles, Basle 394 km./244 miles, Hamburg 795 km./493 miles). If you don't want to drive on the *autobahn,* but would like to enjoy the nature and culture along the way, you can contact your automobile association and get help to plan a suitable route. Those not in a rush might like to follow the Rhine from Koblenz down to Mainz, for some of Germany's most pleasurable scenery, before branching off on the autobahn No. 11 to Munich.

Numerous tour operators in Germany and abroad offer **coach tours** to Munich all year round. Reservations must be booked in advance. The journey from London to Munich direct takes approximately 24 hours.

BY RAIL

Potential rail travellers will find information on trains and reduced-price tickets on pp. 124–125. There are numerous trains a day from

London to Munich via Dover and Ostend, a journey of 17 hours. The service via Harwich and the Hook of Holland (20 hours) is direct, but passengers on the night train must change in Cologne. In the season there's a *Train Auto Couchettes* from Paris to Munich. Seats or sleepers should be booked a couple of days in advance.

When you book your train, you might think of the **rail/road** possibility, where you pick up a rental car at the station on arrival.

When to Go

Whatever the season, Munich has something to offer the visitor. There are, of course, the well-publicized Oktoberfest celebrations in late September and the revelry of Fasching (Carnival) in January. But Munich has many attractions more, from the superb collections of the Alte Pinakothek and Residenzmuseum to the abundance of fine shops and restaurants in streets like Theatinerstrasse. Music events are scheduled year-round, including a season of Mozart operas from December to February and the Münchner Festspiele in July and August. No matter when you visit the capital of Bavaria, there's always a great deal to see and do.

The following chart shows Munich's average daytime temperatures:

	J	F	M	A	M	J	J	A	S	O	N	D
°F	34	37	48	57	64	70	73	73	68	55	45	35
°C	1	3	9	14	18	21	23	23	20	13	7	2

Planning Your Budget

To give you an idea of what to expect, here's a list of average prices in marks (DM). They can only be approximate, however, as even in West Germany inflation creeps relentlessly up.

Airport transfer. Bus to central railway station DM 5, taxi DM 30.

Baby-sitters. DM 10–15 per hour.

Camping. DM 15–18 for two persons with car and tent or caravan (trailer).

Car hire. *Ford Fiesta* DM 65 per day, DM 0.49 per kilometre, DM 687 per week with unlimited mileage. *Opel Kadett L* DM 81 per day, DM 0.62 per kilometre, DM 845 per week with unlimited mileage. *BMW 316* DM 124 per day, DM 1.05 per km., DM 1,404 per week with unlimited mileage. Tax included.

Cigarettes. DM 3.50–4.00 per packet of 20.

Entertainment. Cinema DM 8–12, theatre DM 15–50, discotheque DM 15–30, nightclub DM 20–100.

Hairdressers. *Woman's* haircut DM 15–40, shampoo and set DM 20–50, blow-dry DM 15–25, permanent wave DM 50–70. *Man's* haircut DM 10–25.

Hotels (double room per night). Luxury class DM 300–450, first class DM 230–400, medium class 120–180, budget class DM 90–120. *Boarding house* DM 60–90.

Meals and drinks. Continental breakfast DM 6–10, lunch or dinner in fairly good establishment DM 20–30, bottle of wine (German) DM 20–40, beer (small bottle) DM 2.30–3, soft drinks (small bottle) DM 2.20, coffee DM 2.20–5.

Museums. DM 1–5 (often free).

Shopping bag. 1 kg. of bread DM 3, 250 g. of butter DM 2.60, 6 eggs DM 1.60, 1 kg. of hamburger meat DM 13, ½ kg. of coffee DM 10, 100 g. of instant coffee DM 7, ½ litre of beer DM 1.20, 1 litre of soft drink DM 1–1.40.

Taxis. Initial charge DM 2.90, plus DM 1.50 per km within centre of Munich.

Youth hostels. Single rooms (where available) DM 23–39, double rooms per person DM 20–37, four-bed rooms DM 10–15 per person. Breakfast included.

An A–Z Summary of Practical Information and Facts

> A star (*) following an entry indicates that relevant prices are to be found on p. 105.
>
> Listed after many entries is the appropriate German translation, usually in the singular, plus a number of phrases that should help you when seeking assistance.

A

ACCOMMODATION*. See also CAMPING. The Munich tourist offices provide a free multi-lingual list with full details of amenities and prices of accommodation in the city. They also operate a hotel-booking service at the airport and at the central railway station (no telephone calls) for a small charge; note that part of the room rate must be paid in advance. For a wider selection, consult the *German Hotel Guide*, distributed free by the German National Tourist Board (see TOURIST INFORMATION OFFICES). During the summer, at weekends and in periods with special events, it is advisable to book well ahead. The Allgemeine Deutsche Zimmerreservierung (ADZ) operates a computer reservation system at:

Beethovenstrasse 61, D-6000 Frankfurt am Main: tel. (069) 74 07 67

In addition to hotels, there are inns *(Gasthof)* and boarding houses *(Pension)*. The tourist office can arrange for accommodation in private homes—a nice way to get to know the local people. If you are touring Bavaria by car, look out for "Zimmer frei" (room to let) signs.

A list of hotels and inns in Upper Bavaria is available from Fremdenverkehrsverband München-Oberbayern:

Sonnenstrasse 10/III, D-8000 München 2; tel. (089) 59 73 47/48

Youth hostels. If you are planning to make extensive use of youth hostels during your stay in Munich, obtain an international membership card from your national youth hostel association before departure. For full information about hostels in West Germany, contact the German Youth Hostel Association *(Deutsches Jugendherbergswerk—DJH):*

Bülowstrasse 26, D-4930 Detmold

The above-mentioned organization maintains the following hostels in and around Munich:

DJH München, Wendl-Dietrich-Strasse 20
Jugendgästehaus Thalkirchen, Miesingstrasse 4
Jugendherberge Burg Schwaneck, Burgweg 4–6, D-8023 Pullach

Further possibilities:

Christlicher Verein Junger Männer (YMCA), Landwehrstrasse 13
Haus International, Elisabethstrasse 87 (Schwabing)

I'd like a single room/double room.	**Ich hätte gern ein Einzelzimmer/ Doppelzimmer.**
with bath/shower	**mit Bad/Dusche**
What's the rate per night/week?	**Wieviel kostet es pro Nacht/ Woche?**

AIRPORT* *(Flughafen)*. München-Riem Airport, about 10 kilometres east of the city centre, handles domestic and international flights. You will find banks, car hire desks, restaurants, coffee bars, news- and souvenir-stands, a post office, hairdresser, hotel reservation desk, tourist information office and duty-free shop.

Ground transport. Taxis, buses and suburban trains *(S-Bahn)* shuttle between the airport and the main railway station *(Hauptbahnhof)*. Buses leave from outside the airport arrival hall at frequent intervals. For the return journey to the airport, catch the bus outside the railway station in Arnulfstrasse. The trip takes about 20 minutes. At night, buses run as required.

If you're taking the S-Bahn, get on No. 6 (Tutzing–Erding) from the Hauptbahnhof and change at Riem station to the airport shuttle service (bus No. 37).

Airport information, tel. 92 11 21 27

Lufthansa (Germany's national airline) reservation desks can be reached by dialling 5 11 38.

BICYCLE HIRE *(Fahrradverleih)*. It's not a good idea to ride bikes or mopeds in the city; the pace of Munich traffic is just too fast and furious. Pedal around the English Garden instead. There are bikes for hire on weekends and holidays at the Königinstrasse/Veterinärstrasse entrance. Or ask at the tourist office about special cycle routes.

It's also pleasant to tour the countryside around Munich by bike. Many train and S-Bahn stations in the small outlying towns and villages provide a year-round bicycle hire service. A list of participating stations *(Fahrradbahnhof)* is available at ticket counters and tourist offices. In some places, you can hire a bicycle at one station and return

B it to another. Suggested itineraries are indicated on notice boards at the stations. Railway passengers hiring bikes are entitled to a special discount.

Are there bicycles for hire at this station?	**Kann man an diesem Bahnhof Fahrräder mieten?**
May I return it to another station?	**Kann ich es an einem anderen Bahnhof zurückgeben?**

C **CAMPING★.** Four major campsites are situated within the city limits:

Langwieder See, Eschenrieder Strasse 119 (north-west, along the Augsburg–Stuttgart motorway), open April 1–mid-October.

Campingplatz München-**Ludwigsfeld,** Dachauer Strasse 571 (north-west, on the road to Dachau), open year-round.

München-**Obermenzing,** Lochhausener Strasse 59 (north-west, along the Augsburg–Stuttgart motorway), open mid-March–early November.

Campingplatz München-**Thalkirchen,** Zentralländstrasse 49 (on the Isar river, opposite the Zoo), open mid-March–end-October.

From the end of June through August, the city of Munich runs a campsite for youths, **Jugendlager Kapuzinerhölzl,** at Franz-Schrank-Strasse. A tent large enough for 300 people is set up; bring a sleeping bag and air mattress.

Sites are indicated by the international blue sign with a black tent on a white background. Some sites give reductions to members of the International Camping Association.

For full information about sites and facilities, consult the guides published by the German Automobile Club ADAC or the German Camping Club *(Deutscher Camping-Club—DCC):*

Mandlstrasse 28, D-8000 München 40; tel. (089) 33 40 21

If you camp off the beaten track, be sure to obtain the permission of the proprietor or the police, and note that camping in the rest-areas off the motorways is not permitted.

May we camp here?	**Dürfen wir hier zelten?**
Is there a campsite nearby?	**Gibt es in der Nähe einen Zeltplatz?**

CAR HIRE★ *(Autovermietung).* See also DRIVING. You can arrange to hire a car immediately upon arrival at Munich's airport or central railway station. Otherwise enquire at your hotel or refer to the yellow pages of the telephone directory for addresses of leading firms. It's usually possible to have a car delivered to your hotel if you wish. Larger firms allow you to return cars to another European city for an extra fee. Special weekend and weekly unlimited mileage rates are usually available. Many airlines offer fly/drive holidays to Munich, and the German Federal Railways promote a "Rail-and-Road" car-hire programme.

To hire a car, you'll need a valid driving licence held for at least half a year; the minimum age is 18. Normally a deposit is charged, but holders of major credit cards are exempt.

CIGARETTES, CIGARS, TOBACCO* *(Zigaretten, Zigarren, Tabak)*.

Foreign cigarette brands (manufactured under German licence) and a wide range of cigars and tobacco are sold in specialized tobacco shops, at kiosks and from vending machines. Most of the domestic makes resemble American cigarettes, but there are some with coarser tobacco.

As a rule, smoking is prohibited in theatres, cinemas, buses and trams. Trains have special smoking compartments.

A packet of …	**Eine Schachtel …**
A box of matches, please.	**Eine Schachtel Streichhölzer, bitte.**

CLOTHING.

Munich's climate can go to extremes—from bitter-cold to hot and muggy. During the winter months, you'll need a heavy coat and warm clothing. In summer, lightweight garments are in order. Bring along a bathing suit, too, particularly if you want to take the sun in the English Garden—except, of course, for that restricted area by the river where you need nothing at all. A light wrap can come in handy on cool summer evenings. It may rain in spring and summer, so be prepared with a raincoat or umbrella.

At better hotels and restaurants, more formal clothes are expected, but there are few places where a tie is obligatory.

COMMUNICATIONS

Post offices. Munich's central post office stands just opposite the main railway station, on Bahnhofplatz 1. It remains open 24 hours a day to deal with mail, telegrams and telephone calls. A telex service and currency exchange desk operate from 7 a.m. to 11 p.m.

Branch offices of Germany's Bundespost are generally open from 8 a.m. to 6 p.m., Monday to Friday (till noon on Saturdays). They also handle telegrams and telephone calls.

C

Mail boxes are painted yellow with a black post-horn. Stamps can be purchased at yellow vending machines near mail boxes and at some tobacconists and stationers.

Poste restante (general delivery). This service is taken care of by Munich's central post office: if you have mail addressed to you c/o *Hauptpostlagernd*, it will automatically arrive at the central post office. Be sure to take your passport or identity card when you go to collect your mail.

Telegrams. Go in person to a post office or phone in messages from your hotel or any private telephone (dial 1131). Night letters at a reduced rate for a minimum of 22 words can only be sent overseas.

Telephone. Telephone booths, glass boxes with yellow frames, bear a sign showing a black receiver in a yellow square (national calls) or a green square (national and international calls). Area code numbers are listed in a special telephone book. Communications within Germany and to neighbouring countries are cheaper from 6 p.m. to 8 a.m. weekdays and all day Saturday and Sunday. Calls placed by hotels and restaurants generally carry a considerable surcharge.

Some useful numbers:

Enquiries: domestic 1188, international 00118
Operator: domestic 010, international 0010

A stamp for this letter/postcard, please.	**Eine Briefmarke für diesen Brief/ diese Karte, bitte.**
express (special delivery)	**Eilzustellung**
airmail	**Luftpost**
registered	**Eingeschrieben**
Have you received any mail for ...?	**Ist Post da für ...?**
I want to send a telegram to ...	**Ich möchte ein Telegramm nach ... aufgeben.**
Can I use the telephone?	**Kann ich das Telefon benutzen?**
Can you get me this number in ...	**Können Sie mich mit dieser Nummer in ... verbinden?**
reverse-charge (collect) call	**R-Gespräch**
personal (person-to-person) call	**Gespräch mit Voranmeldung**

COMPLAINTS. If something goes wrong that you cannot take care of yourself, report the matter to the Munich tourist office.

In hotels and restaurants, discuss any problems with the proprietor or manager. If you fail to obtain satisfaction on the spot, contact the Bayerischer Hotel- und Gaststättenverband:

Türkenstrasse 7; tel. 23 68 050

Department stores provide a special counter *(Kundendienst)* to deal with customers' complaints.

If you have a problem with taxi service, call 77 30 77.

CONSULATES *(Konsulat)*

Canada	Maximiliansplatz 9, München 2; tel. 55 85 31
Eire	Mauerkircherstrasse 1a, München 80; tel. 98 57 23/25
South Africa	Sendlinger-Tor-Platz 5, München 2; tel. 260 50 81
United Kingdom	Amalienstrasse 62, München 40; tel. 39 40 15/19
U.S.A.	Königinstrasse 5, München 22; tel. 2 30 11

CRIME and THEFT. Compared to most urban centres, Munich's crime rate is quite low. Nonetheless it's advisable to take all the normal precautions. Don't leave money or valuables in your car or hotel room. Lock them in the hotel safe instead. If you are robbed, report the incident to the hotel receptionist and the nearest police station. The police will provide you with a certificate to present to your insurance company, or to your consulate if your passport has been stolen.

I want to report a theft.	**Ich möchte einen Diebstahl melden.**
My handbag/wallet/my passport has been stolen.	**Meine Handtasche/Brieftasche/ mein Pass ist gestohlen worden.**

CUSTOMS *(Zoll)* **and ENTRY REGULATIONS.** For a stay of up to three months, a valid passport is sufficient for citizens of Australia, Canada, New Zealand, South Africa and U.S.A. Visitors from Eire and the United Kingdom need only an identity card to enter West Germany.

The chart on p. 112 shows what you can take into West Germany duty free and, when returning home, into your own country:

C

111

C

Entering West Germany from:	Cigarettes		Cigars		Tobacco	Spirits	Wine
1)	200	or	50	or	250 g.	1 l. and 2 l.	
2)	300	or	75	or	400 g.	1.5 l. and 5 l.	
3)	400	or	100	or	500 g.	1 l. and 2 l.	
Into:							
Canada	200	and	50	and	900 g.	1.1 l. or 1.1 l.	
Eire	200	or	50	or	250 g.	1 l. and 2 l.	
U.K.	200	or	50	or	250 g.	1 l. and 2 l.	
U.S.A.	200	and	100	and	4)	1 l. or 1 l.	

1) EEC countries with goods bought tax free, and other European countries
2) EEC countries with goods not bought tax free
3) countries outside Europe
4) a reasonable quantity

Currency restrictions. There are no restrictions on the import or export of marks or any other currency.

I've nothing to declare.	**Ich habe nichts zu verzollen.**
It's for personal use.	**Es ist für meinen persönlichen Gebrauch.**

D **DRIVING IN GERMANY**

Entering Germany. To bring your car into Germany you will need:

- a national (or international for those coming from the U.S.A., Australia, South Africa) driving licence
- car registration papers
- a national identity sticker for your car and a red warning triangle in case of breakdown, as well as a first-aid kit

Insurance. Third-party insurance is compulsory. Visitors from abroad, except those from EEC and certain other European countries, will have to present their international insurance certificate (Green Card) or take out third-party insurance at the German border. Seat belts are obligatory, and that includes back-seat passengers if the car is so equipped. If you don't wear them, insurance companies reduce compensation in the event of an accident.

Driving conditions. Traffic jams, lack of parking space, pedestrian areas and one-way streets make driving in Munich a frustrating experience. It's better by far to get around town by public transport, reserving your car for excursions out of the city. Bear in mind that bottlenecks form on major approach roads into Munich at the beginning and end of peak holiday periods. Munich seems to catch most of the North German traffic en route to the Alps and Italian destinations.

Drive on the right, pass on the left. Traffic in Germany follows the same basic rules that apply in most countries, though some may differ:

- on the Autobahn (motorway, expressway): 1) passing another vehicle on the right is prohibited; 2) cars with caravans (trailers) are not allowed to overtake on certain stretches (watch for signs); 3) should police or emergency vehicles need to pass through a traffic jam (*Stau*), cars in the right lane must keep close to the right, and those in the left lane close to the left, thereby opening a passageway down the middle.

- in the absence of traffic lights, stop or yield signs, vehicles coming from the right have priority at intersections, unless otherwise indicated

- at roundabouts (traffic circles), approaching cars must give way to traffic already in mid-stream, unless otherwise indicated

- trams must be passed on the right and never at a stop (unless there's a traffic island)

- at dusk, and in case of bad visibility, headlights or dipped headlights must be used; driving with parking lights only is forbidden, even in built-up areas

Speed limits. The speed limit is 100 kilometres per hour (62 mph) on all open roads except for motorways and dual carriageways (divided highways), where there's no limit unless otherwise indicated (the suggested maximum speed is 130 kph, or 81 mph). In town, speed is restricted to 50 kph (31 mph). Cars towing caravans may not exceed 80 kph (50 mph).

Traffic police (see also POLICE) may confiscate the car keys of persons they consider unfit to drive. Drinking and driving, for example, is a very serious offence in Germany. The permissible level of alcohol in the blood is 0.8 per mille (millilitres), or about two glasses of beer. Be careful, too, to stay within speed limits; the police are getting more and more strict, and radar is used both inside and out of towns.

113

D **Breakdowns.** In the event of a breakdown on the Autobahn and other important roads, use one of the emergency telephones located every second kilometre (the nearest one is indicated by a small arrow on the reflector poles at the roadside). Ask for *Strassenwacht*, a service run jointly by the German automobile clubs ADAC *(Allgemeiner Deutscher Automobil Club)* and AvD *(Automobilclub von Deutschland)*. Assistance is free; towing and spare parts have to be paid for.

For round-the-clock breakdown service, call 19211.

Fuel and oil *(Benzin; Öl).* You'll find service stations everywhere, many of them self-service. It's customary to tip attendants for any extra attention.

Fluid measures

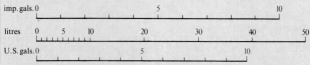

Road signs. Most road signs employed in West Germany are international pictographs, but here are some written ones you might come across:

Einbahnstrasse	One-way street
Einordnen	Get into lane
Fussgänger	Pedestrians
Kurzparkzone	Short-term parking
Links fahren	Keep left
Parken verboten	No parking
Schlechte Fahrbahn	Poor road surface
Strassenarbeiten	Road works (Men working)
Umleitung	Diversion (Detour)
Vorsicht	Caution

(International) Driving Licence	**(Internationaler) Führerschein**
Car Registration Papers	**Kraftfahrzeugpapiere**
Green Card	**Grüne Karte**
Where's the nearest car park?	**Wo ist der nächste Parkplatz?**
Full tank, please.	**Bitte volltanken.**
Check the oil/tires/battery, please.	**Kontrollieren Sie bitte das Öl/ die Reifen/die Batterie.**
I've had a breakdown.	**Ich habe eine Panne.**
There's been an accident.	**Es ist ein Unfall passiert.**

ELECTRIC CURRENT. West Germany has 220–250-volt, 50-cycle AC. Plugs are the standard continental type, for which British and North American appliances need an adaptor.

EMERGENCIES. See also under CONSULATES, DRIVING, HEALTH AND MEDICAL CARE OR POLICE according to the type of emergency.

Emergency telephone numbers:

Police	110
Fire	112
Ambulance	1 92 22

If you don't speak German, try English, or ask the first person you see to help you call.

Please, can you place an emergency call for me to the …?	**Würden Sie bitte … für mich anrufen?**
police/fire brigade/hospital	**die Polizei/die Feuerwehr/ das Krankenhaus**

GUIDES and TOURS. The tourist office will put you in touch with qualified guides and interpreters if you want a personally conducted tour or need linguistic assistance.

City sightseeing tours by bus start from the main entrance of the central railway station. Choose from the variety of different tours on offer, according to your interests. Daily excursions by coach to outlying towns and villages are also organized; enquire at the tourist office for details.

HAIRDRESSERS* *(Damenfriseur)* and **BARBERS** *(Herrenfriseur).* Munich is well supplied with hairdressing establishments. Prices rise to *haute coiffure* levels in elegant Maximilianstrasse or trendy Schwabing; elsewhere in the city, salons are more likely to be moderate. Rates are often displayed in the window. Most establishments close on Saturday afternoons and all day Monday. It's always a good idea to telephone in advance for an appointment. You should tip 10 to 15%.

I'd like a shampoo and set.	**Waschen und Legen, bitte.**
haircut	**Schneiden**
shave	**Rasieren**
blow-dry (brushing)	**mit dem Fön trocknen**
Don't cut it too short.	**Schneiden Sie es nicht zu kurz.**
A little more off (here).	**(Hier) etwas kürzer.**

H **HEALTH and MEDICAL CARE.** Ask your insurance company before leaving home if you are covered for medical treatment in Germany. Visitors who are not reimbursed for medical bills abroad can take out a short-term holiday policy before setting out. Citizens of European Community countries may use the German Health Services for medical treatment. Ask for a copy of the requisite form at your local Health and Social Security Office.

In the event of accident or serious illness, call for an ambulance (222666) or ask the medical emergency service staff (tel. 558661) to recommend a competent doctor. You can also contact the American or British consulates for a list of English-speaking doctors and dentists.

It is perfectly safe to drink the tap water in West Germany; only rarely will you see the sign "Kein Trinkwasser" (usually on public squares).

Pharmacies are open during normal shopping hours. At night and on Sundays and holidays, all chemists display the address of the nearest one open.

Where's the nearest (all-night) pharmacy?	**Wo ist die nächste (Dienst-) Apotheke?**
I need a doctor/dentist.	**Ich brauche einen Arzt/Zahnarzt.**
I have a pain here.	**Ich habe hier Schmerzen.**
stomach ache	**Magenschmerzen**
headache	**Kopfschmerzen**
a fever	**Fieber**
medical emergency service	**Ärztlicher Notdienst**
ambulance	**Rettungsdienst**
hospital	**Krankenhaus**

HITCH-HIKING. There are no laws or regulations prohibiting hitch-hiking, but there's little to encourage it: you'll be lucky if anyone stops for you. In Bavaria, it is permitted to thumb rides at the entrance of access roads to the Autobahn. However, it is strictly forbidden on the Autobahn itself.

Student associations can often arrange for inter-city trips *(Mitfahrgelegenheit)*; try the Mitfahrer-Zentrale at Lämmerstrasse 4 (near the central railway station) or the Känguruh at Amalienstrasse 87.

HOURS. See also under COMMUNICATIONS and MONEY MATTERS.

Museum hours vary, but are usually from 9 a.m. to 4 p.m. Most museums close on Mondays, others on Saturdays and/or Sundays. For exact time-tables, consult the official *Monatsprogramm* or enquire at the tourist office.

Restaurant meals. Breakfast is served until 10 a.m., lunch from noon to 2 p.m. and dinner from 6 to 9.30 p.m.

Shops are generally open from 8.30 or 9 a.m. to 6.30 p.m., Monday to Friday, till 2 p.m. (some only till 12.30) on Saturdays (until 6 p.m. on the first Saturday of the month). Shops outside the city centre usually close between 1 and 3 p.m.

Tourist information offices. The airport office operates from 8.30 a.m. to 10 p.m., Monday to Saturday, and from 1 to 9 p.m. on Sundays. The DB-Reisezentrum office in the central railway station opens daily from 6 a.m. to 11 p.m.

LANGUAGE. About one-third of the Munich population speak some form of Bavarian dialect. Real Bavarian is difficult to understand, even for the many northern Germans who live in Munich; but Bavarians can often be persuaded to speak something closer to High ("normal") German. English is widely understood and spoken, but don't take it for granted. Most of the larger shops, however, have English-speaking staff.

When entering a shop, it's customary to say *Guten Tag* (Good Day) or *Grüss Gott* ("God greet you"), the latter being widely used in Bavaria. When leaving, say *Auf Wiedersehen* (Good-bye); the less formal *Servus*, meaning "Bye" or "See you soon", is a privilege of the autochthons.

The Berlitz phrase book GERMAN FOR TRAVELLERS covers most of the situations you are likely to encounter in Germany, and the German-English/English-German pocket dictionary contains a special menu-reader supplement.

Do you speak English? **Sprechen Sie Englisch?**

LAUNDRY and DRY-CLEANING. Having your laundry washed or cleaned by the hotel is of course the quickest and most convenient method, but prices are correspondingly high; it is therefore worth seeking out a laundromat *(Waschsalon)* or neighbourhood dry-cleaners. Dry-cleaning usually takes two days. Some cleaners offer a quick-service *(Schnellreinigung)* which takes a minimum of two hours and is slightly more expensive.

L **LOST PROPERTY.** Munich's general lost-property office *(Fundbüro)* is at Ruppertstrasse 19 (tel. 23 31).

For property lost on trains, contact the Fundbüro at the central railway station, opposite Platform 26 (tel. 128 66 64), or the S-Bahn office at the east railway station *(Ostbahnhof),* tel. 12 88 44 09.

For anything lost in a post office or telephone call box, enquire at the post office, Arnulfstrasse 195 (tel. 126 25 52).

For property lost at or near the airport, call 921 22 63.

I've lost my wallet/my bag/ my passport.	**Ich habe meine Brieftasche/meine Tasche/meinen Pass verloren.**

M **MAPS.** Excellent free maps of Munich are available at the tourist offices, most banks, car-hire firms and bigger hotels. Falk-Verlag, Hamburg, who prepared the maps for this book, publish a detailed map of the city. For the hiker, there is a series called *Kompass Wanderkarten*—on sale in most bookstores—that will keep you on the right track as you wander through Bavaria.

I'd like a street plan of Munich.	**Ich möchte einen Stadtplan von München.**
a road map/hiking map of this region	**eine Strassenkarte/Wanderkarte dieser Gegend**

MEETING PEOPLE. Bavarians are at their most relaxed in traditional taverns and beer gardens. Just take a place at one of the long tables for a meal or a glass of beer, and you'll soon find yourself chatting to new acquaintances. One of the most popular meeting places in Munich itself is the beer garden at the Chinese Tower in the English Garden. Activity here reaches fever pitch on summer weekends. Students have long been attracted to the Schwabing district with its cafés, bars and restaurants. You'll also find lively open-air cafés around Marienplatz, which has been transformed into a pedestrian zone. And then, of course, there are the two great Bavarian festivals, Fasching and the Oktoberfest, both of which provide plenty of opportunities for celebrating with local people from all walks of life.

MONEY MATTERS

Currency. Germany's monetary unit is the *Deutsche Mark (DM).* The mark is divided into 100 *Pfennig (Pf.).*

Coins: 1, 2, 5, 10 and 50 Pf. and DM 1, 2, 5 and 10.

Notes: DM 5, 10, 20, 50, 100, 500 and 1,000.

Banking hours are usually from 8.15 a.m. to 12.30 p.m. and 1.45 to 3.30 p.m., Monday to Friday (Thursday until 5.30 p.m.). Banks at the airport operate daily from 7 or 7.30 a.m. till around 9 p.m. Banking transactions can also be made at the central railway station from 6 a.m. to 11 p.m. every day.

Changing money. Foreign currency can be changed at ordinary banks *(Bank)*, savings banks *(Sparkasse)* and currency exchange offices *(Wechselstube)*. It can also be done at hotels, travel agencies and Munich's central post office, but rates are not as good. The same is true of currency and traveller's cheques changed in shops or restaurants.

Credit cards, traveller's cheques, eurocheques. Traveller's cheques are welcome almost everywhere, and most major hotels and many restaurants and shops accept credit cards. Eurocheques are widely used in West Germany.

I want to change some pounds/dollars.	**Ich möchte Pfund/Dollars wechseln.**
Do you accept traveller's cheques?	**Nehmen Sie Reiseschecks?**
Can I pay with this credit card?	**Kann ich mit dieser Kreditkarte zahlen?**

NEWSPAPERS and MAGAZINES *(Zeitung; Zeitschrift)*. Major British, American and continental newspapers and magazines are on sale at newsagents in the city centre, as well as at larger hotels, the central railway station and airport.

A guide to forthcoming events *(Monatsprogramm)*, published each month, is available at the tourist office, at hotels and news-stands.

There is an English bookshop with a large selection of English paperbacks in Schellingstrasse, near the university. Other sources of English-language books and newspapers are the:

British Council Library, Bruderstrasse 7 (tel. 22 33 26)
Amerika Haus Library, Karolinenplatz 3 (tel. 59 53 67/68)

Have you any English-language newspapers?	**Haben Sie Zeitungen in englischer Sprache?**

PHOTOGRAPHY. Some of the world's best cameras come from West Germany, so you might even think of getting equipped here. All

P brands of film are easily found. Developing usually takes two to three days, but some shops provide overnight service.

Some airport security machines use X-rays which can ruin your film. Ask that it be hand-checked, or enclose it in a lead-lined bag.

I'd like a roll of film for this camera.	**Ich hätte gern einen Film für diesen Apparat.**
black-and-white film	**Schwarzweissfilm**
colour prints	**Farbfilm**
colour slides	**Diafilm**
How long will it take to develop this film?	**Wie lange dauert das Entwickeln?**
May I take a picture (of you)?	**Darf ich (Sie) fotografieren?**

POLICE *(Polizei).* West Germany's police wear green uniforms. You'll see them on white motorcycles or in green-and-white cars.

Street parking in towns is supervised by police officers in dark-blue uniforms. If you are fined, they have the right to ask you to pay on the spot.

The police emergency number is 110.

Munich's central police station *(Polizeipräsidium)* is at Ettstrasse 2.

Where's the nearest police station? **Wo ist die nächste Polizeiwache?**

PUBLIC HOLIDAYS *(Feiertag).* The chart below shows the public holidays celebrated in Bavaria, when shops, banks, official departments and many restaurants are closed. If a holiday falls on a Thursday, many people make it into a long weekend.

On December 24 (Christmas Eve), shops stay open till midday, but most restaurants, theatres, cinemas and concert halls are closed.

Jan. 1	*Neujahr*	New Year's Day
Jan. 6	*Heilige Drei Könige*	Epiphany
May 1	*Tag der Arbeit*	Labour Day
June 17	*Tag der Deutschen Einheit*	Day of National Unity
Aug. 15	*Mariä Himmelfahrt*	Assumption Day
Nov. 1	*Allerheiligen*	All Saints' Day
Dec. 25, 26	*Weihnachten*	Christmas

Movable dates:	Karfreitag	Good Friday
	Ostermontag	Easter Monday
	Christi Himmelfahrt	Ascension Day
	Pfingstmontag	Whit Monday
	Fronleichnam	Corpus Christi
	Buss- und Bettag	Day of Prayer and
	(3rd Wed. in Nov.)	Repentance

RADIO and TV *(Radio; Fernsehen)*. You can easily pick up the BBC World Service, American Forces Network (AFN) or the Voice of America anywhere in Germany. Shortwave reception is excellent, especially at night. The Bavarian Radio Service *(Bayerischer Rund-funk)* broadcasts the news in English every day. As for television, there are two national channels—ARD (Channel One) and ZDF (Channel Two)—plus a regional station called *Drittes Programm,* affiliated with the Bayerische Rundfunk. Films are sometimes shown in the original English version, and a news bulletin is relayed in English once a week.

RELIGIOUS SERVICES. Almost half of the Munich population are Roman Catholic and about one-third Protestant. There is also a large Jewish community.

The Munich Baptist Church, Holzstrasse 9, holds services in English. There are American Episcopal (Anglican) services at the Emmaus-kirche in Langobardenstrasse, a synagogue at Reichenbachstrasse 27 and a mosque at Wallnerstrasse 1.

TIME DIFFERENCES. West Germany follows Central European Time (GMT + 1). In summer, the clock is put one hour ahead (GMT + 2):

New York	London	**Munich**	Jo'burg	Sydney	Auckland
6 a.m.	11 a.m.	**noon**	noon	8 p.m.	10 p.m.

What time is it, please? **Wie spät ist es, bitte?**

TIPPING. Since a service charge is normally included in hotel and restaurant bills, tipping is not obligatory. However, it's appropriate to give something extra to bellboys, hat-check attendants, etc., for their services. The chart on p. 122 makes some suggestions as to how much to leave.

Porter, per bag	DM 1–2
Maid, per week	DM 5–10
Lavatory attendant	DM 0.50–1
Waiter	optional (round off)
Taxi driver	round off
Hairdresser/Barber	10–15%
Tourist guide	10%

TOILETS. Public toilets are easily found: most museums, all restaurants, bars, cafés, large stores, airports and railway stations provide facilities. If there's an attendant, and hand towels and soap are offered, you should leave a small tip. Always have several 10-Pfennig coins ready in case the door has a slot machine.

Toilets may be labelled with symbols of a man or a woman or the initials *W.C.* Otherwise *Herren* (Gentlemen) and *Damen* (Ladies) or a double zero (00) sign are indicated.

Where are the toilets, please?   **Wo sind die Toiletten, bitte?**

TOURIST INFORMATION OFFICES. The German National Tourist Board—Deutsche Zentrale für Tourismus e. V. (DZT)—can inform you about when to go, where to stay and what to see in Munich. Headquarters is at:

Beethovenstrasse 69, D-6000 Frankfurt am Main: tel (069) 7 57 20

The national tourist organization also maintains offices in many countries throughout the world:

Canada   1290 Bay Street, Toronto, Ont. M5R 2C3; tel. (416) 968-1570
P.O. Box 417, 2 Fundy, Place Bonaventure, Montreal, Que. H5A 1B8; tel. (514) 878-9885

United Kingdom 61, Conduit Street, London WIR OEN; tel. (01) 734-2600

U.S.A.   747 Third Avenue, 33rd floor, New York, NY 10017; tel. (212) 308-3300
Broadway Plaza, Suite 2230, 444 South Flower Street, Los Angeles, CA 90071; tel. (213) 688-7332

Munich's tourist offices are situated in the arrival hall of the airport and near the Bayerstrasse exit of the central railway station. Address enquiries to:

Fremdenverkehrsamt München, Postfach, D-8000 München 2; tel. (089) 2 39 11

In addition to providing free maps, lists and brochures, Munich's tourist offices offer a hotel booking service for a small fee. The official *Monatsprogramm* of events (concerts, theatre, exhibitions) is on sale there, as are the 24-hour tickets for unlimited trips by tram, bus, U-Bahn and S-Bahn.

You can also listen to recorded tourist information in English:

Museums, galleries   23 91 62
Palaces and other sights   23 91 72

For information about Upper Bavaria, contact the

Fremdenverkehrsverband München-Oberbayern, Sonnenstrasse 10/III, D-8000 München 2; tel. (089) 59 73 47/48.

TRANSPORT. Munich is served by an efficient network of **buses, trams, U-Bahn** (underground railway) and **S-Bahn** (suburban railway, a part of the German Federal Railways). The U-Bahn runs north-south through the city; the S-Bahn crosses Munich on an east-west axis and goes out to the surrounding countrysde in all directions. All forms of public transport operate from about 5 a.m. to 1 a.m. daily. Free maps and information are available at the tourist offices.

Tickets are interchangeable between U-Bahn, S-Bahn, buses and trams, and entitle you to free transfers for up to two hours so long as you travel in the same direction. Buy your tickets from the big blue vending machines at U- and S-Bahn stations (or on buses and at tram stops, tobacconists, newsagents and stationers that display a white "K"). Be sure to cancel them in the blue cancelling machines positioned at platform entrances and in buses and trams. Vending machines are marked *Einzelfahrkarte* (single ticket) or *Mehrfahrten-karte* (strip ticket). Munich Transport *(Münchner Verkehrs-Verbund—MVV)* also offer reduced-price 24-hour tickets which can be used throughout the metropolitan area. They are sold by machines marked *24-Stunden-Karte* and at the tourist offices.

Taxis*. Munich taxis are beige in colour. Catch one at a rank, at busy locations such as the central railway station, or hail a driver roaming

T the streets. There never seem to be enough taxis at rush hour, so it would be wise to book in advance if you can, either through your hotel receptionist or by phoning 2 16 11.

Inter-city bus services. Rural areas are served by the Federal Railways *(Bundesbahn)* buses and the Federal Post Office *(Bundespost)* buses, as well as by local companies. Bus terminals are invariably close to a railway station, and there you'll find information about routes and fares.

In Munich, the bus terminal is situated in Arnulfstrasse, in the front of Starnberg Station (on the north side of the central railway station).

Trains. Deutsche Bundesbahn (DB) trains are extremely comfortable and fast, as well as punctual. They are classified thus:

EC *(EuroCity)*	International trains; with supplement; first and second class
IC *(Intercity)*	Long-distance inter-city trains; some only first, others with first and second class; with supplement.
D *(Schnellzug, or D-Zug)* and **FD** *Fern-Express-Zug)*	Intermediate- to long-distance trains; first and second class, with supplement on trips of less than 50 kilometres
E *(Eilzug)*	Trains making local stops.
Nahverkehrszug	Local trains, stop at all stations.

Tickets for distances of up to 50 kilometres are valid for two days, those over 50 kilometres, for two months. A number of special reduced-price offers and bargain tickets are available:

European Money-Spinner Fares offer return (round-trip) journeys from the U.K. to ten destinations within Germany at about 25% off.

DB Tourist Cards for foreign visitors only, through certain travel agencies. Bring along your passport when ordering. The holder can travel for four, nine or 16 consecutive days on the entire network of the Deutsche Bundesbahn. The card also includes coach and river-boat transport and free travel in Munich's suburban areas on the S-Bahn.

Eurailpasses are special rover tickets covering most of Western Europe. For non-European residents only, to be purchased before leaving home.

Anyone under 26 can purchase an *Inter-Rail* card which allows one month of unlimited 2nd-class rail travel on all participating European **124** railways. The *Rail Europ S* card entitles senior citizens to buy train tickets for European destinations at reduced prices, while the *Rail Europ F* card gives reductions for families of 3 to 8 members.

Tourenkarten, regional rail rover tickets for a given area are bought in Germany. They allow ten days' unlimited travel on regional rail services, with 50% reduction on buses; the only requirement is that your rail journey must have covered at least 200 kilometres one way *before* you can obtain it.

Children under 4 travel free, from 4 to 11 inclusive, half price.

DB Junior Passes entitle youths between 12 and 22 and students under 27 to unlimited travel on DB routes of more than 51 kilometres for one year (also on routes under 51 km. for an additional cost).

For further details, ask for the brochure *Discover Germany by Rail* at travel agencies.

When's the next bus/train to…?	**Wann fährt der nächste Bus/Zug nach…?**
I want a ticket to…	**Ich möchte eine Fahrkarte nach…**
single (one-way)	**einfach**
return (round-trip)	**hin und zurück**
first/second class	**erste/zweite Klasse**

SOME USEFUL EXPRESSIONS

yes/no	**ja/nein**
please/thank you	**bitte/danke**
excuse me/you're welcome	**Entschuldigung/gern geschehen**
how long/how far	**wie lange/wie weit**
where/when/how	**wo/wann/wie**
yesterday/today/tomorrow	**gestern/heute/morgen**
day/week/month/year	**Tag/Woche/Monat/Jahr**
cheap/expensive	**billig/teuer**
hot/cold	**heiss/kalt**
open/closed	**offen/geschlossen**
free (vacant)/occupied	**frei/besetzt**
I don't understand.	**Ich verstehe nicht.**
What does this mean?	**Was bedeutet das?**
Waiter/Waitress, please!	**Ober/Fräulein, bitte!**
How much is that?	**Wieviel kostet das?**

Index

An asterisk (*) next to a page number indicates a map reference.

INDEX

127

U-Bahn and S-Bahn System

MVV

Only runs from Monday to Friday in the rush hour

P Free parking space

Lines: S1, S2, S3, S4, S6, S7, S27, U1, U2, U3, U4, U5, U6

Ismaning, Unterföhring, Johanneskirchen, Englschalking, Daglfing, Leuchtenbergring, Berg am Laim

Erding, Altenerding, Aufhausen, St Koloman, Ottenhofen, Markt Schwaben, Poing, Grub, Heimstetten, Feldkirchen, Riem, Trudering, Gronsdorf, Vaterstetten, Baldham, Zorneding, Eglharting, Kirchseeon, Grafing Bahnhof, Grafing Stadt, Ebersberg

Kieferngarten, Freimann, Studentenstadt, Alte Heide, Nordfriedhof, Dietlindenstraße, Münchner Freiheit, Giselastraße, Universität, Odeonsplatz

Bonner Platz, Hohenzollernplatz, Josephsplatz, Theresienstraße, Königsplatz, Karlsplatz (Stachus)

Olympiazentrum, Petuelring, Scheidplatz, Rotkreuzplatz, Mailingerstraße, Donnersbergerbrücke

Westfriedhof, Gern, Moosfeld, Neuperlach Zentrum, Therese-Giehse-Allee, Neuperlach Süd, Neubiberg, Ottobrunn, Hohenbrunn

Innsbrucker Ring, Michaelibad, Quidenstraße

Arabellapark, Richard-Strauss-Str., Böhmerwaldplatz, Prinzregentenplatz, Max-Weber-Platz, Lehel

Rosenheimer Platz, Isartor, Marienplatz, Sendlinger Tor, Goetheplatz, Poccistraße, Brudermühlstraße, Thalkirchen, Obersendling, Siemenswerke, Großhesselohe Isartalbf, Pullach, Höllriegelskreuth, Baierbrunn

Ostbahnhof, St Martinstraße, Karl-Preis-Platz, Perlach, Gleising, Fasangarten, Fasanenpark, Taufkirchen-U., Furth, Deisenhofen, Sauerlach, Otterfing

Kolumbus- Unterberg- platz, straße, Silberhorn- straße, Fraunhofer- straße

Wächterhof, Höhenkirchen-Siegertsbrunn, Dürrnhaar, Aying, Peiß, Großhelfendorf, Kreuzstraße

Hauptbahnhof, Theresienwiese, Heckerbrücke, Hackerbrücke, Messe- gelände, Heimeranplatz, Harras, Mittersendling

Laim, Friedenheimer Straße, Westend- straße, Partnach- platz, Aidenbach- straße, Forstenrieder Allee, Fürstenried West, Machtlfinger Straße, Basler Straße, Hohenschäftlarn, Ebenhausen-Schäftlarn, Icking, Wolfratshausen

Pasing, Leienfelsstr., Westkreuz, Neuaubing, Aubing, Lochham, Gräfelfing, Planegg, Stockdorf, Gauting, Buchenhain, Hohenschäftlarn

Langwied, Lochhausen, Puchheim, Eichenau, Unterpfaffenhofen-Germering, Fürstenfeldbruck, Buchenau, Schöngeising, Grafrath, Türkenfeld, Geltendorf

Nannhofen, Malching, Maisach, Gernlinden, Esting, Olching, Gröbenzell

Peterhausen, Vierkirchen-Esterhofen, Röhrmoos, Walpertshofen, Dachau, Karlsfeld, Altomünster

Freising, Pulling, Neufahrn, Eching, Lohhof, Unterschleißheim, Oberschleißheim, Feldmoching, Fasanerie, Moosach, Allach, Obermenzing

Geiselbullach, Gilching-Argelsried, Neugilching, Weßling, Steinebach, Seefeld-Hechendorf, Herrsching, Possenhofen, Feldafing, Starnberg, Mühlthal, Berg

S   U

Selection of Munich Hotels and Restaurants

Where do you start? Choosing a hotel or restaurant in a place you're not familiar with can be daunting. To help you find your way amid the bewildering variety, we have made a selection from the *Red Guide to Germany 1988* published by Michelin, the recognized authority on gastronomy and accommodation throughout Europe.

Our own Berlitz criteria have been (a) price and (b) location. In the hotel section, for a double room with bath and breakfast, Higher-priced means above DM 250, Medium-priced DM 160–250, Lower-priced below DM 160. As to restaurants, for a meal consisting of a starter, a main course and a dessert, Higher-priced means above DM 60, Medium-priced DM 45–60, Lower-priced below DM 45. Special features (where applicable), plus regular closing days are also given. As a general rule many Munich hotels and restaurants close around Christmas and New Year and restaurants also often a couple of weeks in August. For hotels and restaurants, checking first to make certain that they are open and advance reservations are both advisable. In Munich, hotel and restaurant prices include service and taxes.

For a wider choice of hotels and restaurants, we strongly recommend you obtain the authoritative Michelin *Red Guide to Germany,* which gives a comprehensive and reliable picture of the situation throughout the country.

HOTELS

HIGHER-PRICED
(above DM 250)

Austrotel – Deutscher Kaiser
Arnulfstr. 2
München 2
Tel. 5 38 60; tlx. 522650
174 rooms
View over Munich from 15th-floor restaurant.

Continental
Max-Joseph-Str. 5
München 2
Tel. 55 15 70; tlx. 522603
160 rooms
Outdoor dining. Antique furnishings.

Eden-Hotel-Wolff
Arnulfstr. 4
München 2
Tel. 55 11 50; tlx. 523564
214 rooms

Hilton
Am Tucherpark 7
München 22
Tel. 3 84 50; tlx. 5215740
485 rooms
Outdoor dining. Beer garden. Massage. Sauna. Indoor swimming pool.

Königshof
Karlsplatz 25
München 2
Tel. 55 13 60; tlx. 523616
106 rooms
Restaurant with notably good cuisine and outstanding wine list.

Vier Jahreszeiten Kempinski
Maximilianstr. 17
München 22
Tel. 23 03 90; tlx. 523859
365 rooms
Quiet hotel. Massage. Sauna. Indoor swimming pool. Walterspiel restaurant (notably good cuisine).

Westpark-Hotel
Garmischer Str. 2
München 2
Tel. 5 19 60; tlx. 523680
258 rooms
Sauna.

MEDIUM-PRICED
(DM 160–250)

Ambassador
Mozartstr. 4
München 2
Tel. 53 08 40; tlx. 522445
62 rooms
Outdoor dining. Alfredo restaurant.

An der Oper
Falkenturmstr. 10
München 2
Tel. 22 87 11; tlx. 522588
55 rooms
Bouillabaisse restaurant.

Apollo
Mittererstr. 7
München 2
Tel. 53 95 31; tlx. 5212981
74 rooms
No restaurant.

Ariston
Unsöldstr. 10
München 22
Tel. 22 26 91; tlx. 522437
61 rooms
No restaurant.

Budapest
Schwanthalerstr. 36
München 2
Tel. 55 11 10; tlx. 529213
100 rooms

Drei Löwen
Schillerstr. 8
München 2
Tel. 59 55 21; tlx. 523867
130 rooms

Erzgießerei-Europe
Erzgießereistr. 15
München 2
Tel. 18 60 55; tlx. 5214977
106 rooms

Intercity-Hotel
Bahnhofplatz 2
München 2
Tel. 55 85 71; tlx. 523174
209 rooms

Mercure
Senefelder Str. 7
München 2
Tel. 55 13 20; tlx. 5218428
167 rooms

Metropol
Bayerstr. 43
München 2
Tel. 53 07 64; tlx. 522816
272 rooms

LOWER-PRICED
(below DM 160)

Blauer Bock
Sebastiansplatz 9
München 2
Tel. 2 60 80 43
76 rooms
No restaurant.

Brack
Lindwurmstr. 153
München 2
Tel. 77 10 52; tlx. 524416
50 rooms
No restaurant.

Europäischer Hof
Bayerstr. 31
München 2
Tel. 55 15 10; tlx. 522642
160 rooms
No restaurant.

Stachus
Bayerstr. 7
München 2
Tel. 59 28 81; tlx. 523696
65 rooms
No restaurant.

Uhland
Uhlandstr. 1
München 2
Tel. 53 92 77; tlx. 528368
25 rooms
No restaurant.

GREATER MUNICH

HIGHER-PRICED

Arabella-Hotel
Arabellastr. 5
München 81-Bogenhausen
Tel. 9 23 21; tlx. 529987
478 rooms
View of Munich. Massage. Sauna.
Indoor swimming pool.

Holiday Inn
Leopoldstr. 194
München 40-Schwabing
Tel. 34 09 71; tlx. 5215439
363 rooms
Beer garden. Massage. Sauna.
Indoor swimming pool.

Palace
Trogerstr. 21
München 80-Bogenhausen
Tel. 4 70 50 91; tlx. 528256
73 rooms
Outdoor dining. Sauna.

Preysing
Preysingstr. 1
München 80-Haidhausen
Tel. 48 10 11; tlx. 529044
76 rooms
Sauna. Indoor swimming pool.

Prinzregent
Ismaninger Str. 42
München 80-Bogenhausen
Tel. 4 70 20 81; tlx. 524403
68 rooms
Elegant, rustic decor. No restau-
rant.

Sheraton
Arabellastr. 6
München 81-Bogenhausen
Tel. 92 40 11; tlx. 522391
650 rooms
View of Munich. Beer garden.
Massage. Sauna. Indoor swim-
ming pool. Garden.

MEDIUM-PRICED

Kent
Englschalkinger Str. 245
München 81-Englschalking
Tel. 93 50 73; tlx. 5216716
47 rooms
Sauna. No restaurant.

Novotel
Rudolf-Vogel-Bogen 3
München 83-Neu Perlach
Tel. 63 80 00; tlx. 522030
254 rooms
Outdoor dining. Sauna. Indoor
swimming pool.

Olympiapark-Hotel
Helene-Mayer-Ring 12
München 40-Schwabing
Tel. 3 51 60 71; tlx. 5215231
100 rooms
Free admission to the indoor
swimming pool at the thermal
springs.

Orbis Hotel
Karl-Marx-Ring 87
München 83-Neu Perlach
Tel. 6 32 70; tlx. 5213357
185 rooms
Sauna. Indoor swimming pool.

LOWER-PRICED

Gästehaus Englischer Garten
Liebergesellstr. 8
München 40-Schwabing
Tel. 39 20 34
14 rooms
Quiet hotel. Garden. No restaurant.

Hotel und Gasthof Sollner Hof
Herterichstr. 63
München 71-Solln
Tel. 79 20 90
46 rooms
Beer garden.

Kriemhild
Guntherstr. 16
München 19-Nymphenburg
Tel. 17 00 77
18 rooms
No restaurant.

Obermaier
Truderinger Str. 304B
München 82-Trudering
Tel. 42 90 21
30 rooms
No restaurant.

Parkhotel Neuhofen
Plinganserstr. 102
München 70-Sendling
Tel. 7 23 10 86
30 rooms
Outdoor dining.

Petra
Marschnerstr. 73
München 60-Pasing
Tel. 83 20 41
18 rooms
Garden. No restaurant.

RESTAURANTS

HIGHER-PRICED
(above DM 60)

Aubergine
Maximiliansplatz 5
München 2
Tel. 59 81 71
Superb cuisine. Closed Sunday and Monday.

Boettner
Theatinerstr. 8
München 2
Tel. 22 12 10
Small old-Munich-style restaurant with notably good cuisine. Closed Saturday evening and Sunday.

Le Gourmet
Ligsalzstr. 46
München 2
Tel. 50 35 97
Small elegant restaurant with notably good cuisine. Dinner only. Closed Sunday.

Sabitzer
Reitmorstr. 21
München 22
Tel. 29 85 84
Notably good cuisine. Dinner only on Saturday. Closed Sunday.

MEDIUM-PRICED
(DM 45–60)

Chesa Rüegg
Wurzerstr. 18
München 22
Tel. 29 71 14
Rustic furnishings. Closed Saturday and Sunday.

Csarda Piroschka
Prinzregentenstr. 1
München 22
Tel. 29 54 25
Hungarian restaurant with gypsy music. Open from 6 p.m. Closed Sunday.

Gasthaus Glockenbach
Kapuzinerstr. 29
München 2
Tel. 53 40 43
Formerly Bavarian beer hall. Closed Sunday and Monday.

La Piazzetta
Oskar-v.-Miller-Ring 3
München 3
Tel. 28 29 90
Outdoor dining. Beer garden. Modern Italian restaurant in Florentine style. Dinner only on Saturday.

Mövenpick im Künstlerhaus
Lenbachplatz 8
München 2
Tel. 55 78 65
Outdoor dining.

Spatenhaus-Bräustuben
Residenzstr. 12
München 2
Tel. 22 78 41
Outdoor dining. Alpine-country decor.

Zum Bürgerhaus
Pettenkoferstr. 1
München 2
Tel. 59 79 09
Farmer-style furnishings. Courtyard terrace. Closed Saturday until 6 p.m. and Sunday.

LOWER-PRICED
(below DM 45)

Augustiner Gaststätten
Neuhauser Str. 16
München 2
Tel. 2 60 41 06
Beer garden.

Goldene Stadt
Oberanger 44
München 2
Tel. 26 43 82
Bohemian specialities. Closed Sunday.

Hackerkeller und Schäfflerstuben
Theresienhöhe 4
München 2
Tel. 50 70 04
Beer garden.

Pschorr-Keller
Theresienhöhe 7
München 2
Tel. 50 10 88
Beer garden.

Spatenhofkeller
Neuhauser Str. 26
München 2
Tel. 26 40 10

Zum Pschorrbräu
Neuhauser Str. 11
München 2
Tel. 2 60 30 01
Outdoor dining.

Zum Spöckmeier
Rosenstr. 9
München 2
Tel. 26 80 88
Outdoor dining.

HIGHER-PRICED

da Pippo
Mühlbaurstr. 36
München 80-Bogenhausen
Tel. 4 70 48 48
Italian cuisine. Outdoor dining.
Closed Sunday.

Käfer Schänke
Schumannstr. 1
München 80-Bogenhausen
Tel. 4 16 81
Outdoor dining. Rustic and period
furnishings. Closed Sunday.

La mer
Schraudolphstr. 24
München 40-Schwabing
Tel. 2 72 24 39
Notably good cuisine. Remarkable
decor. Dinner only. Closed
Monday.

Preysing-Keller
Innere-Wiener-Str. 6
München 80-Haidhausen
Tel. 48 10 15
Notably good cuisine. Exceptional
wine list. Vaults with rustic decor.
Dinner only. Closed Sunday.

Tantris
Johann-Fichte-Str. 7
München 40-Schwabing
Tel. 36 20 61
Excellent cuisine. Modern restau-
rant building with elegant decor.
Outdoor dining. Dinner only on
Monday and Saturday. Closed
Sunday.

MEDIUM-PRICED

Passatore
Wasserburger Landstr. 212
München 82-Trudering
Tel. 4 30 30 00
Italian cuisine. Outdoor dining.
Closed Wednesday.

Restaurant 33
Feilitzschstr. 33
München 40-Schwabing
Tel. 34 25 28
Outdoor dining. Dinner only.

Romagna Antica
Elisabethstr. 52
München 40-Schwabing
Tel. 2 71 63 55
Italian cuisine. Outdoor dining.
Closed Sunday.

Seehaus
Kleinhesselohe 3
München 40-Schwabing
Tel. 39 70 72
View. Lakeside terrace.

LOWER-PRICED

La Bambola
Verdistr. 92
München 60-Obermenzing
Tel. 8 11 27 16
Outdoor dining. Closed Wednes-
day.

Tai Tung
Prinzregentenstr. 60
München 80-Bogenhausen
Tel. 47 11 00
Chinese cuisine. Closed Monday.

BERLITZ®

GERMAN
for travellers

By the staff of Berlitz Guides

How best to use this phrase book

● We suggest that you start with the **Guide to pronunciation** (pp. 6–8), then go on to **Some basic expressions** (pp. 9–15). This gives you not only a minimum vocabulary, but also helps you get used to pronouncing the language. The phonetic transcription throughout the book enables you to pronounce every word correctly.

● Consult the **Contents** pages (3–5) for the section you need. In each chapter you'll find travel facts, hints and useful information. Simple phrases are followed by a list of words applicable to the situation.

● Separate, detailed contents lists are included at the beginning of the extensive **Eating out** and **Shopping guide** sections (Menus, p. 39, Shops and services, p. 97).

● If you want to find out how to say something in German, your fastest look-up is via the **Dictionary** section (pp. 164–189). This not only gives you the word, but is also cross-referenced to its use in a phrase on a specific page.

● If you wish to learn more about constructing sentences, check the **Basic grammar** (pp. 159–163).

● Note the **colour margins** are indexed in German and English to help both listener and speaker. And, in addition, there is also an **index in German** for the use of your listener.

● Throughout the book, this symbol ☞ suggests phrases your listener can use to answer you. If you still can't understand, hand this phrase book to the German-speaker to encourage pointing to an appropriate answer. The English translation for you is just alongside the German.

Contents

4

Acknowledgments
We are particularly grateful to Eva Bayer for her help in the preparation of this book, and to Dr. T.J.A. Bennett who devised the phonetic transcription.

Guide to pronunciation

You'll find the pronunciation of the German letters and sounds explained below, as well as the symbols we use for them in the transcriptions.

The imitated pronunciation should be read as if it were English except for any special rules set out below. It is based on Standard British pronunciation, though we have tried to take into account General American pronunciation as well. Of course, the sounds of any two languages are never exactly the same; but if you follow carefully the indications supplied here, you'll have no difficulty in reading our transcriptions in such a way as to make yourself understood.

In the transcriptions, letters shown in bold print should be read with more stress (louder) than the others.

Consonants

Letter	Approximate pronunciation	Symbol	Example	
f, h, k, l, m, n, p, t, x	normally pronounced as in English			
b	1) at the end of a word or between a vowel and a consonant like p in up	p	**ab**	ahp
	2) elsewhere as in English	b	**bis**	biss
c	1) before e, i, ö and ä, like ts in hits	ts	**Celsius**	**tsehl**ziuss
	2) elsewhere like c in cat	k	**Café**	kah**fay**
ch	1) after back vowels (e.g. ah, o, oo) like ch in Scottish loch, otherwise more like h in huge	kh	**doch**	dokh

ch	2) sometimes, especially before **s**, like **k** in **kit**	k	**Wachs**	vahks
d	1) at the end of a word or between a vowel and a consonant like **t** in eat	t	**Rad**	raat
	2) elsewhere, like **d** in **do**	d	**durstig**	**doo**rstikh
g	1) always hard as in **go** but at the end of a word often more like **ck** in tack	g	**gehen**	**gay**ern
		k	**weg**	vehk
	2) when preceded by **i** at the end of a word like **ch** in Scottish loch	kh	**billig**	**bill**ikh
j	like **y** in yes	y	**ja**	yaa
qu	like **k** followed by **v** as in **vat**	kv	**Quark**	kvahrk
r	generally rolled in the back of the mouth	r	**warum**	vah**rum**
s	1) before or between vowels like **z** in zoo	z	**sie**	zee
	2) before **p** and **t** at the beginning of a syllable like **sh** in shut	sh	**spät**	shpait
	3) elsewhere, like **s** in sit	s/ss	**es ist**	ehss ist
ß	always like **s** in sit	s/ss	**heiß**	highss
sch	like **sh** in shut	sh	**schnell**	shnehl
tsch	like **ch** in chip	ch	**deutsch**	doych
tz	like **ts** in hits	ts	**Platz**	plahts
v	1) like **f** in for	f	**vier**	feer
	2) in most words of foreign origin, like **v** in **vice**	v	**Vase**	**vaa**zer
w	like **v** in vice	v	**wie**	vee
z	like **ts** in hits	ts	**zeigen**	**tsigh**gern

Vowels

In German, vowels are generally long when followed by **h** or by one consonant and short when followed by two or more consonants.

a	1) short like u in cut	ah	lassen	lahssern
	2) long like a in car	aa	Abend	aabernt
ä	1) short like e in let	eh	Lärm	lehrm
	2) long like ai in hair	ai	spät	shpait
e	1) short like e in let	eh	sprechen	shprehkhern
	2) long like a in late, but pronounced without moving tongue or lips	ay	geben	gaybern
	3) in unstressed syllables generally like er in other	er*	bitte	bitter
i	1) short like i in hit	i	billig	billikh
	2) long like ee in meet	ee	ihm	eem
ie	like ee in bee	ee	hier	heer
o	1) short like o in got	o	voll	fol
	2) long like o in note, but pronounced without moving tongue or lips	oa	ohne	oaner
ö	like ur in fur (long or short)	ur*	können	kurnern
u	1) short like oo in foot	u	Nuß	nuss
	2) long like oo in moon	oo	gut	goot
ü	like French u in une; round your lips and try to say ea as in mean (long or short)	ew	über	ewber
y	like German ü	ew	typisch	tewpish

Diphthongs

ai, ay, ei, ey	like igh in high	igh	mein	mighn
au	like ow in now	ow	auf	owf
äu, eu	like oy in boy	oy	neu	noy

---

* The r should not be pronounced when reading this transcription.

Some basic expressions

Yes.	**Ja.**	yaa
No.	**Nein.**	nighn
Please.	**Bitte.**	bitter
Thank you.	**Danke.**	dahnker
You're welcome.	**Bitte.**	bitter
Thank you very much.	**Vielen Dank.**	feelern dahnk
That's all right/ Don't mention it.	**Gern geschehen.**	gehrn gershayern

Greetings *Begrüßung*

Good morning.	**Guten Morgen.**	gootern morgern
Good afternoon.	**Guten Tag.**	gootern taag
Good evening.	**Guten Abend.**	gootern aabernt
Good night.	**Gute Nacht.**	gooter nahkht
Good-bye.	**Auf Wiedersehen.**	owf veederrzayern
See you later.	**Bis bald.**	biss bahlt
This is Mr./Mrs./ Miss ...	**Das ist Herr/Frau/ Fräulein ...**	dahss ist hehr/frow/ froylighn
How do you do? (Pleased to meet you.)	**Sehr erfreut.**	zayr ehrfroyt
How are you?	**Wie geht es Ihnen?**	vee gayt ehss eenern
Very well, thanks. And you?	**Sehr gut, danke. Und Ihnen?**	zayr goot dahnker. unt eenern
How's life?	**Wie geht's?**	vee gayts
Fine.	**Gut.**	goot

I beg your pardon?	**Wie bitte?**	vee bitter
Excuse me. (May I get past?)	**Gestatten Sie?**	gershtahtern zee
Sorry!	**Entschuldigung/ Verzeihung!**	ehntshuldiggung/ fehrtsighung

Questions *Fragen*

Where?	**Wo?**	voa
How?	**Wie?**	vee
When?	**Wann?**	vahn
What?	**Was?**	vahss
Why?	**Warum?**	vahrum
Who?	**Wer?**	vayr
Which?	**Welcher/Welche/ Welches?**	vehlkherr/vehlkher/ vehlkherss
Where is ...?	**Wo ist ...?**	voa ist
Where are ...?	**Wo sind ...?**	voa zint
Where can I find/ get ...?	**Wo finde/bekomme ich ...?**	voa finder/berkommer ikh
How far?	**Wie weit?**	vee vight
How long?	**Wie lange?**	vee lahnger
How much?	**Wieviel?**	veefeel
How many?	**Wie viele?**	vee feeler
How much does this cost?	**Wieviel kostet das?**	veefeel kostert dahss
When does ... open/ close?	**Wann öffnet/ schließt ...?**	vahn urfnert/shleest
What do you call this/that in German?	**Wie heißt dies/ das auf deutsch?**	vee highst deess/dahss owf doych
What does that mean?	**Was bedeutet das?**	vahss berdoytert dahss
What does this word mean?	**Was bedeutet dieses Wort?**	vahss berdoytert deezerss vort

Do you speak ...? *Sprechen Sie ...?*

Do you speak English?	**Sprechen Sie Englisch?**	shprehkhern zee ehnglish
Is there anyone here who speaks English?	**Spricht hier jemand Englisch?**	shprikht heer yaymahnt ehnglish
I don't speak (much) German.	**Ich spreche kaum Deutsch.**	ikh shprehkher kowm doych
Could you speak more slowly?	**Könnten Sie bitte langsamer sprechen?**	kurntern zee bitter lahngzaamerr shprehkhern
Could you repeat that?	**Könnten Sie das bitte wiederholen?**	kurntern zee dahss bitter veederrhoalern
Could you spell it?	**Könnten Sie es bitte buchstabieren?**	kurntern zee ehss bitter bookhshtahbeerern
Please write it down.	**Schreiben Sie es bitte auf.**	shrighbern zee ehss bitter owf
Can you translate this for me/us?	**Könnten Sie mir/uns das übersetzen?**	kurntern zee meer/uns dahss ewberrzehtsern
Please point to the phrase/sentence in the book.	**Bitte zeigen Sie mir den Ausdruck/ den Satz im Buch.**	bitter tsighgern zee meer dayn owsdruk/ dayn zahts im bookh
Just a moment. I'll see if I can find it in this book.	**Einen Augenblick bitte, ich schaue mal im Buch nach, ob ich es finde.**	ighnern owgernblik bitter ikh shower maal im bookh naakh op ikh ehss finder
I understand.	**Ich verstehe.**	ikh fehrshtayer
I don't understand.	**Ich verstehe nicht.**	ikh fehrshtayer nikht
Do you understand?	**Verstehen Sie?**	fehrshtayern zee

Can/May ...? *Kann ...?*

Can I have ...?	**Kann ich ... haben?**	kahn ikh ... haabern
Can we have ...?	**Können wir ... haben?**	kurnern veer ... haabern
Can you show me ...?	**Können Sie mir ... zeigen?**	kurnern zee meer ... tsighgern
I can't.	**Leider nicht.**	lighderr nikht

Can you tell me ...?	**Können Sie mir sagen ...?**	**kur**nern zee meer **zaa**gern
Can you help me?	**Können Sie mir helfen?**	**kur**nern zee meer **hehl**fern
Can I help you?	**Kann ich Ihnen helfen?**	kahn ikh **ee**nern **hehl**fern
Can you direct me to ...?	**Können Sie mir den Weg nach/ zu ... zeigen?**	**kur**nern zee meer dayn vayg naakh/ tsoo ... **tsigh**gern

What do you want? *Was wünschen Sie?*

I'd like ...	**Ich hätte gern/ Ich möchte ...**	ikh **hehter** gehrn/ ikh **murkh**ter
We'd like ...	**Wir hätten gern/ Wir möchten ...**	veer **hehtern** gehrn/ veer **murkh**tern
Give me ...	**Geben Sie mir ...**	**gay**bern zee meer
Give it to me.	**Geben Sie es mir.**	**gay**bern zee ehss meer
Bring me ...	**Bringen Sie mir ...**	**bring**ern zee meer
Bring it to me.	**Bringen Sie es mir.**	**bring**ern zee ehss meer
Show me ...	**Zeigen Sie mir ...**	**tsigh**gern zee meer
Show it to me.	**Zeigen Sie es mir.**	**tsigh**gern zee ehss meer
I'm looking for ...	**Ich suche ...**	ikh **zoo**kher
I'm hungry.	**Ich habe Hunger.**	ikh **haa**ber **hung**err
I'm thirsty.	**Ich habe Durst.**	ikh **haa**ber doorst
I'm tired.	**Ich bin müde.**	ikh bin **mew**der
I'm lost.	**Ich habe mich verirrt.**	ikh **haa**ber mikh fehr**eert**
It's important.	**Es ist wichtig.**	ehss ist **vikh**tikh
It's urgent.	**Es ist dringend.**	ehss ist **dring**ernt
Hurry up!	**Beeilen Sie sich!**	be**righ**lern zee zikh

It is / There is ... *Es ist/Es gibt ...*

| It is ... | **Es ist ...** | ehss ist |
| Is it ...? | **Ist es ...?** | ist ehss |

It isn't ...	**Es ist nicht ...**	ehss ist nikht
Here it is.	**Hier ist es.**	heer ist ehss
Here they are.	**Hier sind sie.**	heer zint zee
There it is.	**Dort ist es.**	dort ist ehss
There they are.	**Dort sind sie.**	dort zint zee
There is/are ...	**Es gibt ...**	ehss gipt
Is there/Are there ...?	**Gibt es ...?**	gipt ehss
There isn't (any) ...	**Es gibt keinen/Es gibt keine/Es gibt kein ...**	ehss gipt **kigh**nern/ehss gipt **kigh**ner/ehss gipt **kigh**n
There aren't (any) ...	**Es gibt keine ...**	ehss gipt **kigh**ner

Adjectives *Eigenschaftswörter*

big/small	**groß/klein**	groass/klighn
quick/slow	**schnell/langsam**	shnehl/**lahng**zaam
cheap/expensive	**billig/teuer**	billikh/**toy**err
hot/cold	**heiß/kalt**	highss/kahlt
full/empty	**voll/leer**	fol/layr
easy/difficult	**leicht/schwierig**	lighkht/**shwee**rikh
heavy/light	**schwer/leicht**	shvayr/lighkht
open/shut	**offen/geschlossen**	offern/ger**shlos**sern
right/wrong	**richtig/falsch**	**rikh**tikh/fahlsh
old/new	**alt/neu**	ahlt/noy
old/young	**alt/jung**	ahlt/yung
next/last	**nächste/letzte**	**naikh**ster/**lehts**ter
beautiful/ugly	**schön/häßlich**	shurn/**hehs**likh
free (vacant)/ occupied	**frei/besetzt**	frigh/ber**zehtst**
good/bad	**gut/schlecht**	goot/shlehkht
better/worse	**besser/schlechter**	**behs**serr/**shlehkht**err
early/late	**früh/spät**	frew/shpait
near/far	**nah/weit**	naa/vight
left/right	**linke/rechte**	**link**er/**rehkh**ter

Quantities *Mengen*

a little	**ein wenig**	ighn **vay**nikh
a lot	**eine Menge**	**igh**ner **mehn**ger
few/a few	**wenige/einige**	**vay**nigger/**igh**nigger
much/many	**viel/viele**	feel/**fee**ler
more (than)	**mehr (als)**	mayr (ahlss)
less (than)	**weniger (als)**	**vay**niggerr (ahlss)
enough/too (much)	**genug/zu (viel)**	ger**nook**/tsu (feel)
some/any (sing.)	**etwas**	**eht**vahss
some/any (pl.)	**einige**	**igh**nigger

A few more useful words *Weitere nützliche Wörter*

at	**an/bei**	ahn/bigh
on	**an/auf**	ahn/owf
in	**in**	in
to	**zu**	tsoo
after	**nach**	naakh
before	**vor**	foar
for	**für**	fewr
from	**von**	fon
with	**mit**	mit
without	**ohne**	**oa**ner
through	**durch**	doorkh
towards	**gegen**	**gay**gern
until	**bis**	biss
during	**während**	**vai**rernt
next to	**neben**	**nay**bern
behind	**hinter**	**hin**terr
between	**zwischen**	**tsvi**shern
since	**seit**	zight
above	**oben**	**oa**bern
below	**unten**	**un**tern
over	**über**	**ew**berr
under	**unter**	**un**terr

inside	**drinnen**	drinnern
outside	**draußen**	drowssern
up	**hinauf**	hinnowf
down	**hinunter**	hinnunterr
here	**hier**	heer
there	**dort**	dort
and	**und**	unt
or	**oder**	oaderr
but	**aber**	aaberr
not	**nicht**	nikht
never	**nie**	nee
nothing	**nichts**	nikhts
none	**kein**	kighn
very	**sehr**	zayr
too (also)	**auch**	owkh
yet	**noch**	nokh
soon	**bald**	bahlt
now	**jetzt**	yehtst
only	**nur**	noor
then	**dann**	dahn
perhaps	**vielleicht**	feelighkht

Pronunciation of the German alphabet

A	aa	H	haa	Ö	ur	V	fow
Ä	ai	I	ee	P	pay	W	vay
B	bay	J	yot	Q	koo	X	eeks
C	tsay	K	kaa	R	ehr	Y	ewpsillon
D	day	L	ehl	S	ehss	Z	tseht
E	ay	M	ehm	T	tay		
F	ehf	N	ehn	U	oo		
G	gay	O	oa	Ü	ew		

In addition to these letters there is the **ß** sign, a combination of
s and z. It is pronounced exactly like **ss**.

Arrival

Here's my passport.	**Hier ist mein Paß.**	heer ist mighn pahss
I'll be staying ...	**Ich bleibe ...**	ikh blighber
a few days	**ein paar Tage**	ighn paar taager
a week	**eine Woche**	ighner vokher
a month	**einen Monat**	ighnern moanaht
I don't know yet.	**Ich weiß es noch nicht.**	ikh vighss ehss nokh nikht
I'm here on holiday.	**Ich bin auf Urlaub hier.**	ikh bin owf oorlowp heer
I'm here on business.	**Ich bin geschäftlich hier.**	ikh bin gershehftlikh heer
I'm just passing through.	**Ich bin nur auf der Durchreise.**	ikh bin noor owf derr doorkhrighzer

If things become difficult:

I'm sorry, I don't understand.	**Es tut mir leid, ich verstehe nicht.**	ehss toot meer light ikh fehrshtayer nikht
Is there anyone here who speaks English?	**Spricht hier jemand Englisch?**	shprikht heer yaymahnt ehnglish

Customs *Zoll*

After collecting your baggage at the airport (*der Flughafen*— derr **floog**haafern) you have a choice: use the green exit if you have nothing to declare. Or leave via the red exit if you have items to declare (in excess of those allowed).

ANMELDEFREIE WAREN NOTHING TO DECLARE		**ANMELDEPFLICHTIGE WAREN** GOODS TO DECLARE

The chart below shows what you can bring in duty-free.

	Cigarettes		Cigars		Tobacco		Spirits (Liquor)		Wine
Germany 1)	200	or	50	or	250 g.		1 l.	and	2 l.
2)	300	or	75	or	400 g.		1.5 l.	and	5 l.
3)	400	or	100	or	500 g.		1 l.	and	2 l.
Austria	200	or	50	or	250 g.		1 l.	and	2 l.
Switzerland	200	or	50	or	250 g.		1 l.	and	2 l.

1) Visitors arriving from EEC countries with tax-free items, and visitors arriving from other European countries
2) Visitors arriving from EEC countries with non-tax-free items
3) Visitors arriving from countries outside Europe

I've nothing to declare.	**Ich habe nichts zu verzollen.**	ikh **haa**ber nikhts tsoo fehr**tsol**lern
I've ...	**Ich habe ...**	ikh **haa**ber
a carton of cigarettes	**eine Stange Zigaretten**	**igh**ner **shtahng**er tsiggah**reh**tern
a bottle of gin	**eine Flasche Gin**	**igh**ner **flah**sher "gin"
It's for my personal use.	**Es ist für meinen persönlichen Gebrauch.**	ehss ist fewr **migh**nern pehr**zurn**likhern ger**browkh**
This is a gift.	**Das ist ein Geschenk.**	dahss ist ighn ger**shenk**

Ihren Paß, bitte.	Your passport, please.
Haben Sie etwas zu verzollen?	Do you have anything to declare?
Bitte öffnen Sie diese Tasche.	Please open this bag.
Dies ist zollpflichtig.	You'll have to pay duty on this.
Haben Sie noch mehr Gepäck?	Do you have any more luggage?

18

Baggage—Porters *Gepäck—Gepäckträger*

These days porters are only available at airports or the railway stations of large cities. Where no porters are available you'll find luggage trolleys for the use of the passengers.

Porter!	**Gepäckträger!**	gerpehktraigerr
Please take this luggage.	**Nehmen Sie bitte dieses Gepäck.**	naymern zee bitter deezerss gerpehk
That's mine.	**Das gehört mir.**	dahss gerhurrt meer
That's my suitcase/ (travelling) bag.	**Das ist mein Koffer/ meine (Reise)tasche.**	dahss ist mighn kofferr/ mighner (righzer)tahsher
There is one piece missing.	**Es fehlt ein Gepäck-stück.**	ehss faylt ighn gerpehk-shtewk
Please take this to the ...	**Bringen Sie das bitte ...**	bringern zee dahss bitter
bus/taxi	**zum Bus/Taxi**	tsum buss/tahksi
luggage lockers	**zu den Schließ-fächern**	tsoo dayn shleesfehkherrn
How much is that?	**Wieviel macht das?**	veefeel mahkht dahss
Where are the luggage trolleys (carts)?	**Wo sind die Koffer-kulis?**	voa zint dee kofferr-kooliss

Changing money *Geldwechsel*

Where's the nearest currency exchange office?	**Wo ist die nächste Wechselstube?**	voa ist dee naikhster vehkserlshtoober
Can you change these traveller's cheques (checks)?	**Können Sie diese Reiseschecks einlösen?**	kurnern zee deezer righzershehks ighnlurzern
I want to change some dollars/pounds.	**Ich möchte Dollar/ Pfund wechseln.**	ikh murkhter dollahr/pfunt vehkserln
Can you change this into ...?	**Können Sie das in ... umwechseln?**	kurnern zee dahss in ... umvehkserln
Austrian shillings	**Schilling**	shilling
German marks	**D-Mark**	day-mahrk
Swiss francs	**Schweizer Franken**	shvightserr frahnkern
What's the exchange rate?	**Wie ist der Wechselkurs?**	vee ist derr vehkserl-koors

BANK—CURRENCY, see page 129

Where is ...? *Wo ist ...?*

Where is the ...?	**Wo ist ...?**	voa ist
booking office	**der Reservierungs-schalter**	derr rehzerr**vee**rungs-shahlterr
car hire	**der Autoverleih**	derr **ow**toffehrligh
duty-free shop	**der Duty-free-Shop**	derr "duty-free-shop"
newsstand	**der Zeitungsstand**	derr **tsight**ungsshtahnt
restaurant	**das Restaurant**	dahss rehstor**rahng**
shopping gallery	**die Einkaufsgalerie**	dee **ighn**kowfsgahlehree
How do I get to Stuttgart?	**Wie komme ich nach Stuttgart?**	vee **kom**mer ikh nakh **shtut**gahrt
How do I get to the ... Hotel?	**Wie komme ich zum Hotel ...?**	vee **kom**mer ikh tsum hot**tehl**
Is there a bus into town?	**Fährt ein Bus ins Stadtzentrum?**	fairt ighn buss ins **shtaht**tsehntrum
Where can I get a taxi?	**Wo finde ich ein Taxi?**	voa **fin**der ikh ighn **tahk**si
Where can I hire (rent) a car?	**Wo kann ich ein Auto mieten?**	voa kahn ikh ighn **ow**to **mee**tern

Hotel reservation *Hotelreservierung*

Do you have a hotel guide?	**Haben Sie ein Hotel-verzeichnis?**	**haa**bern zee ighn hot**tehl**-fehrtsighkhniss
Could you reserve a room for me at a hotel/boarding house?	**Können Sie mir bitte ein Hotel-/Pensions-zimmer reservieren?**	**kur**nern zee meer **bit**ter ighn hot**tehl**/pehnzioans-tsimmerr rehzerr**vee**rern
in the centre	**im Zentrum**	im **tsehn**trum
near the railway station	**beim Bahnhof**	bighm **baan**hoaf
a single room	**ein Einzelzimmer**	ighn **ighnt**serltsimmerr
a double room	**ein Doppelzimmer**	ighn **dop**perltsimmerr
not too expensive	**nicht zu teuer**	nikht tsu **toy**err
Where is the hotel/boarding house?	**Wo liegt das Hotel/die Pension?**	voa leegt dahss hot**tehl**/dee pehn**zioan**
Do you have a street map?	**Haben Sie einen Stadtplan?**	**haa**bern zee **igh**nern **shtaht**plaan

HOTEL/ACCOMMODATION, see page 22

Car hire (rental) *Autoverleih*

To hire a car you must produce a valid driving licence (held for at least one year) and your passport. Some firms set a minimum age at 21, other 25. Holders of major credit cards are normally exempt from deposit payments, otherwise you must pay a substantial (refundable) deposit for a car. Third-party insurance is usually automatically included.

I'd like to hire (rent) a car.	Ich möchte ein Auto mieten.	ikh murkhter ighn owto meetern
small/medium-sized/ large	ein kleines/mittleres/ großes	ighn klighnerss/mitlerrerss groasserss
automatic	mit Automatik	mit owtommaatik
I'd like it for a day/a week.	Ich möchte es für einen Tag/eine Woche.	ikh murkhter ehss fewr ighnern taag/ighner vokher
Are there any week-end arrangements?	Gibt es Wochenend-pauschalen?	gipt ehss vokhernehnt-powshaalern
Do you have any special rates?	Haben Sie Sonder-tarife?	haabern zee zonderr-tahreefer
How much does it cost per day/week?	Wieviel kostet es pro Tag/Woche?	veefeel kostert ehss proa taag/vokher
Is mileage included?	Ist das Kilometer-geld inbegriffen?	ist dahss killommayterr-gehlt inbergriffern
What's the charge per kilometer?	Wieviel kostet es pro Kilometer?	veefeel kostert ehss proa killommayterr
I want to hire the car here and leave it in ...	Ich möchte den Wagen hier mieten und in ... zurück-geben.	ikh murkhter dayn vaagern heer meetern unt in ... tsoorewkgaybern
I want full insurance.	Ich möchte eine Vollkasko-versicherung.	ikh murkhter ighner folkahskoffehrzikherrung
What's the deposit?	Wieviel muß ich hinterlegen?	veefeel muss ikh hinterrlaygern
I've a credit card.	Ich habe eine Kreditkarte.	ikh haaber ighner krehditkahrter
Here's my driving licence.	Hier ist mein Führerschein.	heer ist mighn fewrerrshighn

CAR, see page 75

Taxi *Taxi*

A taxi is usually caught at a rank (*der Taxistand*—der **tahk**si-shtahnt). You can also phone for a taxi wherever you are; numbers are listed on a separate page in front of the phone books. All taxis have meters.

Where can I get a taxi?	**Wo finde ich ein Taxi?**	voa finder ikh ighn tahksi
Please get me a taxi.	**Besorgen Sie mir bitte ein Taxi.**	berzorgern zee meer bitter ighn tahksi
What's the fare to ...?	**Was kostet es bis ...?**	vahss kostert ehss biss
How far is it to ...?	**Wie weit ist es bis ...?**	vee vight ist ehss biss
Take me to ...	**Bringen Sie mich ...**	bringern zee mikh
this address	**zu dieser Adresse**	tsoo deezerr ahdrehsser
the airport	**zum Flughafen**	tsum flooghaafern
the railway station	**zum Bahnhof**	tsum baanhoaf
the town centre	**ins Stadtzentrum**	ins shtahttsehntrum
the ... Hotel	**zum Hotel ...**	tsum hottehl
Turn ... at the next corner.	**Biegen Sie an der nächsten Ecke ... ab.**	beegern zee ahn derr naikhstern ehker ... ahp
left/right	**links/rechts**	links/rehkhts
Go straight ahead.	**Geradeaus.**	gerraaderrowss
Please stop here.	**Halten Sie hier, bitte.**	hahltern zee heer bitter
I'm in a hurry.	**Ich habe es eilig.**	ikh haaber ehss ighlikh
Could you drive more slowly?	**Bitte fahren Sie langsamer.**	bitter faarern zee lahngzaamerr
Could you help me carry my luggage?	**Könnten Sie mir bitte beim Gepäcktragen helfen?**	kurntern zee meer bitter bighm gerpehktraagern hehlfern
Will you wait for me, please?	**Würden Sie bitte auf mich warten?**	vewrdern zee bitter owf mikh vahrtern
I'll be back in 10 minutes.	**Ich bin in 10 Minuten zurück.**	ikh bin in 10 minnootern tsoorewk

TIPPING, see inside back-cover

Hotel—Other accommodation

Early reservation and confirmation are essential in most major tourist centres during the high season. Most towns and arrival points have a tourist information office (*Fremdenverkehrsbüro*—**frehm**dernfehrkayrsbewroa), and that's the place to go if you're stuck without a room.

Hotel (hot**teh**l)	Hotel; simple or fancy, your room will be spotless. You'll probably sleep under a guilt filled with duck or goose down. *Hotel garni* means that only a room and breakfast are offered, no other meals.
Schloßhotel (shlos**hot**tehl)	Castle or palace converted into a hotel; often located in the countryside.
Rasthof (**rahst**hoaf)	Wayside lodge; motel; most are located just off a motorway (expressway) or principal route.
Gasthaus/Gasthof (**gahst**howss/**gahst**hoaf)	Inn
Pension/Fremdenheim (pehn**zioan**/**frehm**dernhighm)	Boarding-house; offers full or half board. *Zimmer frei* will tell you there's a room to let, sometimes also in a private home.
Jugendherberge (**yoo**gernthe**hr**behrger)	Youth hostel
Ferienwohnung (**fay**riernvoanung)	Furnished flat (apartment) found in holiday resorts; you'll probably have to reserve it in advance. Otherwise, contact the local tourist office.

Can you recommend a hotel/pension?	**Können Sie mir ein Hotel/eine Pension empfehlen?**	kurnern zee meer ighn hottehl/ighner pehnzioan ehmpfaylern
Do you have a hotel guide?	**Haben Sie ein Hotelverzeichnis?**	haabern zee ighn hottehlfehrtsighkhniss
Are there any flats (apartments) vacant?	**Gibt es noch freie Ferienwohnungen?**	gipt ehss nokh frigher fayriernvoanungern

CAMPING, see page 32

Checking in—Reception *Empfang*

My name is ...	**Mein Name ist ...**	mighn **naa**mer ist
I've a reservation.	**Ich habe reservieren lassen.**	ikh **haa**ber rehzerr**vee**rern **lah**ssern
We've reserved two rooms, a single and a double.	**Wir haben zwei Zimmer reservieren lassen – ein Einzelzimmer und ein Doppelzimmer.**	veer **haa**bern tsvigh **tsim**merr rehzerr**vee**rern **lah**ssern—ighn **ighnt**serltsimmerr unt ighn **dopperl**tsimmerr
Here's the confirmation.	**Hier ist die Bestätigung.**	heer ist dee ber**shtaitig**gung
Do you have any vacancies?	**Haben Sie noch freie Zimmer?**	**haa**bern zee nokh **frigh**er **tsim**merr
I'd like a ...	**Ich hätte gern ein ...**	ikh **heh**ter gehrn ighn
single room	**Einzelzimmer**	**ighnt**serltsimmerr
double room	**Doppelzimmer**	**dopperl**tsimmerr
A room ...	**Ein Zimmer ...**	ighn **tsim**merr
with twin beds	**mit zwei Einzelbetten**	mit tsvigh **ighnt**serlbehtern
with a double bed	**mit einem Doppelbett**	mit **igh**nerm **dopperl**beht
with a bath	**mit Bad**	mit baat
with a shower	**mit Dusche**	mit **dush**er
with a balcony	**mit Balkon**	mit **bahl**koan
with a view	**mit Aussicht**	mit **owss**ikht
facing the lake/ the mountains	**mit Blick auf den See/ auf die Berge**	mit blik owf dayn zay/ owf dee **behr**ger
in the front	**zur Straße**	tsoor **shtraass**er
at the back	**zum Hof**	tsum hoaf
It must be quiet.	**Es muß ruhig sein.**	ehss muss **rooikh** zighn
Is there ...?	**Gibt es ...?**	gipt ehss
air conditioning	**Klimaanlage**	**klee**mahnlaager
a radio/a television in the room	**Radio/Fernsehen im Zimmer**	**raa**dio/**fehrn**zayern im **tsim**merr
laundry service	**einen Wäschedienst**	**igh**nern **vehsh**erdeenst
room service	**Zimmerbedienung**	**tsim**merrberdeenung
hot water	**warmes Wasser**	**vahr**merss **vahss**err
running water	**fließendes Wasser**	**fleess**ernderss **vahss**err
a private toilet	**eine eigene Toilette**	**igh**ner **igh**gerner toah**leht**er
Could you put an extra bed in the room?	**Könnten Sie ein zusätzliches Bett ins Zimmer stellen?**	**kurn**tern zee ighn **tsoo**zehtslikhers beht ins **tsim**merr **shteh**lern

CHECKING OUT, see page 31

How much? *Wieviel?*

What's the price ...?	**Wieviel kostet es ...?**	vee**feel** kostert ehss
per night	**pro Nacht**	proa nahkht
per week	**pro Woche**	proa **vokher**
for bed and breakfast	**für Übernachtung mit Frühstück**	fewr ewber**nahkh**tung mit **frew**shtewk
excluding meals	**ohne Mahlzeiten**	**oa**ner **maalts**ightern
for full board (A.P.)	**mit Vollpension**	mit **fol**pehnzioan
for half board (M.A.P.)	**mit Halbpension**	mit **hahlb**pehnzioan
Does that include ...?	**Ist ... inbegriffen?**	ist ... **in**begriffern
breakfast	**Frühstück**	**frew**shtewk
service	**Bedienung**	ber**dee**nung
Value-Added Tax (VAT)*	**Mehrwertsteuer**	**mayr**vayrtshtoyerr
Is there any reduction for children?	**Gibt es Ermäßigung für Kinder?**	gipt ehss ehr**mai**ssigung fewr **kin**derr
Do you charge for the baby?	**Berechnen Sie etwas für das Baby?**	ber**rehkh**nern zee **eht**vahss fewr dahss ''baby''
That's too expensive.	**Das ist zu teuer.**	dahss ist tsu **toy**err
Haven't you anything cheaper?	**Haben Sie nichts Billigeres?**	**haa**bern zee nikhts **bil**liggerrerss

Decision *Entscheidung*

May I see the room?	**Kann ich das Zimmer sehen?**	kahn ikh dahss **tsim**merr **zay**ern
That's fine. I'll take it.	**Gut, ich nehme es.**	goot ikh **nay**mer ehss
No, I don't like it.	**Nein, es gefällt mir nicht.**	nighn ehss ger**fehlt** meer nikht
It's too ...	**Es ist zu ...**	ehss ist tsu
cold/hot	**kalt/warm**	kahlt/vahrm
dark/small	**dunkel/klein**	**dun**kerl/klighn
noisy	**laut**	lowt
I asked for a room with a bath.	**Ich wollte ein Zimmer mit Bad.**	ikh **vol**ter ighn **tsim**merr mit baat

---

* Americans note: a type of sales tax in Germany and Austria

NUMBERS, see page 147

Do you have anything …?	**Haben Sie etwas …?**	**haab**ern zee **eht**vahss
better/bigger	**Besseres/Größeres**	**behss**errerrs/**grurs**serrerrs
cheaper/quieter	**Billigeres/Ruhigeres**	**billi**ggerrerrs/**rooi**ggerrerrs
higher up/lower down	**weiter oben/weiter unten**	**vighter** oabern/**vighter** untern
Do you have a room with a better view?	**Haben Sie ein Zimmer mit einer besseren Aussicht?**	**haab**ern zee ighn **tsimmer** mit **igh**nerr **behss**errern **owss**ikht

Registration *Anmeldung*

Upon arrival at a hotel or boarding-house you may be asked to fill in a registration form. (*Anmeldeschein*—**ahn**mehldershighn).

Name/Vorname	Name/First name
Wohnort/Straße/Nr.	Home address/Street/Number
Nationalität/Beruf	Nationality/Profession
Geburtsdatum/Geburtsort	Date/Place of birth
Letzter Aufenthaltsort/ Reiseziel	Coming from/Going to
Paßnummer	Passport number
Kraftfahrzeugnummer	Car number
Ort/Datum	Place/Date
Unterschrift	Signature

What does this mean?	**Was bedeutet das?**	vahss ber**doy**tert dahss

Kann ich Ihren Paß sehen?	May I see your passport?
Würden Sie bitte den Anmeldeschein ausfüllen?	Would you mind filling in the registration form?
Unterschreiben Sie hier, bitte.	Please sign here.
Wie lange bleiben Sie?	How long will you be staying?

We'll be staying ...	Wir bleiben ...	veer blighbern
overnight only	nur eine Nacht	noor ighner nahkht
a few days	einige Tage	ighnigger taager
a week (at least)	(mindestens) eine Woche	(mindersterns) ighner vokher
I don't know yet.	Ich weiß es noch nicht.	ikh vighss ehss nokh nikht

Hotel staff *Hotelpersonal*

hall porter	der Portier	derr portyayr
maid	das Zimmermädchen	dahss tsimmermaitkhern
manager	der Direktor	derr dirrehktor
page (bellboy)	der Page	derr paazher
porter	der Hausdiener	derr howsdeenerr
receptionist	der Empfangschef	derr empfahngsshehf
switchboard operator	die Telefonistin	dee taylayfoanistin
waiter	der Kellner	derr kehlnerr
waitress	die Kellnerin	dee kehlnerrin

If you want to address members of the staff, don't say *Herr, Frau* or *Fräulein,* but use an introductory phrase such as:

| Excuse me. Could you please ...? | Entschuldigung. Könnten Sie bitte ...? | ehntshuldiggung. kurntern zee bitter |

General requirements *Allgemeine Fragen*

What's my room number?	Welche Zimmernummer habe ich?	vehlker tsimmernummerr haaber ikh
The key, please.	Den Schlüssel, bitte.	dayn shlewsserl bitter
Where can I park my car?	Wo kann ich meinen Wagen parken?	voa kahn ikh mighnern vaagern pahrkern
Does the hotel have a garage?	Gibt es eine Hotelgarage?	gipt ehss ighner hottehlgahraazher
Will you have our luggage sent up?	Bitte schicken Sie unser Gepäck hinauf.	bitter shikkern zee unzerr gerpehk hinnowf
I'd like to leave this in your safe.	Ich möchte dies in Ihrem Safe lassen.	ikh murkhter deess in eererm "safe" lahssern

Is there a bath on this floor?	Gibt es ein Bad auf dieser Etage?	gipt ehss ighn baat owf deezerr aytaazher
What's the voltage here?	Welche Stromspannung haben Sie hier?	vehlkher shtroamshpahnung haabern zee heer
Where's the outlet for the shaver?	Wo ist die Steckdose für den Rasierapparat?	voa ist dee shtehkdoazer fewr dayn rahzeerahpahraat
Would you please wake me at ...?	Würden Sie mich bitte um ... Uhr wecken?	vewrdern zee mikh bitter um ... oor vehkern
Can we have breakfast in our room?	Können wir im Zimmer frühstücken?	kurnern veer im tsimmerr frewshtewkern
Can you find me a ...?	Können Sie mir ... besorgen?	kurnern zee meer ... berzorgern
babysitter	einen Babysitter	ighnern "babysitter"
secretary	eine Sekretärin	ighner zaykraytairin
typewriter	eine Schreibmaschine	ighner shrighpmahsheener
May I have a/an/some ...?	Kann ich ... haben?	kahn ikh ... haabern
ashtray	einen Aschenbecher	ighnern ahshernbehkherr
bath towel	ein Badetuch	ighn baadertookh
(extra) blanket	eine (extra) Decke	ighner (ekstraa) dehker
envelopes	Briefumschläge	breefumschlaager
(more) hangers	(noch) einige Kleiderbügel	(nokh) ighnigger klighderrbewgerl
hot-water bottle	eine Wärmflasche	ighner vehrmflahsher
ice cubes	Eiswürfel	ighsvewrferl
needle and thread	eine Nadel und etwas Faden	ighner naaderl unt ehtvahss faadern
(extra) pillow	ein (extra) Kopfkissen	ighn(ekstraa) kopfkissern
reading-lamp	eine Leselampe	ighner layzerlahmper
soap	Seife	zighfer
writing-paper	Schreibpapier	shrighppahpeer
Where's the ...?	Wo ist ...?	voa ist
bathroom	das Bad	dahss baat
dining-room	der Speisesaal	derr shpighzerzaal
emergency exit	der Notausgang	derr noatowsgahng
hairdresser's	der Friseur	derr frizurr
lift (elevator)	der Fahrstuhl	derr faarshtool
television room	der Fernsehraum	derr fehrnzayrowm
toilet	die Toilette	dee toahlehter

Telephone—Post (mail) *Telefon – Post*

Can you put me through to Vienna 12 34 56?	**Können Sie mich mit Wien 12 34 56 verbinden?**	kurnern zee mikh mit veen 12 34 56 fehrbindern
Do you have stamps?	**Haben Sie Briefmarken?**	haabern zee breefmahrkern
Would you post this for me, please?	**Würden Sie das bitte für mich aufgeben?**	vewrdern zee dahss bitter fewr mikh owfgaybern
Is there any mail for me?	**Ist Post für mich da?**	ist post fewr mikh daa
Are there any messages for me?	**Hat jemand eine Nachricht für mich hinterlassen?**	haht yaymahnt ighner naakhrikht fewr mikh hinterrlahssern
How much are my telephone charges?	**Wie hoch ist meine Telefonrechnung?**	vee hoakh ist mighner taylayfoanrehkhnung

Difficulties *Schwierigkeiten*

The ... doesn't work.	**... funktioniert nicht.**	... funktsionneert nikht
air conditioner	**die Klimaanlage**	dee kleemahahnlaager
fan	**der Ventilator**	derr vehntillaator
heating	**die Heizung**	dee hightsung
light	**das Licht**	dahss likht
radio	**das Radio**	dahss raadio
television	**der Fernseher**	derr fehrnzayerr
The tap (faucet) is dripping.	**Der Wasserhahn tropft.**	derr vahsserrhaan tropft
There's no hot water.	**Es gibt kein warmes Wasser.**	ehs gipt kighn vahrmers vahsserr
The wash-basin is blocked.	**Das Waschbecken ist verstopft.**	dahss vahshbehkern ist fehrshtopft
The window/The door is jammed.	**Das Fenster/Die Tür klemmt.**	dahss fehnsterr/dee tewr klehmt
The curtain is stuck.	**Der Vorhang klemmt.**	derr foarhahng klehmt
The bulb is burned out.	**Die Birne ist kaputt.**	dee beerner ist kahput
My room has not been made up.	**Mein Zimmer ist nicht gemacht.**	mighn tsimmerr ist nikht germahkht

POST OFFICE AND TELEPHONE, see page 132

The ... is broken.	... ist kaputt.	... ist kahput
blind	das Rollo	dahss rollo
lamp	die Lampe	dee lahmper
plug	der Stecker	derr shtehkerr
shutter	der Fensterladen	derr fehnsterrlaadern
switch	der Schalter	derr shahlterr
Can you get it repaired?	Können Sie es reparieren lassen?	kurnern zee ehss rehpahreerern lahssern

Laundry—Dry cleaner's   *Wäscherei – Reinigung*

I want these clothes ...	Ich möchte diese Kleider ... lassen.	ikh murkhter deezer klighderr ... lahssern
cleaned	reinigen	righniggern
ironed	bügeln	bewgerln
pressed	dampfbügeln	dahmpfbewgerln
washed	waschen	vahshern
When will they be ready?	Wann sind sie fertig?	vahn zint zee fehrtikh
I need them ...	Ich brauche sie ...	ikh browkher zee
today	heute	hoyter
tonight	heute abend	hoyter aabernt
tomorrow	morgen	morgern
before Friday	vor Freitag	foar frightaag
Can you ... this?	Können Sie das ...?	kurnern zee dahss
mend	ausbessern	owsbehsserrn
patch	flicken	flikkern
stitch	nähen	naiern
Can you sew on this button?	Können Sie diesen Knopf annähen?	kurnern zee deezern knopf ahnnaiern
Can you get this stain out?	Können Sie diesen Fleck entfernen?	kurnern zee deezern flehk ehntfehrnern
Is my laundry ready?	Ist meine Wäsche fertig?	ist mighner vehsher fehrtikh
This isn't mine.	Das gehört nicht mir.	dahss gerhurrt nikht meer
There's one piece missing.	Es fehlt ein Stück.	ehss faylt ighn shtewk
There's a hole in this.	Da ist ein Loch drin.	daa ist ighn lokh drin

DAYS OF THE WEEK, see page 151

HOTEL

30

Hairdresser's—Barber's *Damen- und Herrenfriseur*

Is there a hairdresser/beauty salon in the hotel?	Gibt es einen Friseur/Kosmetiksalon im Hotel?	gipt ehss **ighnern** frizurr/kosmaytikzahlong im hottehl
Can I make an appointment for sometime on Thursday?	Kann ich mich für Donnerstag anmelden?	kahn ikh mikh fewr donnerrstaag **ahn**mehldern
I'd like it cut and shaped.	Schneiden und Legen, bitte.	**shnigh**dern unt **layg**ern **bitt**er
The parting (part) left/right, please.	Den Scheitel links/rechts, bitte.	dayn **shight**erl links/rehkhts **bitt**er
I want a haircut, please.	Haare schneiden, bitte.	**haar**er **shnigh**dern **bitt**er
bleach	eine Aufhellung	**ighn**er **owf**hehlung
blow-dry	fönen	**furn**ern
colour rinse	eine Farbspülung	**ighn**er **fahrp**shpewlung
dye	färben	**fehr**bern
face-pack	eine Gesichtsmaske	**ighn**er ger**zikhts**mahsker
manicure	eine Maniküre	**ighn**er **mahni**kewrer
permanent wave	eine Dauerwelle	**ighn**er **dow**errvehler
setting lotion	ein Haarfestiger	ighn **haar**fehstiggerr
shampoo and set	Waschen und Legen	**vahsh**ern unt **layg**ern
with a fringe (bangs)	mit Ponyfransen	mit **ponni**frahnzern
I'd like a shampoo for ... hair.	Ein Haarwaschmittel für ... Haar, bitte.	ighn **haar**vahshmitterl fewr ... haar **bitt**er
normal/dry/greasy (oily)	normales/trockenes/fettiges	nor**maal**erss/**trokk**ernerss/**fehtt**iggerss
Do you have a colour chart?	Haben Sie eine Farbtabelle?	**haa**bern zee **ighn**er **fahrp**tahbehler
Don't cut it too short.	Nicht zu kurz schneiden.	nikht tsu koorts **shnigh**dern
A little more off the ...	Bitte ... etwas kürzer.	**bitt**er ... **eht**vahss **kewrt**serr
back	hinten	**hint**ern
neck	im Nacken	im **nahk**ern
sides	an den Seiten	ahn dayn **zight**ern
top	oben	**oab**ern
I don't want any hairspray.	Kein Haarspray, bitte.	kighn **haar**shpray **bitt**er
I'd like a shave.	Rasieren, bitte.	rah**zeer**ern **bitt**er

DAYS OF THE WEEK, see page 151

Would you please trim my ...?	**Stutzen Sie mir bitte ...**	shtutsern zee meer bitter
beard	**den Bart**	dayn baart
moustache	**den Schnurrbart**	dayn shnoorbaart
sideboards (sideburns)	**die Koteletten**	dee kotlehtern

Checking out *Abreise*

May I please have my bill?	**Kann ich bitte die Rechnung haben?**	kahn ikh bitter dee rehkhnung haabern
I'm leaving early tomorrow. Please have my bill ready.	**Ich reise morgen früh ab. Bereiten Sie bitte meine Rechnung vor.**	ikh righzer morgern frew ahp. berrightern zee bitter mighner rehkhnung foar
I must leave at once.	**Ich muß sofort abreisen.**	ikh muss zoafort ahprighzern
Is everything included?	**Ist alles inbegriffen?**	ist ahlerss inbergriffen
Can I pay by credit card?	**Kann ich mit Kreditkarte bezahlen?**	kahn ikh mit krehditkahrter bertsaalern
You've made a mistake in this bill, I think.	**Ich glaube, Sie haben sich verrechnet.**	ikh glowber zee haabern zikh fehrrehkhnert
Can you get us a taxi?	**Können Sie uns ein Taxi bestellen?**	kurnern zee uns ighn tahksi bershtehlern
Could you have our luggage brought down, please?	**Würden Sie bitte unser Gepäck herunterbringen lassen?**	vewrdern zee bitter unzerr gerpehk hehrunterrbringern lahssern
We're in a great hurry.	**Wir haben es sehr eilig.**	veer haabern ehss zayr ighlikh
Here's the forwarding address.	**Hier ist meine Nachsendeadresse.**	heer ist mighner naakhzehnderahdrehsser
You have my home address.	**Sie haben meine Wohnadresse.**	zee haabern mighner voanahdrehsser
It's been a very enjoyable stay.	**Es war ein sehr angenehmer Aufenthalt.**	ehss vaar ighn zayr ahngernaymerr owfehnthahlt

TIPPING, see inside back-cover

Camping

There are plenty of authorized camp sites in Germany, many
with excellent facilities. Austria and Switzerland also have
well-equipped camp sites, some of them high up in the
mountains. For information apply to any Tourist Office.

Is there a camp site near here?	**Gibt es hier in der Nähe einen Campingplatz?**	gipt ehss heer in derr naier ighnern kehmpingplahts
Can we camp here?	**Können wir hier zelten?**	kurnern veer heer tsehltern
Have you room for a tent/caravan (trailer)?	**Haben Sie Platz für ein Zelt/einen Wohnwagen?**	haabern zee plahts fewr ighn tsehlt/ighnern voanvaagern
Is there/Are there (a) ...?	**Gibt es ...?**	gipt ehss
drinking water	**Trinkwasser**	trinkvahsserr
electricity	**Stromanschluß**	shtroamahnshluss
playground	**einen Spielplatz**	ighnern shpeelplahts
restaurant	**ein Restaurant**	ighn rehstorrahng
shopping facilities	**Einkaufs- möglichkeiten**	ighnkowfsmurglikhkightern
swimming pool	**ein Schwimmbad**	ighn shvimbaat
What's the charge ...?	**Wie hoch sind die Gebühren ...?**	vee hoakh zint dee gerbewrern
per day	**pro Tag**	proa taag
per person	**pro Person**	proa pehrzoan
for a car	**für ein Auto**	fewr ighn owto
for a caravan (trailer)	**für einen Wohn- wagen**	fewr ighnern voan- vaagern
for a tent	**für ein Zelt**	fewr ighn tsehlt
Is the tourist tax included?	**Ist die Kurtaxe inbegriffen?**	ist dee koortahkser inbergriffern
Where are the showers/toilets?	**Wo sind die Duschen/ die Toiletten?**	voa zint dee dushern/ dee toahlehtern
Where can I get butane gas?	**Wo kann ich Butan- gas bekommen?**	voa kahn ikh buttaangaass berkommern
Is there a youth hostel near here?	**Gibt es hier irgend- wo eine Jugend- herberge?**	gipt ehss heer eergerntvoa ighner yoogernthehrbehrger

CAMPING EQUIPMENT, see page 106

Eating out

There are many types of places where you can eat and drink in Germany, Austria and Switzerland.

Beisel (bighzerl)	The Austrian equivalent to a *Gasthaus*.
Bierhalle (beerhahler)	Beer hall; besides beer served from huge barrels, you'll also be able to order hot dishes, sausages, salads and pretzels. The best-known beer halls are those in Munich which has a giant beer festival *(Oktoberfest)* annually in late September.
Bierstube (beershtoober)	The nearest equivalent to an English pub or an American tavern though the atmosphere may be very different; usually only serves a few "dishes of the day".
Café (kahfay)	Coffee shop; besides coffee, you'll be able to get pastries, snacks and drinks. There's a small dance floor in a *Tanzcafé*.
Gasthaus/Gasthof (gahsthowss/gahsthoaf)	Inn, usually in the country. It offers home-cooking and a folksy atmosphere.
Gaststätte (gahstshtehter)	Another word for *Restaurant*.
Kaffeehaus (kahfayhowss)	The Austrian equivalent to a *Café*.
Konditorei (kondeetoarigh)	A pastry shop; will often have a salon for coffee and pastries.
Milchbar (milkhbaar)	A bar serving mainly plain and flavoured milk drinks with pastries. Also called a *Milchstübl*.
Raststätte (rahstshtehter)	Roadside restaurant; also called a *Rasthof* in Austria; it's usually found on a motorway (expressway). Lodging and service-station facilities are on the premises.
Ratskeller (rahtskehlerr)	A restaurant in the cellar of the town-hall (often a very historic, old building); food is generally excellent.
Restaurant (rehstorrahng)	These are generally found only in urban areas. Menus often cater to foreign visitors as well as offering numerous local specialities.

Schnellbuffet (**shnehl**bewfay)	A snack bar; often with counter service.
Schnellimbiß (**shneh**limbiss)	Snack bar; the English term is also seen. The principal fare is beer and sausages. A sausage stand *(Würstchenstand)* is often quite similar.
Tea-room ("tea-room")	The Swiss equivalent to a *Café.*
Weinstube (**vighn**shtoober)	A cozy type of restaurant found in wine-producing districts where you can sample new wine with simple hot dishes and snacks. In Austria, it's called a *Heuriger* and is identified by a wreath hanging over the portal.

Meal times *Essenszeiten*

Breakfast (*das Frühstück*—dahss **frew**shtewk) is served from 7 a.m. to 10 a.m. and is generally included in the hotel arrangement.

Lunch (*das Mittagessen*—dahss **mit**tahgehssern) is generally served from 11.30 a.m. until 2 p.m.

Dinner (*das Abendessen*—dahss **aa**berntehssern) is served from 6.30 to 8.30 p.m., in large restaurants to 10 or 11 p.m. After this it's usually a case of cold snacks or hot sausages only.

Eating habits *Eßgewohnheiten*

Germans start the day early with a meal that is somewhat more substantial than the typical "continental" breakfast, and they like to eat their main meal in the middle of the day. Supper is generally a slightly more copious version of breakfast—cold meat and cheese, with the addition of a salad. Most restaurants will, however, serve a three course dinner in the evening.

On weekends Germans often eat an afternoon snack. It can be either coffee or tea with pastries, or cold meat and cheese.

Fellow diners usually wish each other *"Mahlzeit"* or *"Guten Appetit".*

German cuisine   *Die deutsche Küche*

German cuisine has undergone many changes in the postwar years. Non-fattening, healthy fare has become more popular, and the influence of French, Italian, Greek, Chinese and other cuisines is remarkable. However, rich hearty dishes, mostly with pork and potatoes, are still served. Each region has its own specialities, and almost each town its own beer (or wine), but everywhere you'll find an extraordinary range of sausages, smoked ham, soused fish and many kinds of good bread. Not to mention *Sauerkraut, Schnitzel, Spätzle, Frankfurter, Frikadellen, Rollmops* ... And if you like game, Germany is the place.

Möchten Sie etwas essen?	Would you like to eat something?
Was nehmen Sie?	What would you like?
Ich empfehle Ihnen ...	I recommend ...
Was trinken Sie?	What would you like to drink?
Möchten Sie ...?	Do you want ...?
... haben wir nicht.	We haven't got ...

Hungry?   *Hungrig?*

I'm hungry/I'm thirsty.	**Ich habe Hunger/ Ich habe Durst.**	ikh **haaber hunger**/ikh **haaber doorst**
Can you recommend a good restaurant?	**Können Sie mir ein gutes Restaurant empfehlen?**	kurnern zee meer ighn **gooterss** rehstor**rahng** ehmp**faylern**
Is there an inexpensive restaurant around here?	**Gibt es in der Nähe ein preiswertes Restaurant?**	gibt ehss in derr **naier** ighn **prighs**vehrterss rehstor**rahng**

If you want to be sure of getting a table in well-known restaurants, it may be better to telephone in advance.

I'd like to reserve a table for 4.	Ich möchte einen Tisch für 4 Personen reservieren lassen.	ikh murkhter ighnern tish fewr 4 pehrzoanern rehzehrveerern lahssern
We'll come at 8.	Wir kommen um 8 Uhr.	veer kommern um 8 oor
Could we have a table ...?	Können wir einen Tisch ... haben?	kurnern veer ighnern tish ... haabern
in the corner	in der Ecke	in derr ehker
by the window	am Fenster	ahm fehnsterr
outside	im Freien	im frighern
on the terrace	auf der Terrasse	owf derr tehrahsser
in a nonsmoking area	in der Nichtraucherecke	in derr nikhtrowkherrehker

Asking and ordering *Fragen und Bestellen*

Waiter/Waitress!	Herr Ober/Fräulein, bitte!	hehr oaberr/froylighn bitter
I'd like something to eat/drink.	Ich möchte gerne essen/etwas trinken.	ikh murkhter gehrner ehssern/ehtvahss trinkern
May I have the menu, please?	Kann ich bitte die Speisekarte haben?	kahn ikh bitter dee shpighzerkahrter haabern
Do you have a set menu/local dishes?	Haben Sie ein Gedeck/hiesige Gerichte?	haabern zee ighn gerdehk/heezigger gerrikhter
What do you recommend?	Was würden Sie mir empfehlen?	vahss vewrdern zee meer ehmpfaylern
I'd like ...	Ich hätte gern ...	ikh hehter gehrn
Could we have a/an ..., please?	Könnten wir bitte ... haben?	kurntern veer bitter ... haabern
ashtray	einen Aschenbecher	ighnern ahshernbehkherr
cup	eine Tasse	ighner tahsser
fork	eine Gabel	ighner gaaberl
glass	ein Glas	ighn glaass
knife	ein Messer	ighn mehsserr
napkin (serviette)	eine Serviette	ighner sehrviehter
plate	einen Teller	ighnern tehlerr
spoon	einen Löffel	ighnern lurferl
May I have some ...?	Könnte ich etwas ... haben?	kurnter ikh ehtvahss ... haabern
bread	Brot	broat
butter	Butter	butterr

lemon	**Zitrone**	tsitroaner
mustard	**Senf**	zehnf
pepper	**Pfeffer**	pfehferr
salt	**Salz**	zahlts
seasoning	**Würze**	vewrtser
sugar	**Zucker**	tsukkerr

Some useful expressions for dieters and special requirements:

I'm on a diet.	**Ich muß Diät leben.**	ikh muss deeait laybern
I don't drink alcohol.	**Ich trinke keinen Alkohol.**	ikh trinker kighnern ahlkohoal
I mustn't eat food containing ...	**Ich darf nichts essen, was ... enthält.**	ikh dahrf nikhts ehssern vahss ... ehnthehlt
flour/fat	**Mehl/Fett**	mayl/feht
salt/sugar	**Salz/Zucker**	zahlts/tsukkerr
Do you have ... for diabetics?	**Haben Sie ... für Diabetiker?**	haabern zee ... fewr deeahbaytikkerr
cakes	**Kuchen**	kookhern
fruit juice	**Fruchtsaft**	frukhtzahft
special menu	**ein Spezialmenü**	ighn shpehtsiahlmaynew
Do you have vegetarian dishes?	**Haben Sie vegetarische Gerichte?**	haabern zee vehgehtaarisher gerrikhter
Could I have cheese/fruit instead of the dessert?	**Könnte ich statt der Süßspeise Käse/Obst haben?**	kurnter ikh shtaht derr zewsshpighzer kaizer/opst haabern
Can I have an artificial sweetener?	**Kann ich Süßstoff haben?**	kahn ikh zewsshtof haabern

And ...

I'd like some more.	**Ich möchte etwas mehr.**	ikh murkhter ehtvahss mayr
Can I have more ..., please.	**Kann ich noch ... haben, bitte?**	kahn ikh nokh ... haabern bitter
Just a small portion.	**Nur eine kleine Portion.**	noor ighner klighner portsioan
Nothing more, thanks.	**Nichts mehr, danke.**	nikhts mayr dahnker
Where are the toilets?	**Wo ist die Toilette?**	voa ist dee toahlehter

Breakfast *Frühstück*

A German breakfast is a rather substantial meal. You may
be served cold meat, cheese, a variety of breads—*Schwarz-
brot, Vollkornbrot, Roggenbrot, Weißbrot* (black, whole-
grain, rye, white)—and rolls *(Brötchen* or *Semmeln)* or
croissants *(Hörnchen)* with butter and jam, accompanied by
coffee or tea.

I'd like breakfast, please.	Ich möchte frühstücken, bitte.	ikh murkhter frewshtewkern bitter
I'll have a/an/some ...	Ich hätte gern ...	ikh hehter gehrn
bacon and eggs	Spiegeleier mit Speck	shpeegerligherr mit shpehk
boiled egg	ein gekochtes Ei	ighn gerkokhterss igh
soft/hard	weich/hartgekocht	vighkh/hahrtgerkokht
cereal	Getreideflocken	gertrighderflokkern
cheese	Käse	kaizer
eggs	Eier	igherr
fried eggs	Spiegeleier	shpeegerligherr
scrambled eggs	Rühreier	rewrigherr
grapefruit juice	Grapefruitsaft	grehpfrootzahft
ham and eggs	Spiegeleier mit Schinken	shpeegerligherr mit shinkern
jam	Marmelade	mahrmehlaader
marmalade	Apfelsinenmarmelade	ahpferlzeenernmahrmehlaader
orange juice	Orangensaft	orrahngzhernzahft
toast	Toast	toast
May I have some ...?	Kann ich ... haben?	kahn ikh ... haabern
bread	Brot	broat
butter	Butter	butterr
(hot) chocolate	(heiße) Schokolade	(highsser) shokkollaader
coffee	Kaffee	kahfay
decaffeinated	koffeinfreien Kaffee	koffeheenfrighern kahfay
black	schwarzen Kaffee	shvahrtsern kahfay
with milk	Milchkaffee	milkhkahfay
honey	Honig	hoanikh
milk	Milch	milkh
hot/cold	heiße/kalte	highsser/kahlter
rolls	Brötchen	brurtkhern
tea	Tee	tay
with milk/lemon	mit Milch/Zitrone	mit milkh/tsitroaner
(hot) water	(heißes) Wasser	(highsserss) vahsserr

What's on the menu? *Was steht auf der Speisekarte?*

Most restaurants display a menu *(Speisekarte)* outside. Besides the à la carte menu, they'll usually offer one or more set menus *(Menü* or *Gedeck)*. Value-added tax—a type of sales tax *(Mehrwertsteuer* or *Mwst)*—and a service charge *(Bedienung)* are usually included.

Under the headings below you'll find alphabetical lists of dishes that might be offered on a German menu, with their English equivalent. You can simply show the book to the waiter. If you want some cheese, for instance, let *him* point to what's available on the appropriate list. Use pages 36 and 37 for ordering in general.

Reading the menu *Die Speisekarte entziffern*

Tagesgedeck	Set menu of the day
Tagesgericht	Dish of the day
Spezialität des Hauses	Speciality of the house
Unser Küchenchef empfiehlt ...	The chef recommends ...
Nach ... art	... style
Hausgemacht	Home-made
Dasselbe mit ...	The same served with ...
Nur auf Bestellung	Made to order
Alle Preise sind inklusive Bedienung und Mehrwertsteuer	Service charge and VAT (sales tax) included
... im Preis inbegriffen	... included in the price
Nach Wahl	At your choice
Extraaufschlag	Extra charge

Beilagen	bighlaagern	accompaniments
Eierspeisen	ighershpighzern	egg dishes
Eintopfgerichte	ighntopfgerrikhter	stews
Eis	ighss	ice-cream
Fischgerichte	fishgerrikhter	fish
Fleischgerichte	flighshgerrikhter	meat
Glace	glahsser	ice-cream
Gemüse	germewzer	vegetables
Geflügel	gerflewgerl	poultry
Getränke	gertrainker	drinks
Hauptgerichte	howptgerrikhter	main course
Käse	kaizer	cheese
Meeresfrüchte	mayrersfrewkhter	seafood
Nachspeisen/ Nachtisch	naakhshpighzern/ naakhtish	desserts
Obst	oapst	fruit
Reisgerichte	righsgerrikhter	rice
Salate	zahlaater	salads
Suppen	zuppern	soups
Süßspeisen	zewsshpighzern	desserts
Teigwaren	tighkvaarern	pasta
Vom Rost	fom roast	grilled (broiled)
Vorspeisen	foarshpighzern	first course
Wein	vighn	wine
Wild	vilt	game

Appetizers *Vorspeisen*

If you feel like something to whet your appetite, choose carefully, for the German appetizer can be filling. Starters may also be listed on the menu under *Kleine Gerichte* or *Kalte Platten*.

I'd like an appetizer.	**Ich hätte gern eine Vorspeise.**	ikh **heh**ter gehrn **igh**ner **foar**shpighzer
Aal (in Gelee)	aal in zher**lay**	(jellied) eel
Appetithäppchen	ahpeh**teet**hehpkhern	canapés
Artischocken	ahrti**shok**kern	artichoke
Austern	**ow**sterrn	oysters
Bündnerfleisch	**bewnd**nerrf**ligh**sh	cured, dried beef served in thin slices
Bückling	**bewk**ling	bloater, kipper
Fleischpastete	**fligh**shpahs**tay**ter	meat loaf
Froschschenkel	**froshs**hehn**kerl**	frog's legs
Gänseleberpastete	**gehn**zerlayberr-pahs**tay**ter	pâté, goose liver purée
Hering	**hay**ring	herring
Hummer	**hum**merr	lobster
Hummerkrabben	**hum**merr**krahb**ern	large prawns
Käsehäppchen	**kai**zerhehpkhern	cheese sticks
Krabben	**krahb**ern	prawns, shrimps
Krebs	**krayps**	river crayfish
Lachs	**lahks**	salmon
Languste	**lahng**guster	spiny lobster
Makrele	mah**kray**ler	mackerel
Muscheln	**mush**erln	mussels
Pilze	**pilt**ser	mushrooms
Räucheraal	**royk**herraal	smoked eel
Räucherhering	**royk**herr**hay**ring	smoked herring
Rollmops	**rol**mops	soused herring
Rohschinken	**roa**shinkern	cured ham
Russische Eier	**rus**sisher **igh**err	hard-boiled eggs with mayonnaise
Sardellen	zahr**deh**lern	anchovies
Sardinen	zahr**dee**nern	sardines
Schinken	**shin**kern	ham
Schnecken	**shneh**kern	snails
Spargelspitzen	**shpaar**gerlshpitsern	asparagus tips
Thunfisch	**toon**fish	tunny, tuna
Wurst	**voorst**	sausage
Wurstplatte	**voorst**plahter	assorted cold cuts

Bismarckhering (**bis**mahrkhayring)	soused herring with onions
Frisch geräucherte Gänsebrust auf Toast (frish gerroykherrter gehnzerbrust owf toast)	freshly smoked breast of goose on toast
Hoppel-Poppel (hopperl-popperl)	scrambled eggs with diced sausages or bacon
Königinpastete (kurnigginpahstayter)	puff-pastry shell filled with diced meat and mushrooms
Matjeshering (mahtyehshayring)	salted young herring
Matjesfilet nach Hausfrauenart (mahtyehsfillay nahk howsfrowernahrt)	fillets of herring with apples and onions
Hausgemachte Rehpastete (howsgermakhkter raypahstayter)	home-made venison meatloaf
Schinkenröllchen mit Spargel (shinkernrurlkhern mit shpahrgerl)	rolled ham with asparagus filling
Strammer Max (shtrahmerr mahkss)	slice of bread with highly spiced minced pork served with fried eggs and onions

Soups and stews   *Suppen und Eintopfgerichte*

German soup can be hearty fare and particularly welcome on a cold day. *Eintopf* is a stew and will usually be a meal in itself.

I'd like some soup.	**Ich möchte gern eine Suppe.**	ikh **murkh**ter gehrn **igh**ner **zup**per
Aalsuppe	**aal**zupper	eel soup
Bauernsuppe	**bow**errnzupper	cabbage and frank-furter soup
Bohnensuppe	**boan**ernzupper	bean soup with bacon
Bouillon	**boo**lyong	clear soup
Erbsensuppe	**ehrp**zernzupper	pea soup
Fischsuppe	**fish**zupper	fish soup
Fischbeuschelsuppe	**fish**boysherlzupper	fish roe and vegetable soup
Fridattensuppe	**fridd**ahternzupper	broth with pancake strips

Frühlingssuppe	frewlingssupper	spring vegetable soup
Grießnockerlsuppe	greessnokkerrlzupper	semolina-dumpling soup
Gulaschsuppe	goolahshzupper	spiced soup of stewed beef
Hühnerbrühe	hewnerrbrewer	chicken broth
Kartoffelsuppe	kahrtofferlzupper	potato soup
(Semmel-) Knödelsuppe	(zehmerl-) knurderlzupper	dumpling soup
Königinsuppe	kurnigginzupper	soup with beef, sour cream and almonds
Kraftbrühe	krahftbrewer	beef consommé
mit Ei	mit igh	with raw egg
mit Einlage	mit ighnlaager	with a garnish
Leberknödelsuppe	layberrknurderlzupper	liver-dumpling soup
Linsensuppe	linzernzupper	lentil soup
Nudelsuppe	nooderlzupper	noodle soup
Ochsenschwanz-suppe	oksernshvahntszupper	oxtail soup
Pichelsteiner Eintopf	pikherlshtighnerr ighntopf	meat and vegetable stew
Schildkrötensuppe	shiltkrurternzupper	turtle soup
Serbische Bohnensuppe	zehrbisher boanernzupper	spiced bean soup
Tomatensuppe	tommaaternzupper	tomato soup
Zwiebelsuppe	tsveeberlzupper	onion soup

Backerbsensuppe
(bahkehrpsernzupper)
broth served with pea-sized balls of pasta

Basler Mehlsuppe
(baaslerr maylzupper)
flour soup with grated cheese (Swiss)

Labskaus
(laapskowss)
thick stew of minced and marinated meat with mashed potatoes

Fish and seafood   *Fisch und Meeresfrüchte*

I'd like some fish.	**Ich hätte gern Fisch.**	ikh hehter gehrn fish
What kind of seafood do you have?	**Welche Meeresfrüchte haben Sie?**	vehlkher mayrersfrewkhter haabern zee
Aal	aal	eel
Austern	owsterrn	oysters
Barsch	bahrsh	freshwater perch
Brasse/Brachse	brahsser/brahkser	bream

Dorsch	dorsh	cod
Egli	ehglee	perch
Felchen	fehlkhern	kind of trout
Fischfrikadellen	fishfrikkahdehlern	fish croquettes
Forelle	forehler	trout
Flunder	flunderr	flounder
Garnelen	gahrnaylern	prawns/shrimps
Hecht	hehkht	pike
Heilbutt	highlbut	halibut
Hering	hayring	herring
Hummer	hummerr	lobster
Jakobsmuscheln	yaakopsmusherln	scallops
Kabeljau	kaaberlyow	cod
Kaisergranate	kighzerrgrahnahter	kind of scampi
Karpfen	kahrpfern	carp
Krebs	krayps	river crayfish
Lachs	lahks	salmon
Languste	lahnggooster	spiny lobster
Makrele	mahkrayler	mackerel
Muscheln	musherln	clams/mussels
Rotbarsch	roatbahrsh	red sea-bass
Salm	zahlm	salmon
Schellfisch	shehlfish	haddock
Scholle	sholler	plaice
Seebarsch	zaybahrsh	sea bass
Seebutt	zaybut	brill
Seezunge	zaytsunger	sole
Sprotten	shprottern	sprats
Steinbutt	shtighnbut	turbot
Stint	shtint	smelt
Stör	shturr	sturgeon
Zander	tsahnderr	(giant) pike-perch

baked	**gebacken**	gerbahkern
boiled in bouillon	**blau**	blow
breaded	**paniert**	pahneert
fried	**gebraten**	gerbraatern
deep-fried	**im schwimmenden**	im shvimmerndern
	Fett gebacken	feht gerbahkern
grilled	**gegrillt**	gergrilt
marinated	**mariniert**	mahrinneert
sautéed (in butter)	**(in Butter)**	(in butterr)
	geschwenkt	gershvehnkt
smoked	**geräuchert**	gerroykhert
steamed	**gedämpft**	gerdehmpft

Meat *Fleisch*

Bear in mind that the Germans most often write in one word what would take us two or more. For example, *Rindszunge* is *Rinds-* (beef) and *-zunge* (tongue) or *Kalbsbrust* is breast of veal. So you may have to look under two entries in the following lists to fully understand what's on the menu.

I'd like some ...	Ich hätte gern ...	ikh hehter gehrn
beef	**Rindfleisch**	rintflighsh
lamb	**Lammfleisch**	lahmflighsh
mutton	**Hammelfleisch**	hahmerlflighsh
pork	**Schweinefleisch**	shvighnerflighsh
veal	**Kalbfleisch**	kahlpflighsh
Bauernomelett	bowerrnomleht	diced bacon and onion omelet
(deutsches) Beefsteak	(doytsherss) beef-stayk	hamburger
Beuschel	boysherl	veal offal with lemon sauce
-braten	-braatern	joint, roast
-brust	-brust	breast
Eisbein	ighsbighn	pickled pig's knuckle
Faschiertes	fahsheerterss	minced meat
Filetsteak	fillaystayk	beef steak
Fleischkäse	flighshkaizer	type of bologna sausage
Frikadellen	frikkahdehlern	meat patties
Geschnetzeltes	gershnehtserlterss	chipped veal served in wine sauce
Geselchtes	gerzehlkhterss	smoked or salted meat usually pork
Gulasch	goolahsh	gulash; chunks of beef stewed in a rich paprika gravy
Hackbraten	hahkbraatern	meatloaf
-hachse/haxe	-hahkser	shank
-herz	-hehrts	heart
Kasseler Rippenspeer	kahssehlerr rippernshpayr	smoked pork chops
-klößchen	-klurskhern	meatballs
-kotelett	-kotleht	cutlet, chop
Krenfleisch	kraynflighsh	pork, usually brawn, served with shredded vegetables and horseradish

Kutteln	kutterln	tripe
Leber	layberr	liver
Leberkäse	layberrkaizer	type of meatloaf
Lenden-	lehndern	fillet of beef (tenderloin)
Nieren	neerern	kidneys
Nierenstück	neerernshtewk	loin
-plätzli	-plehtslee	escalope
Pökelfleisch	purkerlflighsh	marinated meat
Rippensteak	rippernshtayk	rib steak
Rostbraten	roastbraatern	rumpsteak
Rouladen	roolaadern	slices of beef or veal filled, rolled and braised (in brown gravy)
Sauerbraten	zowerrbraatern	marinated, brased beef
Schinken	shinkern	ham
Schlachtplatte	shlahkhtplahter	platter of various sausages and cold meats
Schnitzel	shnitserl	escalope
Spanferkel	shpaanfehrkerl	suck(l)ing pig
Speck	shpehk	bacon
-spießchen	-shpeeskhern	skewered meat
Sülze	zewltser	brawn (headcheese)
Wiener Schnitzel	veenerr shnitserl	breaded veal escalope
-zunge	-tsunger	tongue

Here are some hearty dishes you'll certainly want to try:

Bauernschmaus (bowerrnshmowss)	sauerkraut garnished with boiled bacon, smoked pork, sausages, dumplings, potatoes (Austrian)
Berner Platte (behrnerr plahter)	sauerkraut (or green beans) liberally garnished with pork chops, boiled bacon and beef, sausages, tongue and ham (Swiss)
Holsteiner Schnitzel (holshtighnerr shnitserl)	breaded veal escalope topped with fried egg, garnished with vegetables and usually accompanied by bread and butter, anchovies, mussels and smoked salmon
Kohlroulade (koalroolaader)	cabbage leaves stuffed with minced meat
Königsberger Klopse (kurnigsbehrgerr klopser)	Meatballs in white caper sauce

boiled	gekocht	gerkokht
braised	geschmort	gershmoart
fried	(in der Pfanne)	(in derr pfahner)
	gebraten	gerbraatern
grilled (broiled)	gegrillt	gergrilt
roasted	(im Ofen)	(im oafern)
	gebraten	gerbraatern
stewed	gedämpft	gerdehmpft
stuffed	gefüllt	gerfewlt
underdone (rare)	blutig	blootikh
medium	mittel	mitterl
well-done	gut durchgebraten	goot doorchgerbraatern

Sausages   *Würste*

Sausages are produced in dozens of different varieties. Some with more garlic or spices than others. One of the mildest is the Frankfurter.

Bierwurst	beervoorst	smoked, pork and beef
Blutwurst	blootvoorst	black pudding (blood sausage)
Bockwurst	bokvoorst	large frankfurter
Bratwurst	braatvoorst	fried, pork
Jagdwurst	yaagtvoorst	smoked, with garlic and mustard
Leberwurst	layberrvoorst	liver sausage
Katenrauchwurst	kaaternrowkhvoorst	country-style, smoked
Nürnberger Bratwurst	newrnbehrgerr braatvoorst	fried, veal and pork
Regensburger	raygernsburgerr	highly spiced, smoked
Rotwurst	roatvoorst	black pudding (blood sausage)
Weißwurst	vighsvoorst	veal and bacon with parsley and onion
Wienerli	veenerrli	Vienna-style frankfurter
Zervelat(wurst)	zehrvehlaat(voorst)	seasoned, smoked, pork, beef and bacon
Zungenwurst	tsungernvoorst	blood sausage with pieces of tongue and diced fat
Zwiebelwurst	tsveeberlvoorst	liver and onion

Game and poultry   *Wild und Geflügel*

German cuisine is often said to be unimaginative, but this certainly doesn't apply to game. The venison is usually carefully marinated till tender and served with sweet raisin or red currant sauce or a purée of chestnuts *(Maronenpüree)*.

If your meal is prepared *nach Jägerart* (in the hunter's style), it's likely sautéed with mushrooms and root vegetables and served in a wine gravy *(Weinsoße—**vighn**zoasser)*.

Back-	bahk-	fried
Brat-	braat-	roast
-braten	-braatern	joint, roast
Ente	ehnter	duck
Fasan	fahzaan	pheasant
Gans	gahns	goose
Hähnchen	hainkhern	chicken
Hase	haazer	hare
-hendl	-hehndl	chicken
gespickter Hirsch	gershpikterr heersh	larded venison
Huhn	hoon	chicken
Kaninchen	kahneenkhern	rabbit
Kapaun	kahpown	capon
-keule	-koyler	haunch
Masthühnchen	mahsthewnkhern	pullet chicken
-pfeffer	-pfehferr	jugged game
Poulet	poolay	chicken
Rebhuhn	rehphoon	partridge
Reh	ray	venison
-rücken	-rewkern	saddle
Schnepfe	shnehpfer	woodcock
Taube	towber	pigeon, squab
Truthahn	troothaan	turkey
Wachtel	vahkhterl	quail
Wildschwein	viltshvighn	wild boar

Potatoes   *Kartoffeln*

The Germans' favourite accompaniment *(Beilage)* is undoubtedly the potato which can be prepared in a seemingly endless variety of ways.

Bratkartoffeln	braatkahrtofferln	fried potatoes
Geröstete	gerrursterter	hashed-brown potatoes

Kartoffel(n)	kahrtofferl(n)	potato(es)
-bälle	-behler	balls
-brei	-brigh	mashed
-klöße	-klursser	dumplings
-mus	-mooss	mashed
-puffer	-pufferr	fritters
-stock	-shtok	mashed
-kroketten	-kroakehtern	croquettes
Kartoffelsalat	kahrtofferlzahlaat	potato salad
Pellkartoffeln	pehlkahrtofferln	potatoes boiled in their jackets
Petersilienkartoffeln	payterrzeeliern-kahrtofferln	parsley potatoes
Pommes frites	pom frit	chips (french fries)
Reibekuchen	righberkookhern	potato pancake
Rösti	rurshtee	hashed-brown potatoes
Röstkartoffeln	rurstkahrtofferln	fried potatoes
Salzkartoffeln	zahltskahrtofferln	boiled potatoes

Rice and noodles   *Reis und Nudeln*

Butterreis	butterrighss	buttered rice
Curryreis	kurreerighss	curried rice
Knöpfli	knurpflee	kind of gnocchi
Mehlnockerln	maylnokkerrln	small dumplings
Nudeln	nooderln	noodles
Reis	righss	rice
Spätzle	shpehtsler	kind of gnocchi
Teigwaren	tighgvaarern	pasta

Vegetables and salads   *Gemüse und Salate*

What vegetables do you recommend?	**Welches Gemüse empfehlen Sie?**	vehlkhers germewzer ehmpfaylern zee
I'd prefer some salad.	**Ich nehme lieber Salat.**	ikh naymer leeberr zahlaart
Auberginen	oaberrzheenern	aubergines (eggplant)
Blaukraut	blowkrowt	red cabbage
Blumenkohl	bloomernkoal	cauliflower
Bohnen	boanern	beans
grüne	grewner	French (green) beens
weiße	vighsser	haricot beans, white kidney beans
Brokkoli	brokkollee	broccoli

Champignons	shahmpinyong	button mushrooms
Chicorée	sheekorray	endive (Am. chicory)
Endivien	ehndeeviern	chicory (Am. endives)
Erbsen	ehrpsern	peas
Essiggurken	ehssikhgoorkern	gherkins (pickles)
Fenchel	fehnkherl	fennel
Fisolen	feezoalern	french (green) beans
Gemüse	germewzer	vegetables
gemischtes	germishterss	mixed vegetables
grüner Salat	grewnerr zahlaat	green salad
Grünkohl	grewnkoal	kale
Gurken	goorkern	cucumber
Häuptlsalat	hoyptlzahlaat	lettuce salad
Karfiol	kahrfioal	cauliflower
Karotten	kahrottern	carrots
Kohl	koal	cabbage
Kohlrabi	koalraabee	turnips
Kopfsalat	kopfzahlaat	lettuce salad
Krautstiel	krowtshteel	white beet
Kürbis	kewrbiss	pumpkin
Lattich	lahtikh	lettuce
Lauch	lowkh	leeks
Leipziger Allerlei	lighptseegerr ahlerrligh	peas, carrots, asparagus
Mais	mighss	sweet corn
Mohrrüben	moarrewbern	carrots
Paradeiser	pahrahdighzerr	tomatoes
Pfifferlinge	pfifferlinger	chanterelle mushrooms
Pilze	piltser	mushrooms
Radieschen	rahdeeskhern	radishes
Rettich	rehtikh	black radish
Rosenkohl	roazernkoal	Brussels sprouts
rote Beete/Rüben	roater bayter/rewbern	beetroot
Rotkohl	roatkoal	red cabbage
Rüebli	rewblee	carrots
Salat	zahlaat	salad
Sauerkraut	zowerrkrowt	sauerkraut
Schwarzwurzeln	shvahrtsvoortserln	salsify
Sellerie	zehlerree	celery
Spargel	shpaargerl	asparagus
Spargelspitzen	shpaargerlshpitsern	asparagus tips
Spinat	shpeenaat	spinach
Tomaten	tommaatern	tomatoes
Weißkohl	vighskoal	cabbage
Zwiebeln	tsveeberln	onions
Zucchetti	tsuggehtee	courgette (zucchini)

Vegetables may be served ...

oven-browned	**überbacken**	ewberr**bahkern**
boiled	**gekocht**	ger**kokht**
creamed	**-püree**	-**pewray**
diced	**gehackt**	ger**hahkt**
stewed	**gedämpft**	ger**dehmpft**

As for the seasoning ...

Anis	ah**nees**	aniseed
Basilikum	bah**zee**likkum	basil
Dill	dil	dill
Essig	**ehs**sikh	vinegar
Estragon	**ehs**trahgon	tarragon
Gewürz	ger**vewrts**	spice
Ingwer	**ing**verr	ginger
Kapern	**kaa**perrn	capers
Knoblauch	**knop**lowkh	garlic
Kräuter	**kroy**terr	mixture of herbs
Kren	krayn	horseradish
Kresse	**kreh**sser	cress
Kümmel	**kew**merl	caraway
Lorbeer	**loar**bayr	bay leaf
Majoran	**mah**yoraan	marjoram
Meerrettich	**mayr**rehtikh	horseradish
Muskatnuß	mus**kaht**nuss	nutmeg
Nelke	**nehl**ker	clove
Öl	url	oil
Petersilie	payterr**zee**lier	parsley
Pfeffer	**pfeh**ferr	pepper
Pfefferminz	**pfeh**ferrmints	mint
Rosmarin	**ros**mahreen	rosemary
Safran	**zah**fraan	saffron
Salbei	**zahl**bigh	sage
Salz	zahlts	salt
Schnittlauch	**shnit**lowkh	chives
Senf	zehnf	mustard
Süßstoff	**zews**shtof	artificial sweetener
Thymian	**tew**miaan	thyme
Tomatenketchup	tom**maa**ternkehtshup	ketchup
Wacholder	**vahkh**olderr	juniper
Würze	**vewr**tser	seasoning
Zimt	tsimt	cinnamon
Zucker	**tsuk**kerr	sugar

Cheese *Käse*

Most of the cheese produced in Germany, Austria and Switzerland is mild. You may see *Käseteller* (**kai**zertehlerr) on the menu. This means you'll get a plate of three or four varieties of cheese, doubtless including the renowned *Emmentaler* (**eh**merntaalerr), which we call simply Swiss cheese. If you are looking for curd cheese, ask for *Frischkäse*.

| What sort of cheese do you have? | **Welche Käsesorten haben Sie?** | vehlkher kaizerzoartern haabern zee |
| A piece of that one, please. | **Ein Stück von dem da, bitte.** | ighn shtewk fon daym daa bitter |

| mild | Allgäuer Bergkäse (like Swiss cheese), Allgäuer Rahmkäse, Altenburger (made of goat's milk), Appenzeller, Greyerzer, Kümmelkäse (made with caraway seeds), Quark, Räucherkäse (smoked cheese), Schichtkäse, Sahnekäse, Tilsiter, Topfen, Weißkäse. |
| sharp | Handkäse, Harzer Käse, Schabzieger. |

curd	**frisch**	frish
hard	**hart**	hahrt
mild	**mild**	millt
ripe	**reif**	righf
sharp	**scharf**	shahrf
soft	**weich**	vighkh

The following dish in Switzerland makes a meal in itself:

| **fondue** (fong**dew**) | a hot, bubbly mixture of melted cheese, white wine, a drop of kirsch and a hint of garlic; each guest dips a bite-size piece of bread on a fork into the pot of cheese. |

And for a cheesy snack try one of the following specialities:

| **Käsewähe** (**kai**zervaier) | a hot cheese tart |
| **Käseschnitte** (**kai**zershnitter) | an open-faced melted cheese sandwich |

Fruit and nuts *Obst und Nüsse*

Do you have (fresh) fruit?	**Haben Sie (frisches) Obst?**	haabern zee (frisherss) oapst
I'd like a fruit cocktail.	**Ich hätte gern einen Obstsalat.**	ikh hehter gehrn ighnern oapstzahlaat
Ananas	ahnahnahss	pineapple
Apfel	ahpferl	apple
Apfelsine	ahpferlzeener	orange
Aprikosen	ahprekkoazern	apricots
Backpflaumen	bahkpflowmern	prunes
Banane	bahnaaner	banana
Birne	beerner	pear
Blaubeeren	blowbayrern	blueberries
Brombeeren	brombayrern	blackberries
Datteln	dahterln	dates
Erdbeeren	ehrtbayrern	strawberries
Erdnüsse	ehrdnewsser	peanuts
Feigen	fighgern	figs
Haselnüsse	haazerlnewsser	hazelnuts
Heidelbeeren	highderlbayrern	blueberries
Himbeeren	himbayrern	raspberries
Johannisbeeren	yohhahnisbayrern	currants
rote/schwarze	roater/shvahrtser	red/black
Kirschen	keershern	cherries
Kokosnuß	kokkosnuss	coconut
Mandarine	mahndahreener	tangerine
Mandeln	mahnderln	almonds
Marillen	mahrillern	apricots
Melone	mayloaner	melon (cantaloupe)
Mirabellen	meerahbehlern	a variety of plums
Nüsse	newsser	nuts
Pampelmuse	pahmperlmoozer	grapefruit
Pfirsich	pfeerzikh	peach
Pflaumen	pflowmern	plums
Preiselbeeren	prighzerlbayrern	cranberries
Quitte	kvitter	quince
Rhabarber	rahbahrberr	rhubarb
Ribisel	reebeezl	currants
Rosinen	rozeenern	raisins
Stachelbeeren	stahkherlbayrern	gooseberries
Walnüsse	vahlnewsser	walnuts
Wassermelone	vahsserrmayloaner	watermelon
Weintrauben	vighntrowbern	grapes
Zitrone	tsitroaner	lemon
Zwetsch(g)en	tsvehtsh(g)ern	plums

Dessert–Pastries   *Nachtisch–Gebäck*

Desserts may also be listed on the menu under *Nachspeisen* or *Süßspeisen*. If you want an ice-cream, look under *Eis* in Germany and Austria and under *Glace* in Switzerland. The German waiter may ask you if you want your dessert served with *Schlagsahne*, the Austrian will say *Schlagobers* or simply *Schlag* and the Swiss *Schlagrahm*. Wherever you are it means whipped cream.

I'd like a dessert, please.	**Ich hätte gern eine Nachspeise.**	ikh **heh**ter gehrn **igh**ner **naakh**shpighzer
Something light, please.	**Etwas Leichtes, bitte.**	**eht**vahss **lighkh**terss **bit**ter
Just a small portion.	**Nur eine kleine Portion.**	noor **igh**ner **kligh**ner **port**sioan
Nothing more, thanks.	**Nein danke, nichts mehr.**	nighn **dahn**ker nikhts mayr
Götterspeise	**gurterrsh**pighzer	fruit jelly (Jell-O)
Kaltschale	**kahlt**shaaler	chilled fruit soup
Obstsalat	**oapst**zahlaat	fruit cocktail

Here are some basic words you'll need to know if you want to order a dessert. Remember that Germans often write in one word what would take us two. The words below may be combined with a fruit or a flavour, e.g. *Apfelauflauf*, *Erdbeereis*, etc.

-auflauf	-owflowf	soufflé
-creme	-kraym	pudding
-eis, -glace	-ighss -glahsser	ice-cream
-kompott	-kompot	compote
-kuchen	-kookhern	cake
-pudding	-pudding	pudding
-torte	-torter	layer cake

These flavours of ice-cream are very popular:

Erdbeer-	**ehrt**bayr-	strawberry
Karamel-	**kahrah**mehl-	caramel
Mokka-	**mok**kah-	coffee
Schokoladen-	**shokkollaa**dern-	chocolate
Vanille-	**vah**niller-	vanilla
Zitronen-	**tsit**roanern-	lemon

If you'd like to try something more filling with your coffee, we'd recommend ...

Apfelstrudel (ahpferlshtrooderl)	paper-thin layers of pastry filled with apple slices, nuts, raisins and jam
Berliner (behrleenerr)	jam doughnut
Bienenstich (beenernshtikh)	honey-almond cake
Cremeschnitte (kraymshnitter)	millefeuille (napoleon)
Gugelhupf (googerlhupf)	a moulded cake with a hole in the centre, usually filled with raisins and almonds
Hefekranz (hayferkrahnts)	ring-shaped cake of yeast dough, with almonds and sometimes candied fruit
Kaiserschmarren (kighzerrshmahrern)	shredded pancake with raisins served with syrup (Austrian)
Mohrenkopf (moarernkopf)	chocolate meringue with whipped-cream filling
Palatschinken (pahlahtshinkern)	when listed under desserts, pancakes with a jam or white cheese filling, otherwise they are a savoury dish
Schillerlocke (shillerrlokker)	pastry cornet with vanilla cream filling
Schwarzwälder Kirschtorte (shvahrtsvehlderr keershtorter)	chocolate layer cake filled with cream and cherries, flavoured with cherry brandy
Topfenstrudel (topfernshtrooderl)	flaky pastry filled with creamed, vanilla-flavoured white cheese, rolled and baked
Windbeutel (vintboyterl)	cream puff

Here are the names of some favourite biscuits (cookies):

Honigkuchen	hoanikhkookhern	honey biscuits
Leckerli	lehkerrli	ginger biscuits
Makronen	mahkroanern	macaroons
Printen	printern	honey biscuits
Spekulatius	shpehkoolaatsiuss	almond biscuits

Beer *Bier*

Needless to say, beer is the Germans' favourite drink. Almost every town with a sizable population has at least one brewery. You'll want to try some of the local brews. However, Dortmund and Bavarian beer are found throughout the country. *Bier vom Faß* (draught or draft beer) is considered to have a better taste and is less expensive, too, than bottled beer.

I'd like a beer.	**Ich hätte gern ein Bier.**	ikh **heh**ter gehrn ighn beer
a dark beer	**ein Dunkles**	ighn **dunk**lerss
a light beer	**ein Helles**	ighn **heh**lerss
I'd like a ... of beer.	**Ich hätte gern ... Bier.**	ikh **heh**ter gehrn ... beer
bottle	**eine Flasche**	**igh**ner **flah**sher
glass	**ein Glas**	ighn glaass
a small one	**ein kleines**	ighn **kligh**nerss
a large one	**ein großes**	ighn **groa**sserss
mug (a quart)	**eine Maß**	**igh**ner maass
Waiter! Another beer, please!	**Herr Ober, noch ein Bier, bitte!**	hehr **oa**berr nokh ighn beer **bit**ter

Altbier (**ahlt**beer)	a bitter beer with a high hops content
Bockbier, Doppelbock, Märzen, Starkbier (**bok**beer, **dopp**erlbok, **mehrt**sern, **shtahrk**beer)	these are beers with a high alcoholic and malt content
Malzbier (**mahlts**beer)	a dark, sweetish beer with a low alcoholic content but high in calories
Pilsener (**pil**zernerr)	has a particularly strong aroma of hops
Radlermaß (**raad**lerrmaass)	a light beer to which a bit of lemonade is added; in north Germany it's called *Alsterwasser* (**ahl**sterrvahsserr)
Weißbier (**vighs**beer)	a light beer brewed from wheat grain; Berliners love a *Berliner Weiße mit Schuß*—*Weißbier* with a shot of raspberry juice.

Wine *Wein*

The best wine-producing regions of Germany are those round the Rhine and Moselle rivers—the northernmost wine-producing areas of Europe.

More so than French vintners to the west, German wine producers are at the mercy of the vagaries of the country's climatic conditions. One type of wine can have a quite different character from one year to the next depending upon the weather. For this reason, you'll have to learn to recognize a few basic terms on German labels which will tell you something about how you can likely expect a certain wine to taste.

In good years wine may be labeled *naturrein* or *Naturwein* which just means it's been produced under ordinary methods. In a bad year, sugar is sometimes added to increase the alcoholic content. If this is done, *verbessert* (improved) is euphemistically printed on the label.

There are four other words commonly found on German wine labels which you should know. They indicate the ripeness of the grapes when they were picked—or the degree of dryness or sweetness of the wine.

Spätlese (spaitlayzer)	gathered late after the normal harvesting; dry wine
Auslese (owslayzer)	selected gathering of particularly ripe bunches of grapes; slightly dry wine
Beerenauslese (bayrernowslayzer)	selected overripe grapes, slightly sweet wine
Trockenbeerenauslese (trokkernbayrern- owslayzer)	selected dried or raisin-like grapes; one drop of nectar can be squeezed out of each grape; a sweet or dessert wine is produced.

In neighbouring German-speaking Switzerland, mostly red wine is produced. Austria's Wachau region along the fabled Danube riverbanks produces white wine while Burgenland to the east of Vienna has red wine.

Gaststätten

Type of wine	Examples	Accompanies
sweet white wine	Rheinpfalz is noted for wine in this category; bottles labeled *Trockenbeerenauslese* also fall into this section.	desserts, especially puddings and cake
dry white wine	The Rheingau region produces extraordinary white wine in good vintage years; Moselle wine can usually be counted on to be very dry; wine labelled *Spätlese* or *Auslese* can go into this category as well as those with the term *naturrein* or *Naturwein*.	cold meat or shellfish, fish, boiled meat, egg dishes, first courses, fowl, veal, dishes served with sauerkraut, sausages
rosé	Sometimes referred to as *Schillerwein*	goes with almost anything but especially cold dishes, eggs, pork, lamb
light-bodied red wine	Most local red wine fits into this category, particularly the wine of Austria's Burgenland, German-speaking Switzerland, the Ahr region (look for the names *Ahrweiler, Neuenahr* and *Walporzheim* on the label) and Baden-Württemberg.	roast chicken, turkey, veal, lamb, beef steak, ham, liver, quail, pheasant, stews, dishes served with gravy
full-bodied red wine	A difficult wine to find but a *Spätburgunder* from the Ahr Valley is a good example.	duck, goose, kidneys, most game, goulash, in short, any strong-flavoured preparations
sparkling wine	German *Sekt* comes into this category; some of it rivals French champagne in quality.	if it's dry, it goes with anything; may be drunk as an aperitif or as the climax to the dinner; goes well with shellfish, nuts and dried fruit; if it's sweet, it'll go nicely with dessert and pastry like *Strudel*

May I please have the wine list?	**Die Weinkarte, bitte.**	dee **vighn**kahrter **bitter**
I want a bottle of white wine/red wine/ sparkling wine.	**Ich möchte eine Flasche Weißwein/ Rotwein/Schaum- wein.**	ikh **murkhter ighner flahsher vighsvighn/ roat**vighn/**showm**vighn
I'd like a glass/ carafe of ...	**Ich hätte gern ein Glas/eine Karaffe ...**	ikh **hehter** gehrn ighn glaass/**ighner kah**rahfer
Please bring me another ...	**Bitte bringen Sie mir noch ...**	**bitter bringern** zee mir nokh
Where does this wine come from?	**Woher kommt dieser Wein?**	vo**ahayr** komt **dee**zerr vighn

red/white/rosé	**rot/weiß/rosé**	roat/vighss/**ro**zay
(very) dry/sweet	**(sehr) trocken/süß**	(zayr) **trokkern/**zewss
light	**leicht**	lighkht
full-bodied	**vollmundig**	**vol**mundig

A refreshing highball for the ladies is sparkling wine and orange juice, *Damengedeck* (**daa**merngerdehk) or for the men, *Herrengedeck* (**heh**rerngerdehk), which is sparkling wine and beer. The German champagne (*Sekt*—sehkt) is also worth trying.

Other alcoholic drinks   *Andere alkoholische Getränke*

I'd like a/an/some ...	**Ich hätte gern ...**	ikh **hehter** gehrn
aperitif	**einen Aperitif**	**ighnern** ahpayrit**teef**
brandy	**einen Weinbrand**	**ighnern vighn**brahnt
cider	**Apfelwein**	**ahp**ferlvighn
cognac	**einen Kognak**	**ighnern ko**nyahk
liqueur	**einen Likör**	**ighnern** lik**kurr**
mulled wine	**Glühwein**	**glew**vighn
port	**Portwein**	**port**vighn
rum	**einen Rum**	**ighnern** rum
vermouth	**einen Wermut**	**ighnern vayr**moot
vodka	**einen Wodka**	**ighnern vot**kah
whisky	**einen Whisky**	**ighnern** "whisky"
neat (straight)	**pur**	poor
on the rocks	**mit Eis**	mit ighss

You'll certainly want to take the occasion to sip a liqueur or brandy after your meal. The names of some well-known wine-distilled brandies are *Asbach-Uralt*, *Chantré* and *Dujardin*. Here are some other after-dinner drinks:

Are there any local specialities?	**Haben Sie hiesige Spezialitäten?**	haabern zee heezigger shpehtsiahlitaitern
I'd like to try a glass of ..., please.	**Ich möchte ein Glas ... probieren.**	ikh murkhter ighn glaass ... proabeeern
Apfelschnaps	ahpferlshnahps	apple brandy
Aprikosenlikör	ahprikkoazernlikkurr	apricot liqueur
Birnenschnaps	beernernshnahps	pear brandy
Bommerlunder	bommerrlunderr	caraway-flavoured brandy
Doornkaat	dornkaat	German gin, juniper-berry brandy
Eierlikör	igherrlikkurr	eggflip, eggnog
Heidelbeergeist	highderlbayrgighst	blueberry brandy
Himbeergeist	himbayrgighst	raspberry brandy
Himbeerlikör	himbayrlikkurr	raspberry liqueur
Kirschlikör	kirshlikkurr	cherry liqueur
Kirschwasser	kirshvahsserr	cherry brandy
(Doppel)Korn	(dopperl)korn	grain-distilled liquor, akin to whisky
Kümmel	kewmerl	caraway-flavoured liquor
Obstler	oapstlerr	fruit brandy
Pflümli(wasser)	pflewmli(vahsserr)	plum brandy
Steinhäger	shtighnhaigerr	juniperberry brandy, akin to gin
Träsch	traish	pear and apple brandy
Weizenkorn	vightsernkorn	wheat-distilled liquor, akin to whisky
Zwetschgenwasser	tsvehtshgernvahsserr	plum brandy

ZUM WOHL / PROST!
(tsum voal / proast)
YOUR HEALTH / CHEERS!

Nonalcoholic drinks   *Alkoholfreie Getränke*

I'd like a/an ...	Ich hätte gern ...	ikh **hehter** gehrn
apple juice	einen Apfelsaft	**ighnern** ahpferlzahft
currant juice (red or black)	einen Johannisbeer-saft	**ighnern** yohhahnisbayrzaft
fruit juice	einen Fruchtsaft	**ighnern** frukhtzahft
grape juice	einen Traubensaft	**ighnern** trowbernzahft
herb tea	einen Kräutertee	**ighnern** kroyterrtay
iced tea	einen Eistee	**ighnern** ighstay
lemonade	eine Limonade	**ighner** limmonnaader
(glass of) milk	(ein Glas) Milch	(ighn glaass) milkh
milkshake	ein Milchmixgetränk	ighn **milkh**miksgertrehnk
mineral water	ein Mineralwasser	ighn minnerraalvahsserr
fizzy (carbonated)	mit Kohlensäure	mit koalernzoyrer
still	ohne Kohlensäure	oaner koalernzoyrer
orange juice	einen Orangensaft	**ighnern** orrahngzhernzahft
orangeade	eine Orangeade	**ighner** orahngzhaader
tomato juice	einen Tomatensaft	**ighnern** tommaaternzahft
tonic water	ein Tonic	ighn tonnik

Hot beverages   *Warme Getränke*

Perhaps you'd like a coffee after dinner. In Austria, you can't ask for just "a cup of coffee"; the varieties are endless. There, you can ask for anything from a *Nußschwarzer* (**nus**shvahrtserr) or *Neger* (**nay**gerr)—strong black coffee—to an *Einspänner* (**ighn**shpehnerr)—topped with whipped cream—or a *Melange* (may**lahng**zher)—coffee and hot milk.

I'd like a/an ...	Ich hätte gern ...	ikh **hehter** gehrn
(hot) chocolate	eine (heiße) Schokolade	**ighner** (**highs**ser) shokkollaader
coffee	einen Kaffee	**ighnern** kahfay
with cream	mit Sahne	mit zaaner
with milk	einen Milchkaffee	**ighnern** milkhkahfay
black/decaffein-ated coffee	einen schwarzen/ koffeinfreien Kaffee	**ighnern** shvahrtsern/ koffeheenfrighern kah**fay**
espresso coffee	einen Expresso	**ighnern** ehksprehsoa
mokka	einen Mokka	**ighnern** mokkah
tea	einen Tee	**ighnern** tay
cup of tea	eine Tasse Tee	**ighner** tahsser tay
with milk/lemon	mit Milch/Zitrone	mit milkh/tsitroaner

Complaints   *Reklamationen*

There is a plate/glass missing.	**Es fehlt ein Teller/ ein Glas.**	ehss faylt ighn tehlerr/ ighn glaass
I have no knife/fork/ spoon.	**Ich habe kein Messer/ keine Gabel/keinen Löffel.**	ikh haaber kighn mehsserr/ kighner gaaberl/kighnern lurferl
That's not what I ordered.	**Das habe ich nicht bestellt.**	dahss haaber ikh nikht berstehlt
I asked for ...	**Ich wollte ...**	ikh volter
There must be some mistake.	**Es muß ein Irrtum sein.**	ehss muss ighn irtoom zighn
May I change this?	**Können Sie mir dafür etwas anderes bringen?**	kurnen zee meer daafewr ehtvahss ahnderrerss bringern
I asked for a small portion (for the child).	**Ich wollte eine kleine Portion (für das Kind).**	ikh volter ighner klighner portsioan (fewr dahss kint)
The meat is ...	**Das Fleisch ist ...**	dahss flighsh ist
overdone	**zu stark gebraten**	tsu shtahrk gerbraatern
underdone (too rare)	**zu roh**	tsu roa
too tough	**zu zäh**	tsu tsai
This is too ...	**Das ist zu ...**	dahss ist tsu
bitter/sour	**bitter/sauer**	bitter/zowerr
salty/sweet	**salzig/süß**	zahltsikh/zewss
I don't like this.	**Das schmeckt mir nicht.**	dahs shmehkt meer nikht
The food is cold.	**Das Essen ist kalt.**	dahss ehssern ist kahlt
This isn't fresh.	**Das ist nicht frisch.**	dahss ist nikht frish
What's taking you so long?	**Weshalb dauert es so lange?**	vehshahlp dowerrt ehss zoa lahnger
Have you forgotten our drinks?	**Haben Sie unsere Getränke vergessen?**	haabern zee unzerrer gertrehnker fehrgehssern
The wine is corked.	**Der Wein schmeckt nach Korken.**	derr vighn shmehkt naakh koarkern
This isn't clean.	**Das ist nicht sauber.**	dahss ist nikht zowberr
Would you ask the head waiter to come over?	**Würden Sie bitte den Oberkellner rufen?**	vewrdern zee bitter dayn oaberrkehlnerr roofern

The bill (check) *Die Rechnung*

A service charge is generally included automatically in restaurant bills. Anything extra for the waiter is optional. Credit cards may be used in an increasing number of restaurants.

I'd like to pay.	**Ich möchte zahlen.**	ikh murkhter tsaalern
We'd like to pay separately.	**Wir möchten getrennt bezahlen.**	veer murkhtern gehtrehnt bertsaalern
I think you made a mistake in this bill.	**Ich glaube, Sie haben sich verrechnet.**	ikh glowber zee haabern zikh fehrrehkhnert
What is this amount for?	**Wofür ist dieser Betrag?**	voafewr ist deezerr bertraakh
Is service included?	**Ist die Bedienung inbegriffen?**	ist dee berdeenung inbergriffern
Do you accept traveller's cheques?	**Nehmen Sie Reiseschecks?**	naymern zee righzershehks
Can I pay with this credit card?	**Kann ich mit dieser Kreditkarte bezahlen?**	kahn ikh mit deezerr krayditkahrter bertsaalern
That was a very good meal.	**Das Essen war sehr gut.**	dahss ehssern vaar zayr goot

> **BEDIENUNG INBEGRIFFEN**
> SERVICE INCLUDED

Snacks—Picnic *Imbiß – Picknick*

A *Café* (in Austria *Kaffeehaus*) will serve anything from simple pastries to luscious, monumental sweet delicacies and often snacks. For a fast meal the German *Schnellimbiß* (snack bar) is the place. Ordering is easy since most of the snacks are on display. And if you are in a hurry have a sausage at a *Würstchenstand*.

Give me two of these and one of those.	**Geben Sie mir davon zwei und davon eins.**	gaybern zee meer daafon tsvigh unt daafon ighns
to the left/right above/below	**links/rechts darüber/darunter**	links/rehkhts dahrewberr/dahrunterr
It's to take away.	**Es ist zum Mitnehmen.**	ehss ist tsum mitnaymern

TIPPING, see inside back-cover

I'd like a piece of cake.	**Ich hätte gern ein Stück Kuchen.**	ikh **heh**ter gehrn ighn shtewk **kook**hern
fried sausage	**eine Bratwurst**	**igh**ner **braat**voorst
omelet	**ein Omelett**	ighn om**leht**
open sandwich	**ein belegtes Brot**	ighn ber**layg**terss broat
with ham	**mit Schinken**	mit **shin**kern
with cheese	**mit Käse**	mit **kaiz**er
potato salad	**Kartoffelsalat**	kahr**tof**ferlzahlaat
sandwich	**ein Sandwich**	ighn **sehnd**vitsh

Here's a basic list of food and drink that might come in useful when shopping for a picnic.

I'd like a/an/some ...	**Ich hätte gern ...**	ikh **heh**ter gehrn
apples	**Äpfel**	**ehp**ferl
bananas	**Bananen**	bah**naa**nern
biscuits (Br.)	**Kekse**	**kayk**ser
beer	**Bier**	beer
bread	**ein Brot**	ighn broat
butter	**Butter**	**butt**err
cheese	**Käse**	**kaiz**er
chips (Am.)	**Kartoffelchips**	kahr**tof**ferlcheeps
chocolate bar	**eine Tafel Schokolade**	**igh**ner **taa**ferl shokkol**laad**er
coffee	**Kaffee**	kah**fay**
cold cuts	**Aufschnitt**	**owf**shnit
cookies	**Kekse**	**kayk**ser
crisps	**Kartoffelchips**	kahr**tof**ferlcheeps
eggs	**Eier**	**igh**err
gherkins (pickles)	**Essiggurken**	**ehss**ikhgoorkern
grapes	**Trauben**	**trow**bern
ice-cream	**ein Eis**	ighn ighss
milk	**Milch**	milkh
mustard	**Senf**	zehnf
oranges	**Orangen**	or**rahng**zhern
pepper	**Pfeffer**	**pfeh**ferr
rolls	**Brötchen**	**brurt**khern
salt	**Salz**	zahlts
sausage	**eine Wurst**	**igh**ner voorst
soft drink	**ein alkoholfreies Getränk**	ighn **ahl**kohoalfrigherss ger**trehnk**
sugar	**Zucker**	**tsuk**kerr
tea	**Tee**	tay
yoghurt	**Joghurt**	**yoa**goort

Travelling around

Plane *Flugzeug*

Is there a flight to Vienna?	**Gibt es einen Flug nach Wien?**	gipt ehss **igh**nern floog naakh veen
Is it a direct flight?	**Ist es ein Direktflug?**	ist ehss ighn dir**rehkt**floog
When's the next flight to Hamburg?	**Wann ist der nächste Flug nach Hamburg?**	vahn ist derr **naikh**ster **floog** nahkh **hahm**boorg
Do I have to change planes?	**Muß ich umsteigen?**	muss ikh **um**shtighgern
Can I make a connection to Cologne?	**Habe ich Anschluß nach Köln?**	**haa**berr ikh **ahn**shluss nahkh kurln
I'd like a ticket to Zurich.	**Bitte ein Flugticket nach Zürich.**	**bit**ter ighn **floog**tikkert naakh **tsew**rikh
single (one-way) return (roundtrip)	**Hinflug Hin- und Rückflug**	**hin**floog hin unt **rewk**floog
What time does the plane take off?	**Wann ist der Abflug?**	vahn ist derr **ahp**floog
What time do I have to check in?	**Wann muß ich einchecken?**	vahn muss ikh **ighn**shehkern
Is there an airport-bus?	**Gibt es einen Flughafenbus?**	gipt ehss **igh**nern **floog**haafernbuss
What's the flight number?	**Welche Flugnummer ist es?**	**vehl**kher **floog**nummerr ist ehss
What time do we arrive?	**Wann landen wir?**	vahn **lahn**dern veer
I'd like to ... my reservation.	**Ich möchte meine Reservierung ...**	ikh **murkh**ter **migh**ner rehzer**vee**rung
cancel change confirm	**annullieren umbuchen bestätigen**	ahnul**lee**rern **um**bookhern bersh**tai**tiggern

ANKUNFT ARRIVAL	**ABFLUG** DEPARTURE

Train *Eisenbahn*

Travel on the main railway lines is generally fast, and the trains run on time. First-class coaches are comfortable; second-class, more than adequate.

TEE (tay-ay-ay)	Trans-Europ-Express: a luxury international service for which you pay a surcharge; reservation compulsory
Intercity ("intercity")	Long distance inter-city trains; some only first, others with first and second class, with surcharge; in Switzerland the equivalent of the Austrian *Städteschnellzug*
City-D-Zug ("city"-**day**-tsoog)	Short-distance inter-city trains, with few stops at major points only; first and second class with surcharge on trips of less than 50 kilometres (Germany)
D-Zug (**day**-tsoog)	Intermediate- to long-distance trains (Germany)
Schnellzug (**shnehl**tsoog)	Fast trains, stop at big and medium towns (Austria, Switzerland)
Städteschnellzug (**shteh**tershnehltsoog)	Fast trains, connecting the biggest towns (Austria)
Expreßzug (ayks**prehs**tsoog)	Fast trains, stop at big and medium towns (Austria)
Eilzug (**ighl**tsoog)	Medium-distance trains, not stopping at small stations (Germany, Austria)
Nahverkehrszug (**naa**fehrkayrstsoog)	Local trains, stopping at all stations; in Austria called *Personenzug* and in Switzerland *Regionalzug*
Triebwagen (**treep**vaagern)	Small diesel coach used for short runs (Austria, Germany); in Germany sometimes *Schienenbus*

Here are a few more useful terms:

Speisewagen (**shpighz**ervaagern)	Dining-car
Schlafwagen (**shlaaf**vaagern)	Sleeping-car, compartments with wash basins and 1, 2 or 3 berths
Liegewagen (**lee**gervaagern)	Coach containing berths with sheets, blankets and pillows

To the railway station   *Unterwegs zum Bahnhof*

Where's the railway station?	**Wo ist der Bahnhof?**	voa ist derr **baan**hoaf
Taxi, please!	**Taxi bitte!**	**tahk**si **bit**ter
Take me to the ...	**Fahren Sie mich ...**	**faa**rern zee mikh
main railway station	**zum Hauptbahnhof**	tsum **howpt**baanhoaf
railway station	**zum Bahnhof**	tsum **baan**hoaf
What's the fare?	**Was macht das?**	vahss mahkht dahss

EINGANG	ENTRANCE
AUSGANG	EXIT
ZU DEN BAHNSTEIGEN	TO THE PLATFORMS
AUSKUNFT	INFORMATION

Where's the ...?   *Wo ist ...?*

Where is/are the ...?	**Wo ist/sind ...?**	voa ist/zint
booking office	**die Platz-reservierung**	dee **plahts**rehzerrveerung
currency-exchange office	**die Wechselstube**	dee **wehk**zerlshtoober
left-luggage office (baggage check)	**die Gepäckauf-bewahrung**	dee ger**pehk**owfbervaarung
lost property (lost-and-found) office	**das Fundbüro**	dahss **funt**bewroa
luggage lockers	**die Schließfächer**	dee **shlees**fehkherr
newsstand	**der Zeitungsstand**	derr **tsigh**tungsshtahnt
platform 3	**Bahnsteig 3**	**baan**shtighg 3
reservations office	**die Platz-reservierung**	dee **plahts**rehzerrveerung
restaurant	**das Restaurant**	dahss rehstorr**rahng**
snack bar	**der Schnellimbiß**	derr **shneh**limbiss
ticket office	**der Fahrkarten-schalter**	derr **faar**kahrternshahlterr
track 7	**Gleis 7**	glighss 7
waiting room	**der Wartesaal**	derr **vahr**terzaal
Where are the toilets?	**Wo sind die Toiletten?**	voa zint dee toah**leh**tern

TAXI, see page 21

Inquiries *Auskunft*

When is the ... train to Kiel?	**Wann fährt der ... Zug nach Kiel?**	vahn fairt derr ... tsoog naakh keel
first/last/next	**erste/letzte/nächste**	**ehrster/lehtster/naikhster**
What's the fare to Basle?	**Was kostet die Fahrt nach Basel?**	vahss kostert dee faart naakh baazerl
Is it a through train?	**Ist es ein durchgehender Zug?**	ist ehss ighn doorkhgayernderr tsoog
Must I pay a surcharge?	**Muß ich einen Zuschlag bezahlen?**	muss ikh ighnern tsushlaag bertsahlern
Is there a connection to ...?	**Gibt es einen Anschluß nach ...?**	gipt ehss ighnern ahnshluss naakh
Do I have to change trains?	**Muß ich umsteigen?**	muss ikh umshtighgern
Is there sufficient time to change?	**Reicht die Zeit zum Umsteigen?**	righkht dee tsight tsum umshtighgern
Will the train leave on time?	**Fährt der Zug pünktlich ab?**	fairt derr tsoog pewnktlikh ahp
What time does the train arrive at Münster?	**Wann kommt der Zug in Münster an?**	vahn komt derr tsoog in mewnsterr ahn
Is there a dining-car/sleeping-car on the train?	**Führt der Zug einen Speisewagen/Schlafwagen?**	fewrt derr tsoog ighnern shpighzervaagern/shlaafvaagern
Does the train stop at Ingolstadt?	**Hält der Zug in Ingolstadt?**	hehlt derr tsoog in ingolshtaht
What platform does the train for Bonn leave from?	**Auf welchem Bahnsteig fährt der Zug nach Bonn ab?**	owf vehlkherm baanshtighg fairt derr tsoog naakh bon ahp
What track does the train from Hamburg arrive at?	**Auf welchem Gleis kommt der Zug aus Hamburg an?**	owf vehlkherm glighss komt derr tsoog owss hahmboorg ahn
I'd like a time-table.	**Ich hätte gern einen Fahrplan.**	ikh hehter gehrn ighnern faarplaan

ANKUNFT	ABFAHRT
ARRIVAL	DEPARTURE

Es ist ein durchgehender Zug.	It's a through train.
Sie müssen in ... umsteigen.	You have to change at ...
Steigen Sie in Heidelberg in einen Nahverkehrszug um.	Change at Heidelberg and get a local train.
Bahnsteig 7 ist ...	Platform 7 is ...
dort drüben/oben/unten links/rechts	over there/upstairs/downstairs on the left/on the right
Es gibt einen Zug nach Bonn um ...	There's a train to Bonn at ...
Ihr Zug fährt auf Gleis ... ab.	Your train will leave from track ...
Der Zug hat ... Minuten Verspätung.	There'll be a delay of ... minutes.
Erste Klasse an der Spitze/in der Mitte/ am Ende des Zuges.	First class at the front/ in the middle/at the end.

Tickets *Fahrkarten*

I want a ticket to ...	Ich möchte eine Fahrkarte nach ...	ikh murkhter ighner faar-kahrter naakh
single (one-way)	einfach	ighnfahkh
return (roundtrip)	hin und zurück	hin unt stoorewk
first class	erste Klasse	ehrster klahsser
second class	zweite Klasse	tsvighter klahsser
half price	zum halben Preis	tsum hahlbern prighss

Reservation *Reservierung*

I want to book a ...	Ich möchte ... reservieren lassen.	ikh murkhter ... rehzerr-veeern lahssern
seat (by the window)	einen (Fenster)platz	ighnern (fehnsterr)plahts
berth	einen Platz im Liegewagen	ighnern plahts im leegervaagern
upper	oben	oabern
middle	in der Mitte	in derr mitter
lower	unten	untern
berth in the sleeping car	einen Platz im Schlafwagen	ighnern plahts im shlaafvaagern

NUMBERS, see page 147

All aboard *Einsteigen bitte*

Is this the right platform for the train to Vienna?	**Ist das der richtige Bahnsteig für den Zug nach Wien?**	ist dahss derr **rikh**tigger **baan**shtighg fewr dayn tsoog naakh veen
Is this the right train to Graz?	**Ist das der Zug nach Graz?**	ist dahss derr tsoog naakh graats
Excuse me. May I get by?	**Verzeihung. Kann ich vorbei?**	**fehrtsigh**ung. kahn ikh for**bigh**
Is this seat taken?	**Ist dieser Platz besetzt?**	ist **dee**zerr plahts ber**zehtst**

RAUCHER	NICHTRAUCHER
SMOKER	NONSMOKER

I think that's my seat.	**Ich glaube, das ist mein Platz.**	ikh **glow**ber dahss ist mighn plahts
Would you let me know before we get to Bamberg?	**Sagen Sie mir bitte, wenn wir in Bamberg ankommen?**	**zaa**gern zee mir **bit**ter vehn veer in **bahm**behrg **ahn**kommern
What station is this?	**Wie heißt dieser Ort?**	vee highst **dee**zerr ort
How long does the train stop here?	**Wie lange hält der Zug hier?**	vee **lahn**ger hehlt derr tsoog heer
When do we get to Cologne?	**Wann kommen wir in Köln an?**	vahn **kom**mern veer in kurln ahn

Sleeping *Im Schlafwagen*

Are there any free compartments in the sleeping-car?	**Sind im Schlafwagen noch Abteile frei?**	zint im **shlaaf**vaagern nokh **ahp**tighgh frigh
Where's the sleeping-car?	**Wo ist der Schlafwagen?**	voa ist derr **shlaaf**vaagern
Where's my berth?	**Wo ist mein Schlafplatz?**	voa ist mighn **shlaaf**plahts
I'd like a lower berth.	**Ich möchte unten schlafen.**	ikh **murkh**ter untern **shlaa**fern

Would you make up our berths?	**Würden Sie unsere Schlafplätze machen?**	vewrdern zee unzerrer shlaafplehtser mahkhern
Would you call me at 7 o'clock?	**Würden Sie mich um 7 Uhr wecken?**	vewrdern zee mikh um 7 oor vehkern
Would you bring me coffee in the morning?	**Würden Sie mir bitte morgen früh Kaffee bringen?**	vewrdern zee meer bitter morgern frew kahfay bringern

Eating *Im Speisewagen*

You can get snacks and drinks in the buffet-car and in the dining-car when it isn't being used for main meals. On some trains an attendant comes around with a cart with snacks, tea, coffee and soft drinks.

| Where's the dining-car? | **Wo ist der Speisewagen?** | voa ist derr shpighzer-vaagern |

Baggage—Porters *Gepäck – Gepäckträger*

Porter!	**Gepäckträger!**	gerpehktraiger
Can you help me with my luggage?	**Können Sie mir mit meinem Gepäck helfen?**	kurnern zee mir mit mighnerm gerpehk hehlfern
Where are the luggage trolleys (carts)?	**Wo sind die Koffer-kulis?**	voa zint dee kofferr-kooliss
Where are the luggage lockers?	**Wo sind die Schließfächer?**	voa zint dee shleesfehkherr
Where's the left-luggage office (baggage check)?	**Wo ist die Gepäck-aufbewahrung?**	voa ist dee gerpehk-owfbervaarung
I'd like to leave my luggage, please.	**Ich möchte mein Gepäck einstellen.**	ikh murkhter mighn gerpehk ighnshtehlern
I'd like to register (check) my luggage.	**Ich möchte mein Gepäck aufgeben.**	ikh murkhter mighn gerpehk owfgaybern

> **GEPÄCKAUFGABE**
> REGISTERING (CHECKING) BAGGAGE

PORTERS, see also page 18

Coach (long-distance bus) *Überlandbus*

To reach out-of-the-way places, you'll find frequent bus services available including the *Kraftpost* or *Postauto*. You'll find information on destinations and timetables at the coach terminals, usually situated near railway stations.

When's the next coach to ...?	**Wann fährt der nächste Bus nach ...?**	vahn fairt derr naikhster buss naakh
Does the coach stop at ...?	**Hält der Bus in ...?**	hehlt derr buss in
How long does the journey (trip) take?	**Wie lange dauert die Fahrt?**	vee lahnger dowerrt dee faart

Note: Most of the phrases on the previous pages can be used or adapted for travelling on local transport.

Bus—Tram (streetcar) *Bus – Straßenbahn*

In most cities you'll find automatic ticket dispensers at each stop enabling you to buy your ticket in advance. In major cities it may be worthwhile to get a pass or a booklet of tickets.

I'd like a pass/booklet of tickets.	**Ich möchte eine Mehrfahrkarte/ein Fahrscheinheft.**	ikh murkhter ighner mayrfaarkahrter/ighn faarshighnhehft
Which tram (streetcar) goes to the centre of town?	**Welche Straßenbahn fährt ins Stadtzentrum?**	vehlkher shtraassernbaan fairt ins shtahttsehntrum
Where can I get a bus into town?	**Wo hält der Bus, der ins Stadtzentrum fährt?**	voa hehlt derr buss derr ins shtahttsehntrum fairt
What bus do I take for ...?	**Welchen Bus muß ich nach ... nehmen?**	vehlkhern buss muss ikh naakh ... naymern
Where's the ...?	**Wo ist ...?**	voa ist
bus stop	**die Bushaltestelle**	dee busshahltershtehler
terminus	**die Endstation**	dee ehntshtahtsioan
When is the ... bus to ...?	**Wann fährt der ... Bus nach ...?**	vahn fairt derr ... buss naakh
first/last/next	**erste/letzte/nächste**	ehrster/lehtster/naikhster

How often do the buses to the airport run?	**Wie oft fahren die Busse zum Flughafen?**	vee oft **faa**rern dee **buss**er tsum **floog**haafern
How much is the fare to ...?	**Was kostet es nach ...?**	vahss **kos**tert ehss naakh
Do I have to change buses?	**Muß ich umsteigen?**	muss ikh **um**shtighern
How many bus stops are there to ...?	**Wie viele Haltestellen sind es bis ...?**	vee **fee**ler **hahl**tershtehlern zint ehss biss
Will you tell me when to get off?	**Können Sie mir bitte sagen, wann ich aussteigen muß?**	**kur**nern zee meer **bit**ter **zaa**gern vahn ikh **owss**shtighern muss
I want to get off at the next stop.	**Ich möchte an der nächsten Haltestelle aussteigen.**	ikh **murkh**ter ahn derr **naikh**stern **hahl**tershtehler **owss**shtighern

BUSHALTESTELLE	REGULAR BUS STOP
BEDARFSHALTESTELLE	STOPS ON REQUEST

Underground (subway) *U-Bahn*

The *U-Bahn* (**oo**-baan) in Berlin, Bonn, Düsseldorf, Cologne, Frankfurt, Hamburg and Munich corresponds to the London underground or the New York subway. A map showing the various lines and stations is displayed outside every station.

Where's the nearest underground station?	**Wo ist die nächste U-Bahnstation?**	voa ist dee **naikh**ster **oo**-baanshtahtsioan
Does this train go to ...?	**Fährt dieser Zug nach ...?**	fairt **dee**zerr tsoog naakh
Where do I change for ...?	**Wo muß ich nach ... umsteigen?**	voa muss ikh naakh ... **um**shtighern
Is the next station ...?	**Ist die nächste Station ...?**	ist dee **naikh**ster shtahts**ioan**
Which line should I take for ...?	**Welche Linie fährt nach ...?**	**vehl**kher **lee**nier fairt naakh

74

Boat service *Auf dem Schiff*

When does a boat for ... leave?	**Wann fährt ein Schiff nach ...?**	vahn fairt ighn shif naakh
Where's the embarkation point?	**Wo ist der Anlege-platz?**	voa ist derr **ahn**layger-plahts
When do we call at Cologne?	**Wann legen wir in Köln an?**	vahn **lay**gern veer in kurln ahn
I'd like to take a harbour roundtour.	**Ich möchte eine Ha-fenrundfahrt machen.**	ikh **murkh**ter **ighn**er **haa**fernruntfaart **mahkh**ern
boat	**das Schiff/das Boot**	dahss shif/dahss boat
cabin	**die Kabine**	dee kah**bee**ner
single	**Einzelkabine**	**ighnt**serlkah**bee**ner
double	**Zweierkabine**	**tsvigh**errkah**bee**ner
cruise	**die Kreuzfahrt**	dee **kroyts**faart
crossing	**die Überfahrt**	dee **ew**berrfaart
deck	**das Deck**	dahss dehk
ferry	**die Fähre**	dee **fair**er
hydrofoil	**das Tragflächenboot**	dahss **traag**flehkhernboat
life belt	**der Rettungsring**	derr **reh**tungsring
life boat	**das Rettungsboot**	dahss **reh**tungsboat
port	**der Hafen**	derr **haa**fern
river cruise	**die Flußfahrt**	dee **flus**faart
ship	**das Schiff**	dahss shif
steamer	**das Dampfschiff**	dahss **dahmpf**shif

Bicycle hire *Fahrradverleih*

Many railway stations provide a bicycle-hire service.

I'd like to hire a bicycle.	**Ich möchte ein Fahrrad mieten.**	ikh **murkh**ter ighn **faar**raat **mee**tern

Other means of transport *Weitere Transportmittel*

cable car	**die Seilbahn**	dee **zighl**baan
helicopter	**der Hubschrauber**	derr **hoop**shrowberr
moped	**das Moped**	dahss **moa**peht
motorbike	**das Motorrad**	dahss **moa**torraat
scooter	**der Motorroller**	derr **moa**torrollerr

Or perhaps you prefer:

to hike	**wandern**	**vahn**derrn
to hitchhike	**trampen**	**trehm**pern
to walk	**zu Fuß gehen**	tsoo fuss **gay**ern

Car   Das Auto

In general roads are good in Germany, Austria and Switzerland. Motorways (expressways) are free in Germany. In Austria some Alpine roads and tunnels charge tolls *(die Maut)*. If you use the motorways in Switzerland you must purchase a sticker *(die Vignette)* to be displayed on the windscreen.

A red reflector warning triangle must be carried for use in case of a breakdown, and seat-belts *(der Sicherheitsgurt)* are obligatory. In winter snow tyres or chains are compulsory on Alpine passes.

Where's the nearest filling station?	**Wo ist die nächste Tankstelle?**	voa ist dee **naikh**ster **tahnk**shtehler
Full tank, please.	**Volltanken, bitte.**	**volt**ahnkern **bitt**er
Give me ... litres of petrol (gasoline).	**Geben Sie mir ... Liter Benzin.**	**gay**bern zee mir ... **lee**terr behnt**seen**
super (premium)/ regular/lead-free/ diesel	**Super/Normal/ bleifreies Benzin/ diesel**	**zoo**perr/**nor**maal/ **bligh**frigherss behnt**seen**/ **dee**zerl
Please check the ...	**Kontrollieren Sie bitte ...**	kontrol**lee**rern zee **bitt**er
battery	**die Batterie**	dee bahte**hree**
brake fluid	**die Bremsflüssigkeit**	dee **brehms**flewssikhkight
oil	**das Öl**	dahss url
water	**das Wasser**	dahss **vah**sserr
Would you check the tyre pressure?	**Würden Sie bitte den Reifendruck prüfen?**	**vew**rdern zee **bitt**er dayn **righ**ferndruk **prew**fern
1.6 front, 1.8 rear.	**Vorne 1,6, hinten 1,8.**	**for**ner ighns zehks **hint**ern ighns ahkht
Please check the spare tyre, too.	**Prüfen Sie auch den Ersatzreifen, bitte.**	**prew**fern zee owkh dayn ehr**zahts**righfern **bitt**er
Can you mend this puncture (fix this flat)?	**Können Sie diesen Reifen flicken?**	**kur**nern zee **dee**zern **righ**fern **flik**kern
Would you please change the ...?	**Würden Sie bitte ... wechseln?**	**vew**rdern zee **bitt**er ... **vehk**serln
bulb	**die Glühbirne**	dee **glew**birner
fan belt	**den Keilriemen**	dayn **kighl**reemern

CAR HIRE, see page 20

spark(ing) plugs	die Zündkerzen	dee **tsewnt**kehrtsern
tyre	den Reifen	dayn **righ**fern
wipers	die Scheibenwischer	dee **shigh**bernvisherr
Would you clean the windscreen (windshield)?	Würden Sie bitte die Windschutzscheibe reinigen?	vewrdern zee **bitter** dee **vint**shutsshighber **righ**niggern

Asking the way—Street directions *Nach dem Weg fragen*

Can you tell me the way to ...?	Können Sie mir sagen, wie ich nach ... komme?	**kur**nern zee meer **zaa**gern vee ikh naakh ... **kom**mer
How do I get to ...?	Wie komme ich nach ...?	vee **kom**mer ikh naakh
Are we on the right road for ...?	Sind wir auf der richtigen Straße nach ...?	zint veer owf derr **rikh**tiggern **shtraas**ser naakh
How far is the next village?	Wie weit ist es bis zum nächsten Dorf?	vee vight ist ehss biss tsum **nehkh**stern dorf
How far is it to ... from here?	Wie weit ist es von hier nach ...?	vee vight ist ehss fon heer naakh
Is there a motorway (expressway)?	Gibt es eine Autobahn?	gipt ehss **igh**ner **ow**tobbaan
Is there a road with little traffic?	Gibt es eine wenig befahrene Straße?	gipt ehss **igh**ner **vay**nikh berfaarerer **shtraas**ser
How long does it take by car/on foot?	Wie lange dauert es mit dem Auto/zu Fuß?	vee **lahng**er **dow**errt ehss mit daym **ow**to/tsoo fuss
Can I drive to the centre of town?	Kann ich bis ins Stadtzentrum fahren?	kahn ikh biss ins **shtaht**tsehntrum **faa**rern
Can you tell me, where ... is?	Können Sie mir sagen, wo ... ist?	**kur**nern zee meer **zaa**gern voa ... ist
Where can I find this address/place?	Wie komme ich zu dieser Adresse/diesem Ort?	vee **kom**mer ikh tsoo **dee**zerr ah**dreh**sser/**dee**zerm ort
Where's this?	Wo ist das?	voa ist dahss
Can you show me on the map where I am?	Können Sie mir auf der Karte zeigen, wo ich bin?	**kur**nern zee meer owf derr **kahr**ter **tsigh**gern voa ikh bin

Sie sind auf der falschen Straße.	You're on the wrong road.
Fahren Sie geradeaus.	Go straight ahead.
Es ist dort vorne ...	It's down there on the ...
links/rechts	left/right
gegenüber/hinter ...	opposite/behind ...
neben/nach ...	next to/after ...
Nord/Süd/Ost/West	north/south/east/west
Fahren Sie bis zur ersten/ zweiten Kreuzung.	Go to the first/second crossroad (intersection).
Biegen Sie bei der Ampel links ab.	Turn left at the traffic lights.
Biegen Sie bei der nächsten Ecke rechts ab.	Turn right at the next corner.
Nehmen Sie die Straße nach ...	Take the road for ...
Sie müssen zurück nach ...	You have to go back to ...

Parking *Parken*

In town centres there are blue zones for which you need a parking disk (*eine Parkscheibe*—**igh**nerr **pahrk**shighber). You set it to show when you arrived and when you must leave. The disk can be obtained from tourist offices, petrol stations and hotels.

Where can I park?	**Wo kann ich parken?**	voa kahn ikh **pahrk**ern
Is there a car park nearby?	**Gibt es einen Park- platz hier in der Nähe?**	gipt ehss **igh**nern **pahrk**- plahts heer in derr **naier**
May I park here?	**Darf ich hier parken?**	dahrf ikh heer **pahrk**ern
How long can I park here?	**Wie lange kann ich hier parken?**	vee **lahng**er kahn ikh heer **pahrk**ern
What's the charge per hour?	**Wieviel kostet es pro Stunde?**	vee**feel** kostert ehss proa **shtund**er
Do you have some change for the parking meter?	**Haben Sie Kleingeld für die Parkuhr?**	**haab**ern zee **klighng**ehlt fewr dee **pahrk**oor

Breakdown—Road assistance *Panne – Pannendienst*

Where's the nearest garage?	**Wo ist die nächste Reparaturwerkstatt?**	voa ist dee **naikhs**ter raypahrah**toor**vehrkshtaht
Excuse me. My car has broken down.	**Entschuldigung, mein Wagen hat eine Panne.**	ehnts**huld**iggung mighn **vaa**gern haht **igh**ner **pah**ner
I've had a breakdown.	**Ich habe eine Panne.**	ikh **haa**ber **igh**ner **pah**ner
Can you send a mechanic?	**Können Sie einen Mechaniker schicken?**	**kur**nern zee **igh**nern meh**khah**nikkerr **shikk**ern
My car won't start.	**Mein Auto springt nicht an.**	mighn **ow**to shpringt nikht ahn
The battery is dead.	**Die Batterie ist leer.**	dee bah**teh**ree ist layr
I've run out of petrol (gasoline).	**Ich habe eine Benzin-panne.**	ikh **haa**ber **igh**ner behnt**seen**pahner
I have a flat tyre.	**Ich habe einen Platten.**	ikh **haa**ber **igh**nern **plah**tern
The engine is over-heating.	**Der Motor läuft heiß.**	derr **mo**ator loyft highss
There is something wrong with ...	**... ist/sind nicht in Ordnung.**	... ist/zint nikht in **ort**nung
brakes	**die Bremsen**	dee **brehm**zern
carburettor	**der Vergaser**	derr fehr**gaa**zerr
exhaust pipe	**der Auspuff**	derr **ows**puf
radiator	**der Kühler**	derr **kew**lerr
a wheel	**ein Rad**	ighn roat
Can you send a breakdown van (tow truck)?	**Können Sie einen Abschleppwagen schicken?**	**kur**nern zee **igh**nern **ahp**shlehp**vaa**gern **shikk**ern
How long will you be?	**Wie lange dauert es?**	vee **lahn**ger **dow**errt ehss

Accident—Police *Verkehrsunfall – Polizei*

| Please call the police. | **Rufen Sie bitte die Polizei.** | **roo**fern zee **bit**ter dee polli**tsigh** |
| There's been an accident. It's about 2 km. from ... | **Es ist ein Unfall passiert, ungefähr 2 Kilometer von ...** | ehss ist ighn **un**fahl pah**sseert un**gerfair 2 killoam**may**terr fon |

Where's the nearest telephone?	**Wo ist das nächste Telefon?**	voa ist dahss **naikh**ster taylay**foan**
Call a doctor/an ambulance, quickly.	**Rufen Sie schnell einen Arzt/einen Krankenwagen.**	**roo**fern zee shnhel **ighn**ern ahrtst/**ighn**ern **krahn**kernvaagern
There are people injured.	**Es hat Verletzte gegeben.**	ehss haht fehr**leht**ster ger**gay**bern
Here's my driving licence.	**Hier ist mein Führerschein.**	heer ist mighn **few-rerr**shighn
What's your name and address?	**Ihr Name und Ihre Anschrift, bitte?**	eer **naam**er unt **eer**er **ahn**shrift **bitt**er
What's your insurance company?	**Ihre Versicherungs-gesellschaft, bitte?**	**eer**er fehrzee**kehr**rungs-ger**zehl**shahft **bitt**er

Road signs *Verkehrszeichen*

AUSFAHRT	Exit (motorway)
DURCHGANGSVERKEHR	Through traffic
EINBAHNSTRASSE	One-way street
EINORDNEN	Get in lane
FROSTSCHÄDEN	Ice damage
FUSSGÄNGER	Pedestrians
GEFÄHRLICHES GEFÄLLE	Steep descent
GLATTEIS	Icy road
HALT, POLIZEI	Stop, police
HUPEN VERBOTEN	No honking
KURZPARKZONE	Limited parking zone
LANGSAM FAHREN	Slow down
LAWINENGEFAHR	Avalanche area
LKW	Heavy vehicles
NUR FÜR ANLIEGER	Access to residents only
PARKEN VERBOTEN	No parking
RECHTS FAHREN	Keep right
SCHLECHTE FAHRBAHN	Bad road surface
SCHULE	School
STAU	Traffic jam
STEINSCHLAG	Falling rocks
STRASSENARBEITEN	Road works ahead (men working)
UMLEITUNG	Diversion (detour)
... VERBOTEN	No ...
VORFAHRT GEWÄHREN	Give way (yield)
VORSICHT	Caution

Sightseeing

Where's the tourist office?	**Wo ist das Fremdenverkehrsbüro?**	voa ist dahss **frehmdern**fehrkayrsbewroa
What are the main points of interest?	**Was sind die Hauptsehenswürdigkeiten?**	vahss zint dee **howpt**zayernsvewrdikhkightern
We're here for ...	**Wir sind für ... hier.**	veer zint fewr ... heer
a few hours	**ein paar Stunden**	ighn paar **shtundern**
a day	**einen Tag**	**ighnern** taag
a week	**eine Woche**	**ighner** vokher
Can you recommend a sightseeing tour/an excursion?	**Können Sie eine Stadtrundfahrt/einen Ausflug empfehlen?**	kurnern zee **ighner shtaht**runtfaart/**ighnern ows**floog ehmpfaylern
What's the point of departure?	**Von wo fahren wir ab?**	fon voa **fahrern** veer ahp
Will the bus pick us up at the hotel?	**Holt uns der Bus vorm Hotel ab?**	hoalt uns derr buss foarm hot**ehl** ahp
How much does the tour cost?	**Was kostet die Rundfahrt?**	vahss kostert dee **runt**faart
What time does the tour start?	**Wann beginnt die Rundfahrt?**	vahn ber**gint** dee **runt**faart
Is lunch included?	**Ist das Mittagessen inbegriffen?**	ist dahss **mittaag**ehssern **in**bergriffern
What time do we get back?	**Wann werden wir zurück sein?**	vahn **vayr**dern veer tsoo**rewk** zighn
Do we have free time in ...?	**Haben wir in ... Zeit zu freier Verfügung?**	**haa**bern veer in ... tsight tsoo **frigh**err fehr**few**gung
Is there an English-speaking guide?	**Gibt es einen englischsprechenden Fremdenführer?**	gipt ehss **ighnern ehng**lishshprehkherndern **frehm**dernfewrer
I'd like to hire a private guide for ...	**Ich möchte einen Fremdenführer für ...**	ikh **murkh**ter **ighnern frehm**dernfewrer fewr
half a day	**einen halben Tag**	**ighnern hahl**bern taag
a full day	**einen Tag**	**ighnern** taag

Where is/Where are the ...?	Wo ist/Wo sind ...?	voa ist/voa zint
abbey	die Abtei	dee ahptigh
alley	die Gasse	dee gahsser
amusement park	der Vergnügungspark	derr fehrgnewgungspahrk
art gallery	die Kunstgalerie	dee kunstgahlehree
botanical gardens	der Botanische Garten	derr bottaanisher gahrtern
building	das Gebäude	dahss gerboyder
business district	das Geschäftsviertel	dahss gershehftsfeerterl
cathedral	die Kathedrale/der Dom	dee kahtehdraaler/derr doam
cave	die Höhle	dee hurler
cemetery	der Friedhof	derr freethoaf
chapel	die Kapelle	dee kahpehler
church	die Kirche	dee keerkher
city walls	die Stadtmauern	dee shtahtmowerrn
concert hall	die Konzerthalle	dee kontsehrthahler
convent	das Kloster	dahss kloasterr
convention hall	die Kongreßhalle	dee kongrehshahler
court house	das Gericht	dahss gerrikht
downtown area	die Innenstadt	dee innernshtaht
exhibition	die Ausstellung	dee owsshtehlung
factory	die Fabrik	dee fahbrik
fair	die Messe	dee mehsser
flea market	der Flohmarkt	derr floamahrkt
fortress	die Festung	dee fehstung
fountain	der Brunnen/Springbrunnen	derr brunnern/shpringbrunnern
gardens	die Grünanlagen	dee grewnahnlaagern
harbour	der Hafen	derr haafern
lake	der See	derr zay
library	die Bibliothek	dee bibliotayk
market	der Markt	derr mahrkt
memorial	das Denkmal	dahss dehnkmaal
monastery	das Kloster	dahss kloasterr
monument	das Denkmal	dahss dehnkmaal
museum	das Museum	dahss muzayum
old town	die Altstadt	dee ahltshtaht
opera house	das Opernhaus	dahss oaperrnhowss
palace	der Palast/das Schloß	derr pahlahst/dahss shloss
park	der Park	derr pahrk
parliament building	das Parlamentsgebäude	dahss pahrlahmehntsgerboyder
ruins	die Ruinen	dee rueenern
shopping area	das Geschäftsviertel	dahss gershehftsfeerterl

square	der Platz	derr plahts
stadium	das Stadion	dahss shtaadion
statue	die Statue	dee shtaatuer
stock exchange	die Börse	dee burrzer
street	die Straße	dee shtrahsser
theatre	das Theater	dahss tayaaterr
tomb	das Grab	dahss graap
tower	der Turm	derr toorm
town hall	das Rathaus	dahss raathowss
university	die Universität	dee unnivehrzitait
wall	die Mauer	dee mowerr
zoo	der Zoo	derr tsoa

Admission *Eintritt*

Is ... open on Sundays?	Ist ... sonntags geöffnet?	ist ... zontaags gerurfnert
What are the opening hours?	Welches sind die Öffnungszeiten?	vehlkherss zint dee urfnungstsightern
When does it close?	Wann schließt es?	vahn shleest ehss
How much is the entrance fee?	Was kostet der Eintritt?	vahss kostert derr ighntrit
Is there any reduction for ...?	Gibt es Ermäßigung für ...?	gipt ehss ehrmaissiggung fewr
children	Kinder	kinderr
disabled	Behinderte	berhinderrter
groups	Gruppen	gruppern
pensioners	Rentner	rehntnerr
students	Studenten	shtuddehntern
Have you a guide book (in English)?	Haben Sie einen Reiseführer (in Englisch)?	haabern zee ighnern righzerfewrerr (in ehnglish)
Can I buy a catalogue?	Kann ich einen Katalog kaufen?	kahn ikh ighnern kahtahloag kowfern
Is it all right to take pictures?	Darf man fotografieren?	dahrf mahn fottograhfeerern

| **EINTRITT FREI** | ADMISSION FREE |
| **FOTOGRAFIEREN VERBOTEN** | NO CAMERAS ALLOWED |

Who—What—When? *Wer – Was – Wann?*

What's that building?	**Was für ein Gebäude ist das?**	vahss fewr ighn gerboyder ist dahss
Who was the ...?	**Wer war der ...?**	vayr vaar derr
architect	**Architekt**	ahrkhittehkt
artist	**Künstler**	kewnstlerr
painter	**Maler**	maalerr
sculptor	**Bildhauer**	bilthowerr
Who built it?	**Wer hat es gebaut?**	vayr haht ehss gerbowt
Who painted that picture?	**Wer hat das Bild gemalt?**	vayr haht dahss bilt germaalt
When did he live?	**Wann hat er gelebt?**	vahn haht ehr gerlaybt
When was it built?	**Wann wurde es erbaut?**	vahn voorder ehss ehrbowt
Where's the house where ... lived?	**Wo ist das Haus, in dem ... wohnte?**	voa ist dahss howss in daym ... voanter
We're interested in ...	**Wir interessieren uns für ...**	veer intehrehsseerern uns fewr
antiques	**Antiquitäten**	ahntikvittaitern
archaeology	**Archäologie**	ahrkhehollogee
art	**Kunst**	kunst
botany	**Botanik**	bottaanik
ceramics	**Keramik**	kehrraamik
coins	**Münzen**	mewntsern
fine arts	**bildende Künste**	bildernder kewnster
furniture	**Möbel**	murberl
geology	**Geologie**	gayollogee
handicrafts	**Kunsthandwerk**	kunsthahntvehrk
history	**Geschichte**	gershikhter
medicine	**Medizin**	mehditseen
music	**Musik**	muzeek
natural history	**Naturkunde**	nahtoorkunder
ornithology	**Vogelkunde**	foagerlkunder
painting	**Malerei**	maalehrigh
pottery	**Töpferei**	turpfehrigh
religion	**Religion**	rayliggioan
sculpture	**Bildhauerei**	bilthowerrigh
zoology	**Zoologie**	tsoaollogee
Where's the ... department?	**Wo ist die ...-Abteilung?**	voa ist dee ... ahptighlung

It's ...	Es ist ...	ehss ist
amazing	erstaunlich	ehrshtownlikh
awful	scheußlich	shoysslikh
beautiful	schön	shurn
gloomy	düster	dewsterr
impressive	eindrucksvoll	ighndruksfol
interesting	interessant	intehrehssahnt
lovely	wunderschön	voonderrshurn
magnificent	großartig	groassahrtikh
overwhelming	überwältigend	ewberrvehltiggernt
pretty	hübsch	hewpsh
romantic	romantisch	rommahntish
sinister	unheimlich	unhighmlikh
strange	seltsam	zehltzaam
superb	prächtig	prehkhtikh
terrible	schrecklich	shrehklikh
tremendous	außerordentlich	owsserrorderntlikh
ugly	häßlich	hehsslikh

Churches—Religious services   *Kirchen – Gottesdienste*

Most churches and cathedrals are open to the public except, of course, when a service is being conducted.

Services are conducted in English in many towns. Ask the local tourist office for further details.

Is there a ... near here?	Gibt es eine ... in der Nähe?	gipt ehss ighner ... in derr naier
Catholic church	katholische Kirche	kahtoalisher keerkher
Protestant church	evangelische/pro- testantische Kirche	ehvahngaylisher/protteh- shtahntisher keerkher
synagogue	Synagoge	zewnahgoager
mosque	Moschee	moshay
At what time is ...?	Wann beginnt ...?	vahn bergint
mass	die Messe	dee mehsser
the service	der Gottesdienst	derr gottersdeenst
Where can I find a ... who speaks English?	Wo finde ich einen ..., der Englisch spricht?	voa finder ikh ighnern ... derr ehnglish shprikht
priest/minister rabbi	Priester/Pfarrer Rabbiner	preesterr/pfahrerr/ rahbeenerr
I'd like to visit the church.	Ich möchte die Kirche besichtigen.	ikh murkhter dee kirkherr berzikhtiggern

In the countryside *Auf dem Lande*

Is there a scenic route to ...?	**Gibt es eine land-schaftlich schöne Straße nach ...?**	gipt ehss **ighner lahnt-**shahftlikh **shurner** shtraasser naakh
How far is it to ...?	**Wie weit ist es bis ...?**	vee vight ist ehss biss
Can we walk?	**Können wir zu Fuß gehen?**	kurnern veer tsoo fooss gayern
How high is that mountain?	**Wie hoch ist dieser Berg?**	vee hoakh ist **deezerr** behrg
What kind of ... is that?	**Was für ... ist das?**	vahss fewr ... ist dahss
animal/bird	**ein Tier/ein Vogel**	ighn teer/ighn **foagerl**
flower/tree	**eine Blume/ein Baum**	**ighner** bloomer/ighn bowm

Landmarks *Zur Orientierung*

bridge	**die Brücke**	dee **brewker**
castle	**das Schloß/die Burg**	dahss shloss/dee boorg
farm	**der Bauernhof**	derr **bowerrnhoaf**
field	**das Feld**	dahss fehlt
footpath	**der Fußweg**	derr **foosvayg**
forest	**der Wald**	derr vahlt
garden	**der Garten**	derr **gahrtern**
hill	**der Hügel**	derr **hewgerl**
house	**das Haus**	dahss howss
lake	**der See**	derr zay
meadow	**die Wiese**	dee **veezer**
path	**der Weg**	derr vayg
mountain pass	**der Paß**	derr pahss
peak	**die Bergspitze**	dee **behrgshpitser**
pond	**der Teich**	derr tighkh
river	**der Fluß/der Strom**	derr fluss/derr shtroam
rock	**der Felsen**	derr **fehlzern**
road	**die Straße**	dee **shtraasser**
sea	**die See/das Meer**	dee zay/dahss mayr
spring	**die Quelle**	dee **kvehler**
valley	**das Tal**	dahss taal
village	**das Dorf**	dahss dorf
vineyard	**der Weinberg**	derr **vighnbehrg**
waterfall	**der Wasserfall**	derr **vahsserfahl**
well	**der Brunnen**	derr **brunnern**
wood	**der Wald**	derr vahlt

ASKING THE WAY, see page 76

Relaxing

Cinema (movies) — Theatre   *Kino – Theater*

Foreign films are usually dubbed into German, though some cinemas also screen them in the original, with German subtitles, at certain times on certain days. Since cinema showings are seldom continuous you can buy your tickets in advance. Theatre curtain time is about 8 p.m. Advance booking is advisable.

You can find out what's playing from newspapers and bill-boards. In most large towns you can buy a publication of the type "This Week in ...".

What's showing at the cinema tonight?	**Was gibt es heute abend im Kino zu sehen?**	vahss gipt ehss **hoy**ter aabernt im **kee**no tsoo **zay**ern
What's playing at the ... theatre?	**Was wird im ...theater gegeben?**	vahss veert im ... tay**aa**terr ger**gay**bern
What sort of play is it?	**Was für ein Stück ist es?**	vahss fewr ighn **shtewk** ist ehss
Who's it by?	**Von wem ist es?**	fon vaym ist ehss
Can you recommend a ...?	**Können Sie mir ... empfehlen?**	**kur**nern zee meer ... ehm**pfay**lern
good film	**einen guten Film**	**ighn**ern **goo**tern film
comedy	**eine Komödie**	**ighn**er kom**mur**dier
musical	**ein Musical**	ighn "musical"
Where's that new film by ... being shown?	**Wo läuft der neue Film von ...?**	voa loyft derr **noy**er film fon
Who's in it?	**Mit welchen Schauspielern?**	mit **vehl**kherm **show**shpeelerrn
Who's playing the lead?	**Wer spielt die Hauptrolle?**	vayr shpeelt dee **howpt**roller
Who's the director?	**Wer ist der Regisseur?**	vayr ist derr rehzhi**ssurr**
At what theatre is that new play by ... being performed?	**In welchem Theater wird das neue Stück von ... gespielt?**	in **vehl**kherm tay**aa**terr veert dahss **noy**er shtewk fon ... ger**shpeelt**

87

RELAXING

What time does the show begin?	**Wann beginnt die Vorstellung?**	vahn bergint dee foarshtehlung
What time does the performance end?	**Wann ist die Vorstellung zu Ende?**	vahn ist dee foarshtehlung tsoo ehnder
Are there any tickets for tonight?	**Gibt es noch Karten für heute abend?**	gipt ehss nokh kahrtern fewr hoyter aabernt
How much are the tickets?	**Wie teuer sind die Karten?**	vee toyerr zint dee kahrtern
I want to reserve 2 tickets for the show on Friday evening.	**Ich möchte 2 Karten für Freitag abend vorbestellen.**	ikh murkhter 2 kahrtern fewr frightaag aabernt foarbershtehlern
Can I have a ticket for the matinée on ...?	**Kann ich eine Karte für die Nachmittagsvorstellung am ... bekommen?**	kahn ikh ighner kahrter fewr dee nakhmittaagsfoarshtehlung ahm ... berkommern
I want a seat in the stalls (orchestra).	**Ich hätte gern einen Platz im Parkett.**	ikh hehter gehrn ighnern plahts im pahrkeht
Not too far back.	**Nicht zu weit hinten.**	nikht tsu vight hintern
Somewhere in the middle.	**Irgendwo in der Mitte.**	eergerntvoa in derr mitter
How much are the seats in the circle (mezzanine)?	**Wie teuer sind die Plätze im Rang?**	vee toyer zint dee plehtser im rahng
May I please have a programme?	**Kann ich bitte ein Programm haben?**	kahn ikh bitter ighn programm haabern
Where's the cloakroom?	**Wo ist die Garderobe?**	voa ist dee gahrderroaber

Bedaure, es ist alles ausverkauft.	I'm sorry, we're sold out.
Es gibt nur noch ein paar Plätze im Rang.	There are only a few seats left in the circle (mezzanine).
Darf ich Ihre Eintrittskarte sehen?	May I see your ticket?
Hier ist Ihr Platz.	This is your seat.

Unterhaltung

 DAYS OF THE WEEK, see page 151

Opera—Ballet—Concert   *Oper – Ballett – Konzert*

Can you recommend a ...?	**Können Sie mir ... empfehlen?**	kurnern zee meer ehmpfaylern
ballet	**ein Ballett**	ighn bahleht
concert	**ein Konzert**	ighn kontsehrt
opera	**eine Oper**	ighner oaperr
operetta	**eine Operette**	ighner oppehrehter
Where's the opera house/the concert hall?	**Wo ist das Opernhaus/die Konzerthalle?**	voa ist dahss oaperrnhowss/ dee kontsehrthahler
What's on at the opera tonight?	**Was wird heute abend in der Oper gegeben?**	vahss veert hoyter aabernt in derr oaperr gergaybern
Who's singing/ dancing?	**Wer singt/tanzt?**	vayr zingt/tahntst
What orchestra is playing?	**Welches Orchester spielt?**	vehlkhers orkehsterr shpeelt
What are they playing?	**Was wird gespielt?**	vahss veert gershpeelt
Who's the conductor/ soloist?	**Wer ist der Dirigent/ der Solist?**	vayr ist derr dirriggehnt/ derr sollist

Nightclubs   *Nachtlokale*

Can you recommend a good nightclub?	**Können Sie mir ein gutes Nachtlokal empfehlen?**	kurnern zee meer ighn gooterss nahkhtlokkaal ehmpfaylern
Is there a floor show?	**Gibt es Attraktionen?**	gipt ehss ahtrahktsioanern
Is evening dress necessary?	**Wird Abendgarderobe verlangt?**	veert aaberntgahrdehroaber fehrlahngt

Discos   *Diskotheken*

Where can we go dancing?	**Wo können wir tanzen gehen?**	voa kurnern veer tahntsern gayern
Is there a discotheque in town?	**Gibt es hier eine Diskothek?**	gipt ehss heer ighner diskottayk
Would you like to dance?	**Möchten Sie tanzen?**	murkhtern zee tahntsern

Sports *Sport*

You name the sport, and you'll doubtless be able to find it in Germany, Austria and Switzerland. The most popular spectator sport is by far football (soccer).

Is there a football (soccer) game anywhere this Saturday?	**Findet diesen Samstag irgendwo ein Fußballspiel statt?**	findert deezern zahmstaag irgerntvoa ighn foosbahlshpeel shtaht
Which teams are playing?	**Welche Mannschaften spielen?**	vehlkher mahnshahftern shpeelern
Can you get me a ticket?	**Können Sie mir eine Karte besorgen?**	kurnern zee meer ighner kahrter berzorgern

basketball	**Basketball**	baaskertbahl
boxing	**Boxen**	boksern
car racing	**Autorennen**	owtorrehnern
cycling	**Radfahren**	raatfaarern
football (soccer)	**Fußball**	foosbahl
horse racing	**Pferderennen**	pfayrderrehnern
horseback riding	**Reiten**	rightern
mountaineering	**Bergsteigen**	behrgshtighgern
skiing	**Skifahren**	sheefaarern
swimming	**Schwimmen**	shvimmern
tennis	**Tennis**	tehniss
volleyball	**Volleyball**	vollibbahl

I'd like to see a boxing match.	**Ich möchte gern einen Boxkampf sehen.**	ikh murkhter gehrn ighnern bokskahmpf zayern
What's the admission charge?	**Was kostet der Eintritt?**	vahss kostert derr ighntrit
Where's the nearest golf course?	**Wo ist der nächste Golfplatz?**	voa ist derr naikhster golfplahts
Where are the tennis courts?	**Wo sind die Tennisplätze?**	voa zint dee tehnisplehtser
Can I hire (rent) rackets?	**Kann ich Tennisschläger mieten?**	kahn ikh tehnisshlaigerr meetern
What's the charge per ...?	**Wieviel kostet es pro ...**	veefeel kostert ehss proa
day/round/hour	**Tag/Spiel/Stunde**	taag/shpeel/shtunder

DAYS OF THE WEEK, see page 151

Unterhaltung

Where's the nearest race course (track)?	**Wo ist die nächste Pferderennbahn?**	voa ist dee **naikh**ster pfehrderrehnbaan
Is there any good fishing around here?	**Kann man hier in der Nähe angeln?**	kahn mahn heer in derr naier ahngerln
Do I need a permit?	**Brauche ich einen Angelschein?**	browkher ikh **igh**nern ahngerlshighn
Where can I get one?	**Wo bekomme ich einen?**	voa berkommer ikh **igh**nern
Can one swim in the lake/river?	**Kann man im See/Fluß baden?**	kahn mahn im zay/fluss **baa**dern
Is there a swimming pool here?	**Gibt es hier ein Schwimmbad?**	gipt ehss heer ighn **shvim**baat
Is it open-air or indoor?	**Ist es ein Freibad oder ein Hallenbad?**	ist ehss ighn **frigh**baat oaderr ighn **hah**lernbaat
Is it heated?	**Ist es geheizt?**	ist ehss ger**hightst**
What's the temperature of the water?	**Welche Temperatur hat das Wasser?**	**vehl**kher tehmperrah**toor** haht dahss **vah**sser
Is there a sandy beach?	**Gibt es einen Sandstrand?**	gipt ehss **igh**nern **zahnt**shtrahnt

On the beach *Am Strand*

The sea is very calm.	**Das Meer ist sehr ruhig.**	dahss mayr ist zayr **rooikh**
There are some big waves.	**Das Meer hat hohen Wellengang.**	dahss mayr haht **hoa**ern **vehl**erngahng
Is it safe for swimming?	**Kann man hier gefahrlos schwimmen?**	kahn mahn heer ger**faar**loass **shvim**mern
Is there a lifeguard?	**Gibt es einen Rettungsdienst?**	gipt ehss **igh**nern **reh**tungsdeenst
Is it safe for children?	**Ist es für Kinder ungefährlich?**	ist ehss fewr **kin**derr **un**gerfairlikh
Are there any dangerous currents?	**Gibt es gefährliche Strömungen?**	gipt ehss ger**fair**likher **shtrur**mungern
What time is high tide/low tide?	**Wann ist Flut/Ebbe?**	vahn ist floot/**ehb**ber

I want to hire (rent) a/an/some ...	Ich möchte ... mieten.	ikh murkhter ... meetern
bathing hut (cabana)	eine Badekabine	ighner baaderkahbeener
deck-chair	einen Liegestuhl	ighnern leegershtool
motorboat	ein Motorboot	ighn moatorboat
rowing-boat	ein Ruderboot	ighn rooderrboat
sailboard	einen Windsurfer	ighnern vintsurrferr
sailing-boat	ein Segelboot	ighn zaygerlboat
skin-diving equipment	eine Taucher- ausrüstung	ighner towkherr- owsrewstung
sunshade (umbrella)	einen Sonnenschirm	ighnern zonnernsheerm
surfboard	ein Surfbrett	ighn surfbreht
water-skis	Wasserski	vahssershee

| PRIVATSTRAND | PRIVATE BEACH |
| BADEN VERBOTEN | NO SWIMMING |

Winter sports *Wintersport*

Is there a skating- rink near here?	Gibt es hier in der Nähe eine Eisbahn?	gipt ehss heer in derr naier ighner ighsbaan
I'd like to ski.	Ich möchte skifahren.	ikh murkhter sheefaarern
downhill/cross- country skiing	Abfahrtslauf/ Langlauf	ahpfahrtslowf/ lahnglowf
Are there any ski runs for ...?	Gibt es Skipisten für ...?	gipt ehss sheepistern fewr
beginners	Anfänger	ahnfaingerr
good skiers	Fortgeschrittene	fortgershritterner
Can I take skiing lessons?	Kann ich Ski- unterricht nehmen?	kahn ikh sheeunterrrikht naymern
Are there ski lifts?	Gibt es Skilifte?	gipt ehss sheelifter
I want to hire a/ some ...	Ich möchte ... mieten.	ikh murkhter ... meetern
poles	Skistöcke	sheeshturker
skates	Schlittschuhe	shlitshooer
ski boots	Skischuhe	sheeshooer
skiing equipment	eine Skiausrüstung	ighner sheeowsrewstung
skis	Skier	sheeerr

Making friends

Introductions *Vorstellen*

May I introduce ...?	**Darf ich ... vorstellen?**	dahrf ikh ... **foar**shtehlern
John, this is ...	**John, das ist ...**	John dahss ist
My name is ...	**Ich heiße ...**	ikh **high**sser
Glad to know you.	**Sehr erfreut.**	zayr ehr**froyt**
What's your name?	**Wie heißen Sie?**	vee **high**ssern zee
How are you?	**Wie geht es Ihnen?**	vee gayt ehss **ee**nern
Fine, thanks. And you?	**Danke, gut. Und Ihnen?**	**dahn**ker goot. unt **ee**nern

Follow-up *Näheres Kennenlernen*

How long have you been here?	**Wie lange sind Sie schon hier?**	vee **lahng**er zint zee shoan heer
We've been here a week.	**Wir sind seit einer Woche hier.**	veer zint zight **igh**nerr **vo**kher heer
Is this your first visit?	**Sind Sie zum ersten Mal hier?**	zint zee tsum **ehr**stern maal heer
No, we came here last year.	**Nein, wir waren schon letztes Jahr hier.**	nighn veer **vaa**rern shoan **lehts**terss yaar heer
Are you enjoying your stay?	**Gefällt es Ihnen hier?**	ger**fehlt** ehss **ee**nern heer
Yes, I like it very much.	**Ja, mir gefällt es sehr gut.**	yaa meer ger**fehlt** ehss zayr goot
I like the landscape a lot.	**Die Landschaft gefällt mir sehr.**	dee **lahnt**shahft ger**fehlt** meer zayr
What do you think of the country/ the city?	**Wie gefällt Ihnen das Land/die Stadt?**	vee ger**fehlt** **ee**nern dahss lahnt/dee shtaht
Where do you come from?	**Woher kommen Sie?**	vo**ahyr** kommern zee
I'm from ...	**Ich bin aus ...**	ikh bin owss

COUNTRIES, see page 146

I'm ...	Ich bin ...	ikh bin
American	Amerikaner(in)	ahmehrikkaanerr(in)
British	Brite (Britin)	britter (brittin)
Canadian	Kanadier(in)	kahnaadierr(rin)
English	Engländer(in)	ehnglehnderr(in)
Irish	Ire (Irin)	eerer (eerin)
Where are you staying?	Wo wohnen Sie?	voa voanern zee
Are you on your own?	Sind Sie allein hier?	zint zee ahlighn heer
I'm with my ...	Ich bin mit ... hier.	ikh bin mit ... heer
wife	meiner Frau	mighnerr frow
husband	meinem Mann	mighnerm mahn
family	meiner Familie	mighnerr fahmeelier
parents	meinen Eltern	mighnern ehlterrn
boyfriend	meinem Freund	mighnerm froynt
girlfriend	meiner Freundin	mighnerr froyndin

father/mother	der Vater/die Mutter	derr faaterr/dee mutterr
son/daughter	der Sohn/die Tochter	derr zoan/dee tokhterr
brother/sister	der Bruder/die Schwester	derr brooderr/dee shvehsterr
uncle/aunt	der Onkel/die Tante	derr onkerl/dee tahnter
nephew/niece	der Neffe/die Nichte	derr nehfer/dee neekhter
cousin	der Cousin/die Cousine	derr kuzehng/dee kuzeener

Are you married/ single?	Sind Sie verheiratet/ ledig?	zint zee fehrhighraatert/ laydikh
Do you have children?	Haben Sie Kinder?	haarbern zee kinderr
What's your occupation?	Was machen Sie beruflich?	vahss mahkhern zee berrooflikh
I'm a student.	Ich bin Student(in).	ikh bin shtuddehnt(in)
What are you studying?	Was studieren Sie?	vahss shtuddeerern zee
I'm here on a business trip.	Ich bin auf einer Geschäftsreise hier.	ikh bin owf ighnerr gershehftsrighzer heer
Do you travel a lot?	Reisen Sie viel?	righzern zee feel
Do you play cards/ chess?	Spielen Sie Karten/ Schach?	shpeelern zee kahrtern/ shahkh

The weather *Das Wetter*

What a lovely day!	**Was für ein herrlicher Tag!**	vahss fewr ighn hehrlikherr taag
What awful weather!	**Was für ein scheußliches Wetter!**	vahss fewr ighn shoysslikherss vehterr
Isn't it cold/hot today?	**Welche Kälte/Hitze heute!**	vehlkher kehlter/hitser hoyter
Is it usually as warm as this?	**Ist es immer so warm?**	ist ehss immerr zoa vahrm
Do you think it's going to ... tomorrow?	**Glauben Sie, es wird morgen ...?**	glowbern zee ehss veert morgern
be a nice day	**schön sein**	shurn zighn
rain	**regnen**	raygnern
snow	**schneien**	shnighern
What is the weather forecast?	**Was sagt der Wetterbericht?**	vahss zahgt derr vehterrberrikht

cloud	**die Wolke**	dee volker
fog	**der Nebel**	derr nayberl
frost	**der Frost**	derr frost
ice	**das Eis**	dahss ighss
lightning	**der Blitz**	derr blits
moon	**der Mond**	derr moant
rain	**der Regen**	derr raygern
sky	**der Himmel**	derr himmerl
snow	**der Schnee**	derr shnay
star	**der Stern**	derr shtehrn
sun	**die Sonne**	dee zonner
thunder	**der Donner**	derr donnerr
thunderstorm	**das Gewitter**	dahss gervitterr
wind	**der Wind**	derr vint

Invitations *Einladungen*

Would you like to have dinner with us on ...?	**Möchten Sie am ... mit uns zu Abend essen?**	murkhtern zee ahm ... mit uns tsoo aabernt ehssern
May I invite you for lunch?	**Darf ich Sie zum Mittagessen einladen?**	dahrf ikh zee tsum mittaagehssern ighnlaadern

DAYS OF THE WEEK, see page 151

Can you come over for a drink this evening?	Kommen Sie heute abend auf ein Gläschen zu uns?	kommern zee hoyter aabernt owf ighn glaiskhern tsoo uns
There's a party. Are you coming?	Es gibt eine Party. Kommen Sie auch?	ehss gipt ighner paartee. kommern zee owkh
That's very kind of you.	Das ist sehr nett von Ihnen.	dahss ist zayr neht fon eenern
Great. I'd love to come.	Prima, ich komme sehr gerne.	preemaa ikh kommer zayr gehrner
What time shall we come?	Wann sollen wir da sein?	vahn zollern veer daa zighn
May I bring a friend/ a girlfriend?	Kann ich einen Freund/eine Freundin mitbringen?	kahn ikh ighnern froynt/ighnner froyndin mitbringern
I'm afraid we've got to leave now.	Leider müssen wir jetzt gehen.	lighderr mewssern veer yehtst gayern
Next time you must come to visit us.	Nächstes Mal müssen Sie uns besuchen.	naikhsterss maal mewssern zee uns berzookhern
Thanks for the evening. It was great.	Vielen Dank für den schönen Abend.	feelern dahnk fewr dayn shurnern aabernt

Dating *Verabredung*

Do you mind if I smoke?	Stört es Sie, wenn ich rauche?	shturt ehss zee vehn ikh rowkher
Would you like a cigarette?	Möchten Sie eine Zigarette?	murkhtern zee ighner tsiggahrehter
Do you have a light, please?	Können Sie mir bitte Feuer geben?	kurnern zee meer bitter foyerr gaybern
Why are you laughing?	Warum lachen Sie?	vahroom lahkhern zee
Is my German that bad?	Ist mein Deutsch so schlecht?	ist mighn doych zoa shlehkht
Can I get you a drink?	Möchten Sie etwas trinken?	murkhtern zee ehtvahss trinkern
Are you waiting for someone?	Warten Sie auf jemanden?	vahrtern zee owf yaymahndern
Are you free this evening?	Sind Sie heute abend frei?	zint zee hoyter aabernt frigh

Would you like to go out with me tonight?	**Möchten Sie heute abend mit mir ausgehen?**	murkhtern zee hoyter aabernt mit meer owsgayern
Would you like to go dancing?	**Möchten Sie gern tanzen gehen?**	murkhtern zee gehrn tahntsern gayern
I know a good discotheque.	**Ich kenne eine gute Diskothek.**	ikh kehner ighner gooter diskottayk
Shall we go to the cinema (movies)?	**Wollen wir ins Kino gehen?**	vollern veer ins keeno gayern
Would you like to go for a drive?	**Wollen wir ein bißchen durch die Gegend fahren?**	vollern veer ighn bisskhern doorkh dee gaygernt faarern
Where shall we meet?	**Wo treffen wir uns?**	voa trehfern veer uns
I'll pick you up at your hotel.	**Ich hole Sie in Ihrem Hotel ab.**	ikh hoaler zee in eererm hottehl ahp
I'll call for you at 8.	**Ich hole Sie um 8 Uhr ab.**	ikh hoaler zee um 8 oor ahp
May I take you home?	**Darf ich Sie nach Hause bringen?**	dahrf ikh zee naakh howzer bringern
Can I see you again tomorrow?	**Kann ich Sie morgen wiedersehen?**	kahn ikh zee morgern veederrzayern
What's your telephone number?	**Wie ist Ihre Telefonnummer?**	vee ist eerer taylayfoannummerr

... and you might answer:

I'd love to, thank you.	**Danke, sehr gern.**	dahnker zayr gehrn
Thank you, but I'm busy.	**Vielen Dank, aber ich habe keine Zeit.**	feelern dahnk aaberr ikh haaber kighner tsight
No, I'm not interested, thank you.	**Nein, das interessiert mich nicht.**	nighn dahss intehrehsseert mikh nikht
Leave me alone, please.	**Lassen Sie mich bitte in Ruhe!**	lahssern zee mikh bitter in rooer
Thank you. It's been a wonderful evening.	**Danke, es war ein wunderbarer Abend.**	dahnker ehss vaar ighn voonderrbaarerr aabernt
I've enjoyed myself.	**Ich habe mich gut unterhalten.**	ikh haaber mikh goot unterrhahltern

Shopping guide

This shopping guide is designed to help you find what you want with ease, accuracy and speed. It features:

1. a list of all major shops, stores and services (p. 98)
2. some general expressions required when shopping to allow you to be specific and selective (p. 100)
3. full details of the shops and services most likely to concern you. Here you'll find advice, alphabetical lists of items and conversion charts listed under the headings below.

<table>
<tr><td></td><td></td><td>page</td></tr>
<tr><td>Bookshop/
Stationer's</td><td>books, magazines, newspapers, stationery</td><td>104</td></tr>
<tr><td>Camping equipment</td><td>all items required for camping</td><td>106</td></tr>
<tr><td>Chemist's (drugstore)</td><td>medicine, first-aid, cosmetics, toilet articles</td><td>108</td></tr>
<tr><td>Clothing</td><td>clothes, shoes, accessories</td><td>112</td></tr>
<tr><td>Electrical appliances</td><td>radios, cassette recorders, shavers</td><td>119</td></tr>
<tr><td>Grocery</td><td>some general expressions, weights, measures and packaging</td><td>120</td></tr>
<tr><td>Jeweller's/
Watchmaker's</td><td>jewellery, watches, watch repairs</td><td>121</td></tr>
<tr><td>Optician</td><td>glasses, lenses, binoculars</td><td>123</td></tr>
<tr><td>Photography</td><td>cameras, films, developing, accessories</td><td>124</td></tr>
<tr><td>Tobacconist's</td><td>smoker's supplies</td><td>126</td></tr>
<tr><td>Miscellaneous</td><td>souvenirs, records, cassettes, toys</td><td>127</td></tr>
</table>

LAUNDRY, see page 29/HAIRDRESSER'S, see page 30

Einkaufsführer

Shops, stores and services   *Geschäfte, Läden usw.*

Shops in Germany, Austria and Switzerland usually open
around 8 or 9 a.m. and close at 6 or 6.30 p.m. Some close for
an hour or two at noon—but never department stores. On
Saturdays shops in Germany and Austria remain open until
noon or 2 p.m. (the first Saturday of the month German
shops are open until 6 p.m.). In Switzerland most shops
remain open until 4 or 5 p.m. on Saturdays, usually taking
Monday morning off.

Where's the nearest ...?	Wo ist der/die/das nächste ...?	voa ist derr/dee/dahss naikhster
antique shop	das Antiquitätengeschäft	dahss ahntikvittayterngershehft
art gallery	die Kunstgalerie	dee kunstgahlehree
baker's	die Bäckerei	dee behkerrigh
bank	die Bank	dee bahnk
barber's	der Friseur	derr frizurr
beauty salon	der Kosmetiksalon	derr kosmaytikzahlong
bookshop	die Buchhandlung	dee bukhhahndlung
butcher's	die Fleischerei/ Metzgerei	dee flighsherrigh/ mehtsgerrigh
cake shop	die Konditorei	dee kondittorrigh
camera shop	das Fotogeschäft	dahss foatogershehft
chemist's	die Apotheke	dee ahpottayker
dairy	die Milchhandlung	dee milkhhahndlung
delicatessen	das Delikatessengeschäft	dahss dehlikkatehsserngershehft
dentist	der Zahnarzt	derr tsaanahrtst
department store	das Warenhaus	dahss vaarernhowss
doctor	der Arzt	derr ahrtst
dress shop	das Modengeschäft	dahss moaderngershehft
drugstore	die Apotheke	dee ahpottayker
dry cleaner's	die chemische Reinigung	dee khaymisher righniggung
electrician	der Elektriker	derr aylehktrikkerr
fishmonger's	die Fischhandlung	dee fishhahndlung
flea market	der Flohmarkt	derr floamahrkt
florist's	das Blumengeschäft	dahss bloomerngershehft
furrier's	das Pelzgeschäft	dahss pehltsgershehft
greengrocer's	die Gemüsehandlung	dee germewzerhahndlung
grocery	das Lebensmittelgeschäft	dahss laybernsmitterlgershehft

hairdresser's (ladies/men)	der Damenfriseur/ Herrenfriseur	derr **daa**mernfrizurr/ **heh**rernfrizurr
hardware store	die Eisenwaren-handlung	dee **igh**zernvaarern-hahndlung
health food shop	das Reformhaus	dahss reh**form**howss
hospital	das Krankenhaus	dahss **krahn**kernhowss
ironmonger's	die Eisenwaren-handlung	dee **igh**zernvaarern-hahndlung
jeweller's	der Juwelier	derr yuuveh**leer**
launderette	der Waschsalon	derr **vahsh**zahlong
laundry	die Wäscherei	dee vehsher**righ**
library	die Bibliothek	dee bibliot**tayk**
market	der Markt	derr mahrkt
newsagent's	der Zeitungshändler	derr **tsigh**tungshehndlerr
newsstand	der Zeitungsstand	derr **tsigh**tungsshtahnt
optician	der Optiker	derr **op**tikkerr
pastry shop	die Konditorei	dee konditto**righ**
photographer	der Fotograf	derr foato**graaf**
police station	die Polizeiwache	dee pollit**sigh**vahkher
post office	das Postamt	dahss **post**ahmt
second-hand shop	der Gebrauchtwaren-laden	derr ger**browkht**vaarern-laadern
shoemaker's (repairs)	der Schuhmacher	derr **shoo**mahkherr
shoe shop	das Schuhgeschäft	dahss **shoo**gershehft
shopping centre	das Einkaufszentrum	dahss **ighn**kowfstsehntrum
souvenir shop	der Andenkenladen	derr **ahn**dehnkernlaadern
sporting goods shop	das Sportgeschäft	dahss **shport**gershehft
stationer's	das Schreibwaren-geschäft	dahss **shrighp**vaarern-gershehft
supermarket	der Supermarkt	derr **zoo**perrmahrkt
tailor's	der Schneider	derr **shnigh**derr
telegraph office	das Telegrafenamt	dahss taylay**graaf**ernahmt
tobacconist's	der Tabakladen	derr **tah**bahklaadern
toy shop	das Spielwaren-geschäft	dahss **shpeel**vaarern-gerhehft
travel agency	das Reisebüro	dahss **righ**zerbewroa
vegetable store	die Gemüsehandlung	dee ger**mew**zerhahndlung
veterinarian	der Tierarzt	derr **teer**ahrtst
watchmaker's	der Uhrmacher	derr **oor**mahkherr
wine merchant's	die Weinhandlung	dee **vighn**hahndlung

EINGANG	ENTRANCE
AUSGANG	EXIT
NOTAUSGANG	EMERGENCY EXIT

General expressions *Allgemeine Redewendungen*

Where? *Wo?*

Where's there a good ...?	**Wo gibt es einen guten/eine gute/ ein gutes ...?**	voa gipt ehss **igh**nern **goo**tern/**igh**ner **goo**ter/ ighn **goo**terss
Where can I find ...?	**Wo finde ich ...?**	voa **fin**der ikh
Where's the main shopping area?	**Wo ist das Geschäftsviertel?**	voa ist dahss ger**shehfts**feerterl
Is it far from here?	**Ist es weit von hier?**	ist ehss vight fon heer
How do I get there?	**Wie komme ich dorthin?**	vee **kom**mer ikh dort**hin**

Service *Bedienung*

Can you help me?	**Können Sie mir helfen?**	**kur**nern zee meer **hehl**fern
I'm just looking.	**Ich sehe mich nur um.**	ikh **zay**er mikh noor um
I want ...	**Ich möchte ...**	ikh **murkh**ter
Can you show me some ...?	**Können Sie mir einige ... zeigen?**	**kur**nern zee meer **igh**nigger ... **tsigh**gern
Do you sell ...?	**Verkaufen Sie ...?**	fehr**kow**fern zee
I'd like to buy ...	**Ich möchte ... kaufen.**	ikh **murkh**ter ... **kow**fern
Do you have any ...?	**Haben Sie ...?**	**haa**bern zee
Where's the ... department?	**Wo ist die ... -Abteilung?**	voa ist dee ... **ahp**tighlung
Where is the lift (elevator)/escalator?	**Wo ist der Fahrstuhl/ die Rolltreppe?**	voa ist derr **faar**shtool/ dee **rolt**rehper

That one *Das da*

Can you show me ...?	**Können Sie mir ... zeigen?**	**kur**nern zee meer ... **tsigh**gern
that/those	**das da/die dort**	dahss daa/dee dort
the one in the window/in the display case	**das im Schaufenster/ in der Vitrine**	dahss im **show**fehnsterr/ in derr vi**tree**ner

Defining the article   *Beschreibung des Artikels*

It must be ...	**Es muß ... sein.**	ehss muss ... zighn
big	**groß**	groass
cheap	**billig**	billikh
dark	**dunkel**	dunkerl
good	**gut**	goot
heavy	**schwer**	shvayr
large	**groß**	groass
light (weight)	**leicht**	lighkht
light (colour)	**hell**	hehl
oval	**oval**	oavaal
rectangular	**rechteckig**	rehkhtehkikh
round	**rund**	runt
small	**klein**	klighn
square	**viereckig**	feerehkikh
sturdy	**robust**	robbust
I don't want any-thing too expensive.	**Ich möchte nichts allzu Teures.**	ikh murkhter nikhts ahlltsu toyrerss

Preference   *Ich hätte lieber ...*

Can you show me some more?	**Können Sie mir noch andere zeigen?**	kurnern zee meer nokh ahnderrer tsighgern
Haven't you anything ...?	**Haben Sie nichts ...?**	haabern zee nikhts
cheaper/better	**Billigeres/Besseres**	billiggerrerss/behsserrerss
larger/smaller	**Größeres/Kleineres**	grursserrerss/klighnerrerss

How much?   *Wieviel?*

How much is this?	**Wieviel kostet das?**	veefeel kostert dahss
I don't understand.	**Ich verstehe nicht.**	ikh fehrshtayer nikht
Please write it down.	**Schreiben Sie es bitte auf.**	shrighbern zee ehss bitter owf
I don't want to spend more than ... marks.	**Ich möchte nicht mehr als ... Mark ausgeben.**	ikh murkhter nikht mayr ahlss ... mahrk owsgaybern

---

AUSVERKAUF   SALE

COLOURS, see page 113

Decision *Entscheidung*

It's not quite what I want.	**Es ist nicht ganz das, was ich möchte.**	ehss ist nikht gahnts dahss vahss ikh murkhter
No, I don't like it.	**Nein, das gefällt mir nicht.**	nighn dahss gerfehlt meer nikht
I'll take it.	**Ich nehme es.**	ikh naymer ehss

Ordering *Bestellen*

| Can you order it for me? | **Können Sie es mir bestellen?** | kurnern zee ehss meer bershtehlern |
| How long will it take? | **Wie lange dauert es?** | vee lahnger dowerrt ehss |

Delivery *Lieferung*

I'll take it with me.	**Ich nehme es mit.**	ikh naymer ehss mit
Deliver it to the ... Hotel.	**Liefern Sie es bitte ins Hotel ...**	leefern zee ehss bitter ins hottehl
Please send it to this address.	**Senden Sie es bitte an diese Anschrift.**	zehndern zee ehss bitter ahn deezer ahnshrift
Will I have any difficulty with the customs?	**Werde ich Schwierigkeiten mit dem Zoll haben?**	vayrder ikh shveerikhkightern mit daym tsol haabern

Paying *Bezahlen*

Where do I pay?	**Wo ist die Kasse?**	voa ist dee kahsser
How much is it?	**Wieviel kostet es?**	veefeel kostert ehss
Can I pay with this credit card?	**Kann ich mit dieser Kreditkarte bezahlen?**	kahn ikh mit deezerr krayditkahrter bertsaalern
Do you accept ...?	**Nehmen Sie ...?**	naymern zee
dollars	**Dollar**	dollahr
pounds	**Pfund**	pfunt
traveller's cheques	**Reiseschecks**	righzershehks
Do I have to pay the VAT (sales tax)?	**Muß ich die Mehrwertsteuer bezahlen?**	muss ikh dee mayrvayrtshtoyerr bertsaalern
Haven't you made a mistake in the bill?	**Haben Sie sich nicht verrechnet?**	haabern zee zikh nikht fehrrehkhnet

Anything else? *Sonst noch etwas?*

No, thanks, that's all.	**Nein danke, das ist alles.**	nighn **dahn**ker dahss ist **ah**lerss
Yes. I want ...	**Ja, ich möchte ...**	yaa ikh **murkh**ter
Show me ...	**Zeigen Sie mir ...**	**tsigh**gern zee meer
May I have a bag, please?	**Kann ich bitte eine Tragetasche haben?**	kahn ikh **bitter** **igh**ner **traa**gertahsher **haa**bern

Dissatisfied *Unzufrieden*

Can you please exchange this?	**Können Sie das bitte umtauschen?**	**kur**nern zee dahss **bitter** **um**towshern
I want to return this.	**Ich möchte das zurückgeben.**	ikh **murkh**ter dahss tsoo**rewk**gaybern
I'd like a refund. Here's the receipt.	**Ich möchte das Geld zurückerstattet haben. Hier ist die Quittung.**	ikh **murkh**ter dahss gehlt tsoo**rewk**ehrshtahtert **haa**bern. heer ist dee **kvit**tung

Kann ich Ihnen helfen?	Can I help you?
Was wünschen Sie?	What would you like?
Welche ... möchten Sie?	What ... would you like?
Farbe/Form	colour/shape
Qualität/Menge	quality/quantity
Es tut mir leid, das haben wir nicht.	I'm sorry, we haven't any.
Das haben wir nicht vorrätig.	We're out of stock.
Sollen wir es für Sie bestellen?	Shall we order it for you?
Nehmen Sie es mit oder sollen wir es Ihnen senden?	Will you take it with you or shall we send it?
Sonst noch etwas?	Anything else?
Das macht ... Mark, bitte.	That's ... marks, please.
Die Kasse ist dort drüben.	The cash desk is over there.

Bookshop *Buchhandlung*

In Germany, bookshops and stationers' are usually separate shops, though the latter will often sell paperbacks. Newspapers and magazines are sold at newsstands.

Where's the nearest ...?	Wo ist der/die/ das nächste ...?	voa ist derr/dee/dahss naikhster
bookshop	die Buchhandlung	dee bukhhahndlung
stationer's	das Schreibwaren-geschäft	dahss shrighpvaarern-gershehft
newsstand	der Zeitungsstand	derr tsightungsshtahnt
Where can I buy an English-language newspaper?	Wo kann ich eine englische Zeitung kaufen?	voa kahn ikh ighner ehnglisher tsightung kowfern
Where's the guide-book section?	Wo stehen die Reiseführer?	voa shtayern dee righzerfewrerr
Where do you keep the English books?	Wo stehen die englischen Bücher?	voa shtayern dee ehnglishern bewkherr
Have you any of ... 's books in English?	Haben Sie ein Buch von ... in Englisch?	haabern zee ighn bookh fon ... in ehnglish
Do you have second-hand books?	Haben Sie auch anti-quarische Bücher?	haaben zee owkh ahnti-kvaarisher bewkherr
I want a/an/ some ...	Ich möchte ...	ikh murkhter
address book	ein Adressen-büchlein	ighn ahdrehssern-bewkhlighn
ball-point pen	einen Kugelschreiber	ighnern koogerlshrighberr
book	ein Buch	ighn bukh
calendar	einen Kalender	ighnern kahlehnderr
carbon paper	Durchschlagpapier	doorkhshlaagpahpeer
cellophane tape	Klebstreifen	klaypshtrighfern
crayons	Buntstifte	buntshtifter
dictionary	ein Wörterbuch	ighn vurrterrbookh
German-English	deutsch-englisch	doych-ehnglish
pocket dictionary	ein Taschen-wörterbuch	ighn tahshernvurrterr-bookh
drawing paper	Zeichenpapier	tsighkhernpahpeer
drawing pins	Reißzwecken	righstsvehkern
envelopes	Briefumschläge	breefumshlaiger
eraser	einen Radiergummi	ighnern rahdeergummi
exercise book	ein Schreibheft	ighn shrighphehft

felt-tip pen	einen Filzstift	ighnern filtsshtift
fountain pen	einen Füllfeder-halter	ighnern fewlfayderrhahlterr
glue	Leim	lighm
grammar book	eine Grammatik	ighner grahmahtik
guidebook	einen Reiseführer	ighnern righzerfewrerr
ink	Tinte	tinter
black/red/blue	schwarz/rot/blau	shvahrts/roat/blow
(adhesive) labels	(selbstklebende) Etikette	(zehlpstklaybernder) ehtikkehter
magazine	eine Illustrierte	ighner illustreerter
map	eine Landkarte	ighner lahntkahrter
map of the town	einen Stadtplan	ighnern shtahtplaan
road map of ...	eine Straßenkarte von ...	ighner shtraassernkahrter fon
mechanical pencil	einen Drehbleistift	ighnern drayblighshtift
newspaper	eine Zeitung	ighner tsightung
American	amerikanische	ahmehrikkaanisher
English	englische	ehnglisher
notebook	ein Notizheft	ighn nottitshehft
note paper	Briefpapier	breefpahpeer
paintbox	einen Malkasten	ighnern maalkahstern
paper	Papier	pahpeer
paperback	ein Taschenbuch	ighn tahshernbookh
paperclips	Büroklammern	bewroaklahmmern
paper napkins	Papierservietten	pahpeerzehrviehtern
paste	Klebstoff	klaypshtof
pen	eine Feder	ighner fayderr
pencil	einen Bleistift	ighnern blighshtift
pencil sharpener	einen Bleistift-spitzer	ighnern blighshtiftshpitserr
playing cards	Spielkarten	shpeelkahrtern
pocket calculator	einen Taschenrechner	ighnern tahshernrehkhnerr
postcard	eine Postkarte	ighner postkahrter
propelling pencil	einen Drehbleistift	ighnern drayblighshtift
refill (for a pen)	eine Ersatzmine	ighner ehrzahtsmeener
rubber	einen Radiergummi	ighnern rahdeergummi
ruler	ein Lineal	ighn linnayaal
staples	Heftklammern	hehftklahmmern
string	Bindfaden/Schnur	bintfaadern/shnoor
thumbtacks	Reißzwecken	rightstsvehkern
tissue paper	Seidenpapier	zighdernpahpeer
typewriter ribbon	ein Farbband	ighn fahrpbahnt
typing paper	Schreibmaschinen-papier	shrighpmahsheenern-pahpeer
writing pad	einen Schreibblock	ighnern shrighpblok

Camping equipment *Campingausrüstung*

I'd like a/an/some ...	Ich hätte gern ...	ikh **heh**ter gehrn
bottle-opener	einen Flaschenöffner	**igh**nern **flah**shernurfnerr
bucket	einen Eimer	**igh**nern **igh**merr
butane gas	Butangas	**buttaan**gaass
campbed	ein Feldbett	ighn **fehlt**beht
can opener	einen Büchsenöffner	**igh**nern **bewk**sernurfnerr
candles	Kerzen	**kehrt**sern
chair	einen Stuhl	**igh**nern shtool
folding chair	Klappstuhl	**klahp**shtool
charcoal	Holzkohle	**holts**koaler
clothes pegs	Wäscheklammern	**vehsh**erklahmmerrn
compass	einen Kompaß	**igh**nern **kom**pahss
cool box	eine Kühltasche	**igh**ner **kewl**tahsher
corkscrew	einen Korkenzieher	**igh**nern **korkernt**seeherr
crockery	Geschirr	ger**shir**
cutlery	Besteck	ber**shtehk**
deckchair	einen Liegestuhl	**igh**nern **leeger**shtool
dishwashing detergent	Spülmittel	**shpewl**mitterl
first-aid kit	einen Verbandkasten	**igh**nern fehr**bahnt**kahstern
fishing tackle	Angelzeug	**ahng**erltsoyg
flashlight	eine Taschenlampe	**igh**ner **tahsh**ernlahmper
food box	einen Proviantbehälter	**igh**nern provvi**ahnt**berhehlterr
frying-pan	eine Bratpfanne	**igh**ner **braat**pfahner
groundsheet	einen Zeltboden	**igh**nern **tsehlt**boadern
hammer	einen Hammer	**igh**nern **hah**merr
hammock	eine Hängematte	**igh**ner **hehng**ermahter
haversack	eine Provianttasche	**igh**ner provvi**ahnt**tahsher
ice pack	einen Kühlbeutel	**igh**nern **kewl**boyterl
kerosene	Petroleum	pay**troa**layum
lamp	eine Lampe	**igh**ner **lahm**per
lantern	eine Laterne	**igh**ner lah**tehr**ner
matches	Streichhölzer	**shtrighkh**hurltserr
mattress	eine Matratze	**igh**ner mah**traht**ser
methylated spirits	Brennspiritus	**brehn**shpeerittuss
mosquito net	ein Mückennetz	ighn **mewk**ernnehts
pail	einen Eimer	**igh**nern **igh**merr
paper napkins	Papierservietten	pah**peer**zehrviehtern
paraffin	Petroleum	pay**troa**layum
penknife	ein Taschenmesser	ighn **tahsh**ernmehsserr
picnic basket	einen Picknickkorb	**igh**nern **pik**nikkorp
plastic bag	einen Plastikbeutel	**igh**nern **plahs**tikboyterl

CAMPING, see page 32

rope	ein Seil	ighn zighl
rucksack	einen Rucksack	ighnern rukzahk
saucepan	einen Kochtopf	ighnern kokhtopf
scissors	eine Schere	ighner shayrer
screwdriver	einen Schrauben-zieher	ighnern shrowbern-tseeherr
sleeping bag	einen Schlafsack	ighnern shlaafzahk
stew pot	einen Schmortopf	ighnern shmoartopf
table	einen Tisch	ighnern tish
folding table	Klapptisch	klahptish
tent	ein Zelt	ighn tsehlt
tent pegs	Heringe	hayringer
tent pole	eine Zeltstange	ighner tsehltshtahnger
tinfoil	Aluminiumfolie	ahlumeeniumfoalier
tin opener	einen Büchsenöffner	ighnern bewksenurfnerr
tongs	eine Zange	ighner tsahnger
torch	eine Taschenlampe	ighner tahshernlahmper
vacuum flask	eine Thermosflasche	ighner tehrmosflahsher
washing powder	Waschpulver	vahshpulferr
washing-up liquid	Spülmittel	shpewlmitterl
water carrier	einen Wasserkanister	ighnern vahsserkahnisterr
water flask	eine Feldflasche	ighner fehltflahsher
wood alcohol	Brennspiritus	brehnshpeerittuss

Crockery *Geschirr*

cups	Tassen	tahssern
mugs	Becher	behkherr
plates	Teller	tehlerr
saucers	Untertassen	unterrtahssern
tumblers	Wassergläser	vahsserrglaizerr

Cutlery *Besteck*

forks	Gabeln	gaaberln
knives	Messer	mehsserr
dessert knives	Dessertmesser	dehssayrmehsserr
spoons	Löffel	lurferl
teaspoons	Teelöffel	taylurferl
made of plastic	aus Plastik	owss plahstik
made of stainless steel	aus rostfreiem Stahl	owss rostfrigherm shtaal

Chemist's (drugstore) *Apotheke*

In German, a chemist's is called *Apotheke* (ahpot**tay**ker). They don't sell cameras, books and the like. At night and on Sundays all chemists' display the address of the nearest one open. If you're looking for toiletries, household articles or film, try a *Drogerie* (drogeh**ree**). You'll also find non-prescription medicine available in a *Drogerie*.

This section has been divided into two parts:

1. Pharmaceutical—medicine, first-aid, etc.
2. Toiletry—toilet articles, cosmetics

General *Allgemeines*

Where's the nearest (all-night) chemist's?	**Wo ist die nächste Apotheke (mit Nachtdienst)?**	voa ist dee **naikh**ster ahpot**tay**ker (mit **nahkht**deenst)
What time does the chemist's open/ close?	**Um wieviel Uhr öffnet/schließt die Apotheke?**	um **vee**feel oor **urf**nert/**shleest** dee ahpot**tay**ker

1—Pharmaceutical *Arzneien*

I want something for ...	**Ich möchte etwas gegen ...**	ikh **murkh**ter **eht**vahss **gay**gern
a cold	**eine Erkältung**	**igh**ner ehr**kehl**tung
a cough	**Husten**	**hoos**tern
a hangover	**einen Kater**	**igh**nern **kaa**terr
hay fever	**Heuschnupfen**	**hoy**shnupfern
insect bites	**Insektenstiche**	in**zehk**ternshtikher
sunburn	**Sonnenbrand**	**zon**nernbrahnt
travel sickness	**Reisekrankheit**	**righ**zerkrahnk-hight
an upset stomach	**Magenverstimmung**	**maa**gernfehrshtimmung
Can you make up this prescription for me?	**Können Sie mir dieses Rezept machen?**	**kur**nern zee meer **dee**zerss reht**sehpt** **mahkh**ern
Can I get it without a prescription?	**Kann ich das ohne Rezept bekommen?**	kahn ikh dahss **oa**ner reht**sehpt** ber**kom**mern
Shall I wait?	**Soll ich warten?**	zol ikh **vahr**tern

DOCTOR, see page 137

Do you have homoeo-pathic remedies?	Haben Sie homöo-pathische Mittel?	haabern zee hommurop-pahtisher mitterl
Can I have a/an/some ...?	Kann ich ... haben?	kahn ikh ... haabern
analgesic	ein Schmerzmittel	ighn shmehrtsmitterl
antiseptic cream	eine Wundsalbe	ighner vuntzahlber
aspirin	Aspirin	ahspireen
bandage	einen Verband	ighnern fehrbahnt
elastic bandage	eine elastische Binde	ighner ehlahstisher binder
Band-Aids	Heftpflaster	hehftpflahsterr
contraceptives	ein Verhütungs-mittel	ighn fehrhewtungsmitterl
corn plasters	Hühneraugen-pflaster	hewnerrowgernpflahsterr
cotton wool (absorbent cotton)	Watte	vahter
cough drops	Hustenpastillen	hoosternpahstillern
disinfectant	ein Desinfektions-mittel	ighn dehsinfehktsioans-mitterl
ear drops	Ohrentropfen	oarerntropfern
Elastoplast	Heftpflaster	hehftpflahsterr
eye drops	Augentropfen	owgerntropfern
gauze	Verbandmull	fehrbahntmul
insect repellent/spray	einen Insektenschutz/ein Insektizid	ighnern inzehkternshuts/ighn inzehktitseet
iodine	Jod	yoat
laxative	ein Abführmittel	ighn ahpfewrmitterl
mouthwash	Mundwasser	muntvahsserr
nose drops	Nasentropfen	naazerntropfern
painkiller	ein Schmerzmittel	ighn shmehrtsmitterl
sanitary towels (napkins)	Damenbinden	daamernbindern
sleeping pills	Schlaftabletten	shlaaftahblehtern
suppositories	Zäpfchen	tsehpfkhern
tampons	Tampons	tahmpongs
thermometer	ein Thermometer	ighn tehrmommayterr
throat lozenges	Halspastillen	hahlspahstillern
tranquillizers	Beruhigungsmittel	berrooiggungsmitterl
vitamin pills	Vitamintabletten	vittahmeentahblehtern

| GIFT | POISON |
| NICHT EINNEHMEN | FOR EXTERNAL USE ONLY |

2—Toiletry *Toilettenartikel*

I'd like a/an/some ...	Ich hätte gern ...	ikh hehter gehrn
acne cream	eine Aknesalbe	ighner ahknerzahlber
after-shave lotion	ein Rasierwasser	ighn rahzeervahsserr
astringent	ein Adstringens	ighn ahdstringehns
bath salts	Badesalz	baaderzahlts
bubble bath	ein Schaumbad	ighn showmbaat
cologne	ein Kölnischwasser	ighn kurlnishvahsserr
cream	eine Creme	ighner kraym
cleansing cream	Reinigungscreme	righniggungskraym
for greasy/	für fettige/normale/	fewr fehtigger/normahler/
normal/dry skin	trockene Haut	trokkehner howt
foundation cream	Grundierungs-creme	grundeerungskraym
moisturizing cream	Feuchtigkeitscreme	foykhtikhkightskraym
night cream	Nachtcreme	nahkhtkraym
cuticle remover	Nagelhautentferner	naagerlhowtehntfehrnerr
deodorant	ein Deodorant	ighn dehoddoarahnt
depilatory cream	Haarentfernungs-mittel	haarehntfehrnungsmitterl
emery board	eine Sandpapierfeile	ighner zahntpahpeerfighler
eye liner	einen Lidstift	ighnern leedshtift
eye pencil	einen Augenbrauen-stift	ighnern owgernbrowern-shtift
eye shadow	einen Lidschatten	ighnern leedshahtern
face powder	Gesichtspuder	gerzikhtspooderr
foot cream	Fußcreme	fooskraym
foot powder	Fußpuder	foospooderr
hand cream	Handcreme	hahntkraym
interdental cleaners	medizinische Zahn-stocher	mayditseenisher tsaan-shtokherr
lipsalve	eine Lippenpomade	ighner lippernpommaader
lipstick	einen Lippenstift	ighnern lippernshtift
make-up remover pads	Abschminkwatte	ahpshminkvahter
mascara	Wimperntusche	vimperrntusher
nail brush	eine Nagelbürste	ighner naagerlbewrster
nail clippers	eine Nagelzange	ighner naagerltsahngerr
nail file	eine Nagelfeile	ighner naagerlfighler
nail polish	Nagellack	naagerllahk
nail polish remover	Nagellackentferner	naagerllahkehntfehrnerr
nail scissors	eine Nagelschere	ighner naagerlshayrer
perfume	ein Parfüm	ighn pahrfewm
powder	Puder	pooderr
razor	einen Rasierapparat	ighnern rahzeerahpahraat
razor blades	Rasierklingen	rahzeerklingern

rouge	**Rouge**	roozh
safety pins	**Sicherheitsnadeln**	zikherrhightsnaaderln
shaving brush	**einen Rasierpinsel**	ighnern rahzeerpinzerl
shaving cream	**Rasiercreme**	rahzeerkraym
soap	**eine Seife**	ighner zighfer
sponge	**einen Schwamm**	ighnern shvahm
sun-tan cream	**Sonnencreme**	zonnernkraym
sun-tan oil	**Sonnenöl**	zonnernurl
talcum powder	**Körperpuder**	kurrperrpooderr
tissues	**Papiertücher**	pahpeertewkherr
toilet paper	**Toilettenpapier**	toahlehternpahpeer
toilet water	**ein Toilettenwasser**	ighn toahlehternvahsserr
toothbrush	**eine Zahnbürste**	ighner tsaanbewrster
toothpaste	**Zahnpasta**	tsaanpahstah
towel	**ein Handtuch**	ighn hahnttukh
tweezers	**eine Pinzette**	ighner pintsehter

For your hair   *Für Ihr Haar*

bobby pins	**Haarklemmen**	haarklehmern
colour shampoo	**ein Tönungsshampoo**	ighn turnungsshahmpoo
comb	**einen Kamm**	ighnern kahm
curlers	**Lockenwickler**	lokkernviklerr
dry shampoo	**ein Trockenshampoo**	ighn trokkernshahmpoo
hairbrush	**eine Haarbürste**	ighner haarbewrster
hair dye	**ein Haarfärbemittel**	ighn haarfehrbermitterl
hairgrips	**Haarklemmen**	haarklehmern
hair lotion	**Haarwasser**	haarvahsserr
hairpins	**Haarnadeln**	haarnaaderln
hair slide	**eine Haarspange**	ighner haarshpahnger
hair spray	**einen Haarspray**	ighnern haarshpray
setting lotion	**einen Haarfestiger**	ighnern haarfehstiggerr
shampoo	**ein Haarwaschmittel**	ighn haarvahshmitterl
for dry/greasy	** für trockenes/**	fewr trokkernerss/
(oily) hair	** fettiges Haar**	fehtiggerss haar
tint	**ein Tönungsmittel**	ighn turnungsmitterl
wig	**eine Perücke**	ighner pehrewker

For the baby   *Für den Säugling*

baby food	**Säuglingsnahrung**	zoyglingsnaarung
dummy (pacifier)	**einen Schnuller**	ighnern shnullerr
feeding bottle	**eine Saugflasche**	ighner zowgflahsher
nappies (diapers)	**Windeln**	vinderln

Clothing *Bekleidung*

If you want to buy something specific, prepare yourself in advance. Look at the list of clothing on page 116. Get some idea of the colour, material and size you want. They're all listed on the next few pages.

General *Allgemeines*

I'd like ...	**Ich möchte ...**	ikh murkhter ...
I want ... for a 10-year-old boy/girl.	**Ich möchte ... für einen Jungen/ein Mädchen von 10 Jahren.**	ikh murkhter ... fewr ighnern yungern/ighn maitkhern fon 10 yaarern
I want something like this.	**Ich möchte etwas in dieser Art.**	ikh murkhter ehtvahss in deezerr aart
I like the one in the window.	**Das im Schaufenster gefällt mir.**	dahss im showfehnsterr gerfehlt meer
How much is that per metre?	**Wieviel kostet der Meter?**	veefeel kostert derr mayterr

1 centimetre (cm.) = 0.39 in.	1 inch = 2.54 cm.
1 metre (m.) = 39.37 in.	1 foot = 30.5 cm.
10 metres = 32.81 ft.	1 yard = 0.91 m.

Colour *Farbe*

I want something in ...	**Ich möchte etwas in ...**	ikh murkhter ehtvahss in
I want a darker/lighter shade.	**Ich möchte es etwas dunkler/heller.**	ikh murkhter ehss etvahss dunklerr/hehlerr
I want something to match this.	**Ich möchte etwas hierzu Passendes.**	ikh murkhter ehtvahss heertsoo pahssernderss
I don't like the colour.	**Die Farbe gefällt mir nicht.**	dee fahrber gerfehlt meer nikht
Is it colour fast?	**Ist es farbecht?**	ist ehss fahrpehkht

NUMBERS, see page 147

beige	**beige**	bayzh
black	**schwarz**	shvahrts
blue	**blau**	blow
brown	**braun**	brown
fawn	**hellbraun**	hehlbrown
golden	**golden**	goldern
green	**grün**	grewn
grey	**grau**	grow
mauve	**lila**	leelah
orange	**orange**	orrahngzher
pink	**rosa**	roazah
purple	**violett**	violleht
red	**rot**	roat
scarlet	**scharlachrot**	shahrlahkhroat
silver	**silbern**	zilberrn
turquoise	**türkisfarben**	tewrkeesfahrbern
white	**weiß**	vighss
yellow	**gelb**	gehlp
light ...	**hell ...**	hehl
dark ...	**dunkel ...**	dunkerl

| **uni** | **gestreift** | **gepunktet** | **kariert** | **gemustert** |
| (unni) | (gershtrighft) | (gerpunktert) | (kahreert) | (germusterrt) |

Fabric *Stoff*

Do you have anything in ...?	**Haben Sie etwas in ...?**	**haa**bern zee **eht**vahss in
Is that ...?	**Ist das ...?**	ist dahss
handmade	**Handarbeit**	**hahn**tahrbight
imported	**importiert**	impor**teert**
made here	**inländisches Fabrikat**	**in**lehndisherss fahbrik**kaat**
I want something thinner.	**Ich möchte etwas Dünneres.**	ikh **murkh**ter ehtvahss **dew**nerrerss
Do you have any better quality?	**Haben Sie eine bessere Qualität?**	**haa**bern zee **igh**ner **behs**serrer kvahlit**tait**

cambric	**Batist**	bahtist
camel-hair	**Kamelhaar**	kahmaylhaar
corduroy	**Kordsamt**	kortzahmt
cotton	**Baumwolle**	bowmvoller
crepe	**Krepp**	krehp
denim	**Drillich**	drillikh
felt	**Filz**	filts
flannel	**Flanell**	flahnehl
gabardine	**Gabardine**	gahbahrdin
lace	**Spitze**	shpitser
leather	**Leder**	layderr
linen	**Leinen**	lighnern
poplin	**Popeline**	popperleen
rayon	**Kunstseide**	kunstzighder
satin	**Satin**	zahtehng
silk	**Seide**	zighder
suede	**Wildleder**	viltlayderr
towelling (terrycloth)	**Frottee**	frottay
velvet	**Samt**	zahmt
velveteen	**Manchester**	mahnshehsterr
wool	**Wolle**	voller
worsted	**Kammgarn**	kahmgahrn

Is it ...?	**Ist es ...?**	ist ehss
pure cotton	**reine Baumwolle**	righner bowmvoller
synthetic	**synthetisch**	zewntaytish
wash and wear	**bügelfrei**	bewgerlfrigh
crease (wrinkle) resistant	**knitterfrei**	knitterrfrigh
Is it hand washable/ machine washable?	**Kann man es mit der Hand/in der Maschine waschen?**	kahn mahn ehss mit derr hahnt/in derr mahsheener vahshern
Will it shrink?	**Läuft es beim Waschen ein?**	loyft ehss bighm vahshern ighn

Size *Größe*

I take size 38.	**Ich habe Größe 38.**	ikh haaber grursser 38
Could you measure me?	**Können Sie mir Maß nehmen?**	kurnern zee meer maass naymern
I don't know the German sizes.	**Ich kenne die deutschen Größen nicht.**	ikh kehner dee doychern grurssern nikht

Sizes can vary somewhat from one manufacturer to another, so be sure to try on shoes and clothing before you buy.

Women *Damen*

Dresses/Suits						
American	8	10	12	14	16	18
British	10	12	14	16	18	20
Continental	36	38	40	42	44	46

Stockings							Shoes			
American	8	8½	9	9½	10	10½	6	7	8	9
British							4½	5½	6½	7½
Continental	0	1	2	3	4	5	37	38	40	41

Men *Herren*

Suits/Overcoats							Shirts			
American	36	38	40	42	44	46	15	16	17	18
British										
Continental	46	48	50	52	54	56	38	41	43	45

Shoes									
American	5	6	7	8	8½	9	9½	10	11
British									
Continental	38	39	41	42	43	43	44	44	45

A good fit? *Paßt es?*

Can I try it on?	**Kann ich es anprobieren?**	kahn ikh ehss ahnprobbeerern
Where's the fitting room?	**Wo ist die Umkleidekabine?**	voa ist dee umklighderkahbeener
Is there a mirror?	**Gibt es einen Spiegel?**	gipt ehss ighnern shpeegerl
It fits very well.	**Es paßt sehr gut.**	ehss pahst zayr goot
It doesn't fit.	**Es paßt nicht.**	ehss pahst nikht

NUMBERS, see page 147

It's too ...	Es ist zu ...	ehss ist tsu
short/long	kurz/lang	koorts/lahng
tight/loose	eng/weit	ehng/vight
How long will it take to alter?	Wie lange brauchen Sie, um es zu ändern?	vee lahnger browkhern zee um ehss tsoo ehnderrn

Clothes and accessories *Kleidungsstücke und Zubehör*

I would like a/an/ some ...	Ich hätte gern ...	ikh hehter gehrn
bathrobe	einen Bademantel	ighnern baadermahnterl
bathing cap	eine Badekappe	ighner baaderkahper
bathing suit	einen Badeanzug	ighnern baaderahntsook
blouse	eine Bluse	ighner bloozer
bow tie	eine Fliege	ighner fleeger
bra	einen Büstenhalter	ighnern bewsternhahlterr
braces	Hosenträger	hoazerntraigerr
briefs	eine Unterhose	ighner unterrhoazer
cap	eine Mütze	ighner mewtser
cardigan	eine Wolljacke	ighner volyahker
coat	einen Mantel	ighnern mahnterl
dress	ein Kleid	ighn klight
dressing gown	einen Morgenrock	ighnern morgernrok
evening dress (woman's)	ein Abendkleid	ighn aaberntklight
frock	ein Kleid	ighn klight
fur coat	einen Pelzmantel	ighnern pehltsmahnterl
girdle	einen Hüfthalter	ighnern hewfthahlterr
gloves	Handschuhe	hahntshooer
handbag	eine Handtasche	ighner hahnttahsher
handkerchief	ein Taschentuch	ighn tahsherntookh
hat	einen Hut	ighnern hoot
jacket	ein Jackett/eine Jacke	ighn zhahkeht/ighner yahker
jeans	Jeans	"jeans"
jersey	eine Strickjacke	ighner shtrikyahker
jumper (Br.)	einen Pullover	ighnern pulloaverr
leather trousers	eine Lederhose	ighner layderrhoazer
nightdress	ein Nachthemd	ighn nahkhthehmt
pair of ...	ein Paar ...	ighn paar
panties	einen Schlüpfer	ighnern shlewpferr
pants (Am.)	eine Hose	ighner hoazer
panty girdle	ein Strumpf-halterhöschen	ighn shtrumpfhahlterr-hurskhern
panty hose	eine Strumpfhose	ighner shtrumpfhoazer

pullover	einen Pullover	ighnern pulloaverr
roll-neck (turtle-neck)	mit Rollkragen	mit rolkraagern
round-neck	mit rundem Ausschnitt	mit runderm owsshnit
V-neck	mit V-Ausschnitt	mit fowowsshnit
with long/short sleeves	mit langen/kurzen Ärmeln	mit lahngern/koortsern ehrmerln
without sleeves	ärmellos	ehrmerlloass
pyjamas	einen Schlafanzug	ighnern shlaafahntsoog
raincoat	einen Regenmantel	ighnern raygernmahnterl
scarf	ein Halstuch	ighn hahlstookh
shirt	ein Hemd	ighn hehmt
shorts	Shorts	"shorts"
skirt	einen Rock	ighnern rok
slip	einen Unterrock	ighnern unterrrok
socks	Socken	zokkern
stockings	Strümpfe	shtrewmpfer
suit (man's)	einen Anzug	ighnern ahntsoog
suit (woman's)	ein Kostüm	ighn kostewm
suspenders (Am.)	Hosenträger	hoazerntraigerr
sweater	einen Pullover	ighnern pulloaverr
sweatshirt	ein Sweatshirt	ighn "sweatshirt"
swimming trunks	eine Badehose	ighner baaderhoazer
swimsuit	einen Badeanzug	ighnern baaderahntsoog
T-shirt	ein T-Shirt	ighn "T-shirt"
tie	eine Krawatte	ighner krahvahter
tights	eine Strumpfhose	ighner shtrumpfhoazer
tracksuit	einen Trainingsanzug	ighnern trainingsahntsoog
trousers	eine Hose	ighner hoazer
umbrella	einen Regenschirm	ighnern raygernshirm
underpants	eine Unterhose/einen Slip	ighner unterrhoazer/ighnern "slip"
undershirt	ein Unterhemd	ighn unterrhehmt
vest (Am.)	eine Weste	ighner vehster
vest (Br.)	ein Unterhemd	ighn unterrhehmt
waistcoat	eine Weste	ighner vehster

belt	der Gürtel	derr gewrterl
buckle	die Schnalle	dee shnahler
button	der Knopf	derr knopf
pocket	die Tasche	dee tahsher
press stud (snap fastener)	der Druckknopf	derr drukknopf
zip (zipper)	der Reißverschluß	derr righsfehrshluss

Shoes *Schuhe*

I'd like a pair of ...	Ich möchte ein Paar ...	ikh murkhter ighn paar
boots	Stiefel	shteeferl
moccasins	Mokassins	mokkahssins
plimsolls (sneakers)	Turnschuhe	toornshooer
rain boots	Gummistiefel	gummishteeferl
sandals	Sandalen	zahndaalern
shoes	Schuhe	shooer
flat	flache	flahkher
with a heel	mit hohen Absätzen	mit hoaern ahpzehtsern
with leather soles	mit Ledersohlen	mit layderzoalern
with rubber soles	mit Gummisohlen	mit gummizoalern
slippers	Hausschuhe	howsshooer
These are too ...	Diese sind zu ...	deezer zint tsu
narrow/wide	eng/weit	ehng/vight
large/small	groß/klein	groass/klighn
Do you have a larger/smaller size?	Haben Sie eine größere/kleinere Nummer?	haabern zee ighner grursserrer/klighnerrer nummerr
Do you have the same in black?	Haben Sie die gleichen in Schwarz?	haabern zee dee glighkhern in shvahrts
cloth/leather	Stoff/Leder	shtof/layderr
rubber/suede	Gummi/Wildleder	gummi/viltlayderr
Is it genuine leather?	Ist es echtes Leder?	ist ehss ehkhters layderr
I need some shoe polish/shoelaces.	Ich brauche Schuhcreme/ Schnürsenkel.	ikh browkher shookraym/ shnewrzehnkerl

Shoes worn out? Here's the key to getting them fixed again:

Can you repair these shoes?	Können Sie diese Schuhe reparieren?	kurnern zee deezer shooer rehpahreerern
Can you stitch this?	Können Sie das nähen?	kurnern zee dahss naiern
I want new soles and heels.	Ich möchte neue Sohlen und Absätze.	ikh murkhter noyer zoalern unt ahpzehtser
When will they be ready?	Wann sind sie fertig?	vahn zint zee fehrtikh

COLOURS, see page 113

Electrical appliances   *Elektrische Geräte*

220 volt, 50-cycle A.C. is almost universal in Germany as well as in Austria and Switzerland.

What's the voltage?	**Welche Spannung haben Sie hier?**	vehlkher shpahnung haabern zee heer
Do you have a battery for this?	**Haben Sie eine Batterie hierfür?**	haabern zee ighner bahterree heerfewr
This is broken. Can you repair it?	**Das ist kaputt. Können Sie es reparieren?**	dahss ist kahput. kurnern zee ehss rehpahreerern
Can you show me how it works?	**Können Sie mir zeigen, wie es funktioniert?**	kurnern zee meer tsighern vee ehss funktsionneert
I'd like a video cassette.	**Ich möchte eine Videokassette.**	ikh murkhter ighner veedehokkahssehter
I'd like a/an/ some ...	**Ich möchte ...**	ikh murkhter
adaptor	**einen Zwischenstecker**	ighnern tsvishern-shtehkerr
amplifier	**einen Verstärker**	ighnern fehrshtairkerr
bulb	**eine Glühbirne**	ighner glewbeerner
clock-radio	**einen Radiowecker**	ighnern raadiovehkerr
electric toothbrush	**eine elektrische Zahnbürste**	ighner aylehktrisher tsaanbewrster
extension lead (cord)	**eine Verlängerungsschnur**	ighner fehrlehngerrungs-shnoor
hair dryer	**einen Haartrockner**	ighnern haartroknerr
headphones	**einen Kopfhörer**	ighnern kopfhurrerr
(travelling) iron	**ein (Reise)bügeleisen**	ighn (righzer)bewgerlighzern
lamp	**eine Lampe**	ighner lahmper
plug	**einen Stecker**	ighnern shtehkerr
portable ...	**Koffer- ...**	kofferr
radio	**ein Radio**	ighn raadio
car radio	**Autoradio**	owtorraadio
record player	**einen Plattenspieler**	ighnern plahternshpeelerr
shaver	**einen Rasierapparat**	ighnern rahzeerahpahraat
speakers	**Lautsprecher**	lowtshprehkherr
(cassette) tape recorder	**einen Kassettenrecorder**	ighnern kahssehtern-rehkorderr
(colour) television	**einen (Farb)fernseher**	ighnern (fahrp)fehrnzayerr
transformer	**einen Transformator**	ighnern trahnsformaator
video-recorder	**einen Videorecorder**	ighnern veedehorrehkorderr

Grocery   *Lebensmittelgeschäft*

I'd like some bread, please.	**Ich möchte ein Brot, bitte.**	ikh **murkh**ter ighn broat **bit**ter
What sort of cheese do you have?	**Welche Käsesorten haben Sie?**	**vehl**kher **kai**zerzortern **haa**bern zee
A piece of ...	**Ein Stück von ...**	ighn shtewk fon
this one	**diesem**	**dee**zerm
the one on the shelf	**dem auf dem Regal**	daym owf daym reh**gaal**
I'll have one of those, please.	**Ich möchte einen von denen, bitte.**	ikh **murkh**ter **igh**nern fon **day**nern **bit**ter
May I help myself?	**Kann ich mich selbst bedienen?**	kahn ikh mikh **zehl**pst ber**dee**nern
I'd like ...	**Ich möchte ...**	ikh **murkh**ter
a kilo of apples	**ein Kilo Äpfel**	ighn **kee**lo **ehp**ferl
half a kilo of tomatoes	**ein halbes Kilo Tomaten**	ighn **hahl**bers **kee**lo tom**maa**tern
100 grams of butter	**100 Gramm Butter**	100 grahm **but**terr
a litre of milk	**einen Liter Milch**	**igh**nern **lee**terr milkh
half a dozen eggs	**ein halbes Dutzend Eier**	ighn **hahl**bers **dut**sernd **igh**err
4 slices of ham	**4 Scheiben Schinken**	4 **shigh**bern **shin**kern
a box of chocolate	**eine Schachtel Schokolade**	**igh**ner **shahkh**terl shokko**laa**der
a jar of jam	**ein Glas Marmelade**	ighn glaass mahr**mer**laader
a tin (can) of peaches	**eine Büchse Pfirsiche**	**igh**ner **bewk**ser **pfeer**ziker
a tube of mustard	**eine Tube Senf**	**igh**ner **too**ber zehnf
a packet of tea	**eine Packung Tee**	**igh**ner **pah**kung tay

---

Weights and measures

1 kilogram or kilo (kg.) = 1000 grams (g.)

100 g. = 3.5 oz.	½ kg. = 1.1 lb.
200 g. = 7.0 oz.	1 kg. = 2.2 lb.

1 oz. =   28.35 g.
1 lb. = 453.60 g.

---

1 litre (l.) = 0.88 imp. quarts = 1.06 U.S. quarts

1 imp. quart = 1.14 l.	1 U.S. quart = 0.95 l.
1 imp. gallon = 4.55 l.	1 U.S. gallon = 3.8 l.

FOOD, see also page 64

Jeweller's—Watchmaker's   *Juwelier – Uhrmacher*

I want a small present for ...	**Ich möchte ein kleines Geschenk für ...**	ikh **murkh**ter ighn **kligh**nerss ger**shehnk** fewr
Could I please see that?	**Könnte ich das bitte sehen?**	**kurn**ter ikh dahss **bitter zay**ern
Do you have anything in gold?	**Haben Sie etwas in Gold?**	**haa**bern zee **eht**vahss in golt
How many carats is this?	**Wieviel Karat hat es?**	vee**feel** kah**raat** haht ehss
Is this real silver?	**Ist das Echtsilber?**	ist dahss **ekht**zilberr
Can you repair this watch?	**Können Sie diese Uhr reparieren?**	**kurn**ern zee **dee**zer oor rehpah**ree**rern
I'd like a/an/some ...	**Ich möchte ...**	ikh **murkh**ter
alarm clock	**einen Wecker**	**igh**nern **veh**kerr
bangle	**einen Armreif**	**igh**nern **ahrm**righf
battery	**eine Batterie**	**igh**ner bahter**ree**
bracelet	**ein Armband**	ighn **ahrm**bahnt
chain bracelet	**Gliederarmband**	**glee**derr**ahrm**bahnt
charm bracelet	**Amulettarmband**	ahmul**leht**ahrmbahnt
brooch	**eine Brosche**	**igh**ner **bro**sher
chain	**eine Kette**	**igh**ner **keh**ter
charm	**ein Amulett**	ighn ahmul**leht**
cigarette case	**ein Zigarettenetui**	ighn tsiggahreht**ten**ehtvee
cigarette lighter	**ein Feuerzeug**	ighn **foy**errtsoyg
clip	**einen Klipp**	**igh**nern klip
clock	**eine Uhr**	**igh**ner oor
cross	**ein Kreuz**	ighn kroyts
cuckoo clock	**eine Kuckucksuhr**	**igh**ner **kuk**kuksoor
cuff links	**Manschettenknöpfe**	mahn**sheh**ternknurpfer
cutlery	**Tafelbesteck**	**taa**ferlbershtehk
earrings	**Ohrringe**	**oar**ringer
gem	**einen Edelstein**	**igh**nern **ay**derlshtighn
jewel box	**ein Schmuckkästchen**	ighn **shmuk**kehstkhern
music box	**eine Spieldose**	**igh**ner **shpeel**doazer
necklace	**eine Halskette**	**igh**ner **hahls**kehter
pendant	**einen Anhänger**	**igh**nern **ahn**hehngerr
pin	**eine Anstecknadel**	**igh**ner **ahn**shtehknaaderl
pocket watch	**eine Taschenuhr**	**igh**ner **tahsh**ernoor
powder compact	**eine Puderdose**	**igh**ner **poo**derrdoazer

ring	einen Ring	ighnern ring
engagement ring	Verlobungsring	fehrloabungsring
signet ring	Siegelring	zeegerlring
wedding ring	Ehering	ayerring
rosary	einen Rosenkranz	ighnern roazernkrahnts
silverware	Tafelsilber	taaferlzilberr
tie clip	einen Krawatten-klipp	ighnern krahvahternklip
tie pin	eine Krawatten-nadel	ighner krahvahternnaaderl
watch	eine Uhr	ighner oor
automatic	automatische	owtomaatisher
digital	Digital-	diggitaal
quartz	Quarz-	kvahrts
with a second hand	mit Sekundenzeiger	mit zehkunderntsighgerr
waterproof	wasserdicht	wahsserrdikht
watchstrap	ein Uhrarmband	ighn oorahrmbahnt
wristwatch	eine Armbanduhr	ighner ahrmbahntoor

amber	Bernstein	behrnshtighn
amethyst	Amethyst	ahmehtist
chromium	Chrom	kroam
copper	Kupfer	kupferr
coral	Koralle	korrahler
crystal	Kristall	kristahl
cut glass	geschliffenes Glas	gershliffernerss glahss
diamond	Diamant	diahmahnt
emerald	Smaragd	smahrahgt
enamel	Email	ehmahi
gold	Gold	golt
gold-plated	vergoldet	fehrgoldert
ivory	Elfenbein	ehlfernbighn
jade	Jade	yaader
onyx	Onyx	oaniks
pearl	Perle	pehrler
pewter	Zinn	tsin
platinum	Platin	plaateen
ruby	Rubin	rubeen
sapphire	Saphir	zahfeer
silver	Silber	zilberr
silver-plated	versilbert	fehrzilbert
stainless steel	rostfreier Stahl	rostfrigherr shtaal
topaz	Topas	toppaass
turquoise	Türkis	tewrkeess

Optician *Optiker*

I've broken my glasses.	**Meine Brille ist zerbrochen.**	mighner briller ist tsehrbrokhern
Can you repair them for me?	**Können Sie sie reparieren?**	kurnern zee zee rehpahreerern
When will they be ready?	**Wann ist sie fertig?**	vahn ist zee fehrtikh
Can you change the lenses?	**Können Sie die Gläser auswechseln?**	kurnern zee dee glaizerr owsvehkserln
I want tinted lenses.	**Ich möchte getönte Gläser.**	ikh murkhter gerturnter glaizerr
The frame is broken.	**Das Gestell ist zerbrochen.**	dahss gershtehl ist tsehrbrokhern
I'd like a spectacle case.	**Ich möchte ein Brillenetui.**	ikh murkhter ighn brillernehtvee
I'd like to have my eyesight checked.	**Ich möchte meine Augen kontrollieren lassen.**	ikh murkhter mighner owgern kontrolleerern lahssern
I'm short-sighted/long-sighted.	**Ich bin kurzsichtig/weitsichtig.**	ikh bin kurtszikhtikh/vightzikhtikh
I want some contact lenses.	**Ich möchte Kontaktlinsen.**	ikh murkhter kontahktlinzern
I've lost one of my contact lenses.	**Ich habe eine Kontaktlinse verloren.**	ikh haaber ighner kontahktlinzer fehrloarern
Could you give me another one?	**Können Sie mir eine Ersatzlinse geben?**	kurnern zee meer ighner errzahtslinzer gaybern
I have hard/soft lenses.	**Ich habe harte/weiche Linsen.**	ikh haaber hahrter/vighkher linzern
Have you any contact-lens liquid?	**Haben Sie eine Flüssigkeit für Kontaktlinsen?**	haabern zee ighner flewssikhkight fewr kontahktlinzern
I'd like to buy a pair of sunglasses.	**Ich hätte gern eine Sonnenbrille.**	ikh hehter gehrn ighner zonnernbriller
May I look in a mirror?	**Kann ich mich im Spiegel sehen?**	kahn ikh mikh im shpeegerl zayern
I'd like to buy a pair of binoculars.	**Ich hätte gern ein Fernglas.**	ikh hehter gehrn ighn fehrnglaass

124

Photography   *Fotogeschäft*

I want a(n) ... camera.	**Ich möchte einen ... Fotoapparat.**	ikh murkhter ighnern ... foatoahpahraat
automatic	**automatischen**	owtommaatishern
inexpensive	**billigen**	billiggern
simple	**einfachen**	ighnfahkhern
Show me some cine (movie) cameras, please.	**Zeigen Sie mir bitte einige Filmkameras.**	tsighgern zee meer bitter ighnigger filmkahmehraass
Show me that one in the window.	**Zeigen Sie mir die im Schaufenster.**	tsighgern zee meer dee im showfehnsterr
I'd like to have some passport photos taken.	**Ich möchte Paßbilder machen lassen.**	ikh murkhter pahssbilderr mahkhern lahssern

Film   *Filme*

I'd like a film for this camera.	**Ich hätte gern einen Film für diese Kamera.**	ikh hehter gehrn ighnern film fewr deezer kahmehraa
black and white	**Schwarzweißfilm**	shvahrtsvighsfilm
colour	**Farbfilm**	fahrpfilm
colour negative	**Farbnegativfilm**	fahrpnehgahteeffilm
colour slide	**Film für Farbdias**	film fewr fahrpdeeahss
cartridge	**eine Kassette**	ighner kahssehter
roll film	**ein Rollfilm**	ighn rolfilm
24/36 exposures	**vierundzwanzig/ sechsunddreißig Aufnahmen**	feerunttsvahntsikh/ zehksuntdrighssikh owfnaamern
this size	**dieses Format**	deezers formaat
this ASA/DIN number	**diese ASA/DIN-Zahl**	deezer aazaa/deen tsaal
artificial light type	**Kunstlichtfilm**	kunstlikhtfilm
daylight type	**Tageslichtfilm**	taagerslikhtfilm
fast (high speed)	**hochempfindlich**	hoakhehmpfintlikh
fine grain	**Feinkorn**	fighnkorn

Processing   *Entwickeln*

| How much do you charge for developing? | **Was kostet das Entwickeln?** | vahss kostert dahss ehntvikkerln |

NUMBERS, see page 147

I want ... prints of each negative.	Ich möchte ... Abzüge von jedem Negativ.	ikh murkhter ... ahptsewger fon yayderm nehgahteef
with a mat finish	matt	maht
with a glossy finish	Hochglanz	hohkglahnts
Will you please enlarge this?	Können Sie das bitte vergrößern?	kurnern zee dahss bitter fehrgrursserrn
When will the photos be ready?	Wann sind die Fotos fertig?	vahn zint dee foatoss fehrtikh

Accessories and repairs *Zubehör und Reparaturen*

I want a/an/some ...	Ich möchte ...	ikh murkhter
battery	eine Batterie	ighner bahterree
cable release	einen Drahtauslöser	ighnern draatowslurzer
camera case	eine Fototasche	ighner foatotahsher
(electronic) flash	einen (Elektronen) blitz	ighnern (aylehktroanern) blits
filter	einen Filter	ighnern filterr
for black and white	für schwarzweiß	fewr shvahrtsvighss
for colour	für Farbe	fewr fahrber
lens	ein Objektiv	ighn obyehkteef
telephoto lens	ein Teleobjektiv	ighn taylerobyehkteef
wide-angle lens	ein Weitwinkelobjektiv	ighn vightvinkerlobyehkteef
lens cap	einen Objektivdeckel	ighnern obyehkteefdehkerl
Can you repair this camera?	Können Sie diesen Fotoapparat reparieren?	kurnern zee deezern foatoahpahraat rehpahreerern
The film is jammed.	Der Film klemmt.	derr film klehmt
There's something wrong with the ...	Mit ... stimmt etwas nicht.	mit ... shtimt ehtvahss nikht
exposure counter	dem Bildzählwerk	daym bilttsailvehrk
film winder	dem Filmtransport	daym filmtrahnsport
flash attachment	dem Blitzgerät	daym blitsgerrait
lens	dem Objektiv	daym obyehkteef
light meter	dem Belichtungsmesser	daym berlikhtungsmehsserr
rangefinder	dem Entfernungsmesser	daym ehntfehrnungsmehsser
shutter	dem Verschluß	daym fehrshluss

Tobacconist's *Tabakladen*

Cigarettes are sold in specialized tobacco shops, at kiosks and from vending machines. In Switzerland you can also buy cigarettes in restaurants, supermarkets, etc.

A packet of cigarettes, please.	**Eine Schachtel Zigaretten, bitte.**	ighner shahkhterl tsiggahrehtern bitter
Do you have any American/English cigarettes?	**Haben Sie amerikanische/ englische Zigaretten?**	haabern zee ahmehrikkaanisher ehnglisher tsiggahrehtern
I'd like a carton.	**Ich möchte eine Stange.**	ikh murkhter ighner shtahnger
Give me a/some ..., please.	**Geben Sie mir bitte ...**	gaybern zee meer bitter
candy	**Bonbons**	bongbongs
chewing gum	**Kaugummi**	kowgummi
chewing tobacco	**Kautabak**	kowtahbahk
chocolate	**Schokolade**	shokkollaader
cigarette case	**ein Zigarettenetui**	ighn tsiggahrehternehtvee
cigarette holder	**eine Zigaretten-spitze**	ighner tsiggahrehtern-shpitser
cigarettes	**Zigaretten**	tsiggahrehtern
filter-tipped	**mit Filter**	mit filterr
without filter	**ohne Filter**	oaner filterr
light/dark tobacco	**heller/dunkler Tabak**	hehlerr/dunklerr tahbahk
mild/strong	**milder/starker**	milderr/shtahrkerr
menthol	**Menthol-**	mehntoal
king-size	**extra lang**	ehkstraa lahng
cigars	**Zigarren**	tsiggahrern
lighter	**ein Feuerzeug**	ighn foyerrtsoyg
lighter fluid/gas	**Benzin/Gas fürs Feuerzeug**	behntseen/gaass fewrs foyerrtsoyg
matches	**Streichhölzer**	shtrighkhhhurltserr
pipe	**eine Pfeife**	ighner pfighfer
pipe cleaners	**Pfeifenreiniger**	pfighfernrighniggerr
pipe tobacco	**Pfeifentabak**	pfighferntahbahk
pipe tool	**ein Pfeifenbesteck**	ighn pfighfernbershtehk
postcard	**eine Postkarte**	ighner postkahrter
snuff	**Schnupftabak**	shnupftahbahk
stamps	**Briefmarken**	breefmahrkern
sweets	**Bonbons**	bongbongs
wick	**einen Docht**	ighnern dokht

Miscellaneous *Verschiedenes*

Souvenirs *Andenken*

Here are some suggestions for articles which you might like
to bring back as a souvenir or a gift from Germany.

Bavarian peasant dress	**das Dirndl(kleid)**	dahss deerndl(klight)
beer stein	**der Bierkrug**	derr beerkroog
glassware	**die Glaswaren**	dee glahsvaarern
leather goods	**die Lederwaren**	dee layderrvaarern
music box	**die Spieldose**	dee shpeeldoazer
porcelain	**das Porzellan**	dahss portsehlaan
waterproof woollen overcoat	**der Lodenmantel**	derr loadernmahnterl
wood carving	**die Holzschnitzarbeit**	dee holtsshnitsahrbight

The high quality of Austrian and Swiss winter sports equipment is well known. But petit-point embroidery and porcelain in Austria and linens and organdies in Switzerland are
also good buys. Consider leather goods and *Lederhosen*
(knee-length leather trousers) in Austria, and don't miss the
fabulous array of watches and luscious chocolate in Switzerland.

chocolate	**die Schokolade**	dee shokkollaader
cuckoo clock	**die Kuckucksuhr**	dee kukkuksoor
embroidery	**die Stickerei**	dee shtikkerrigh
linen	**das Leinenzeug**	dahss lighnerntsoyg
ski equipment	**die Skiausrüstung**	dee sheeowsrewstung
Swiss army knife	**Schweizer Armee- messer**	shvightserr ahrmay- mehsserr
Tyrolean hat	**der Tirolerhut**	derr teeroalerrhoot
Tyrolean pipe	**die Tiroler Pfeife**	dee teeroalerr pfighfer
watch	**die Uhr**	dee oor

Records—Cassettes *Schallplatten – Kassetten*

Do you have any records by ...?	**Haben Sie Schall- platten von ...?**	haabern zee shahl- plahtern fon
Can I listen to this record?	**Kann ich diese Platte hören?**	kahn ikh deezer plahter hurrern

L.P. (33 rpm)	**die Langspielplatte (33 UpM)**	dee **lahng**shpeelplahter (**drig**huntdrighssikh oo pay ehm)
E.P. (45 rpm)	**45 UpM**	**fewnf**untfeertsikh oo pay ehm
single	**die Single**	dee "single"

Have you any songs by ...?	**Haben Sie Lieder von ...?**	**haa**bern zee **lee**derr fon
I'd like a ...	**Ich hätte gern ...**	ikh **heh**ter gehrn
cassette	**eine Kassette**	**igh**ner kahs**seh**ter
video cassette	**eine Videokassette**	**igh**ner **vee**dehokkahssehter
compact disc	**eine Compact Disc**	**igh**ner "compact disc"
chamber music	**die Kammermusik**	dee **kah**merrmuzeek
classical music	**die klassische Musik**	dee **klah**ssisher mu**zeek**
folk music	**die Volksmusik**	dee **folks**muzeek
instrumental music	**die Instrumental-musik**	dee instru**mehn**taalmuzeek
jazz	**der Jazz**	derr dzhaiss
light music	**die Unterhaltungs-musik**	dee unter**rahl**tungsmuzeek
orchestral music	**die Orchestermusik**	dee or**keh**sterrmuzeek
pop music	**die Popmusik**	dee **pop**muzeek

Toys *Spielwaren*

I'd like a toy/game ...	**Ich möchte ein Spiel-zeug/Spiel ...**	ikh **murkh**ter ighn **shpeel**-tsoyg/shpeel
for a boy	**für einen Jungen**	fewr **igh**nern **yung**ern
for a 5-year-old girl	**für ein 5-jähriges Mädchen**	fewr ighn 5**yai**riggerss **mait**khern
ball	**einen Ball**	**igh**nern bahl
bucket and spade (pail and shovel)	**Eimer und Schaufel**	**igh**merr unt **show**ferl
building blocks	**einen Baukasten**	**igh**nern **bow**kahstern
card game	**ein Kartenspiel**	ighn **kahr**ternshpeel
chess set	**ein Schachspiel**	ighn **shahkh**shpeel
doll	**eine Puppe**	**igh**ner **pup**per
electronic game	**ein elektronisches Spiel**	ighn aylek**troa**nishers shpeel
roller skates	**Rollschuhe**	**rol**shooer

NUMBERS, see page 147

Your money: banks—currency

Banking hours in Germany are usually from 8.30 a.m. to 1 p.m. and from 2.30 to 4 p.m., Monday to Friday (Thursday until 5.30 p.m.). Hours are slightly different in Austria and Switzerland. Small currency-exchange offices, indicated by the words *Geldwechsel* or *Wechselstube* are sometimes open outside regular banking hours.

The *Deutsche Mark* (abbreviated to *DM* and called *D-Mark* —**day** mahrk) is the unit of currency in Germany. It's divided into 100 *Pfennig* (**pfeh**nikh), abbreviated *Pf*.
　　Coins: 1, 2 and 5 marks; 1, 2, 5, 10 and 50 pfennigs.
　　Banknotes: 5, 10, 20, 50, 100, 500 and 1,000 marks.

In Austria, the basic unit is the *Schilling* (**shil**ling), abbreviated *S*. It's divided into 100 *Groschen* (**gro**shern), abbreviated *g*.
　　Coins: 1, 5, 10 and 20 schillings; 10 and 50 groschen.
　　Banknotes: 20, 50, 100, 500 and 1,000 schillings.

The *Franken* (**frahn**kern), usually abbreviated *Fr.,* is the Swiss unit of currency. There are 100 *Rappen* (**rah**pern), abbreviated *Rp.,* to a franc.
　　Coins: 1, 2 and 5 francs; 5, 10, 20 and 50 Rappen.
　　Banknotes: 10, 20, 50, 100, 500 and 1,000 francs.

Credit cards may be used in an increasing number of hotels, restaurants, shops, etc. Signs are posted indicating which cards are accepted.

Traveller's cheques are accepted by hotels, travel agents and many shops, although the exchange rate is invariably better at a bank. Eurocheques are also accepted.

| Where's the nearest bank? | **Wo ist die nächste Bank?** | voa ist dee **naikh**ster bahnk |
| Where is the currency exchange office? | **Wo ist die Wechsel-stube?** | voa ist dee **vehk**serl-shtoober |

At the bank *In der Bank*

I want to change some dollars/pounds.	**Ich möchte Dollar/Pfund wechseln.**	ikh **murkh**ter **dollahr**/pfunt **vehk**serln
I want to cash a traveller's cheque.	**Ich möchte einen Reisescheck einlösen.**	ikh **murkh**ter **igh**nern **righ**zershehk **ighn**lurzern
What's the exchange rate?	**Wie ist der Wechselkurs?**	vee ist derr **vehk**serl**koorss**
How much commission do you charge?	**Welche Gebühr erheben Sie?**	**vehl**kher ger**bewr** ehr**hay**bern zee
Can you telex my bank in London?	**Können Sie meiner Bank in London ein Telex schicken?**	**kur**nern zee **migh**nerr bahnk in **london** ighn **tay**lehks **shik**kern
I have a/an/some ...	**Ich habe ...**	ikh **haa**ber
bank card	**eine Kontokarte**	**igh**ner **konto**kahrter
credit card	**eine Kreditkarte**	**igh**ner kray**dit**kahrter
Eurocheques	**Eurocheques**	**oyro**shehks
introduction from ...	**einen Empfehlungsbrief von ...**	**igh**nern ehm**pfay**lungsbreef fon
letter of credit	**einen Kreditbrief**	**igh**nern kray**dit**breef
I'm expecting some money from New York. Has it arrived yet?	**Ich erwarte Geld aus New York. Ist es schon angekommen?**	ikh ehr**vahr**ter gehlt owss "New York". ist ehss shoan **ahn**gerkommern
Please give me ... notes (bills) and some small change.	**Geben Sie mir bitte ... Scheine und etwas Kleingeld.**	**gay**bern zee meer **bit**ter ... **shigh**ner unt **eht**vahss **kligh**ngehlt
Give me ... large notes and the rest in small notes.	**Geben Sie mir ... große Scheine und den Rest in kleinen Scheinen.**	**gay**bern zee meer ... **groass**er **shigh**ner unt dayn rehst in **kligh**nern **shigh**nern

Depositing—Withdrawing *Einzahlen – Abheben*

I want to ...	**Ich möchte ...**	ikh **murkh**ter
open an account	**ein Konto eröffnen**	ighn **konto** ehr**urf**nern
withdraw ...	**... abheben**	... **ahp**haybern
Where should I sign?	**Wo muß ich unterschreiben?**	voa muss ikh unterr**shrigh**bern

NUMBERS, see page 147

| I want to deposit this in my account. | **Ich möchte das auf mein Konto einzahlen.** | ikh murkhter dahss owf mighn konto ighntsaalern |

Business terms *Geschäftsausdrücke*

My name is ...	**Ich heiße ...**	ikh highsser
Here's my card.	**Hier ist meine Karte.**	heer ist mighner kahrter
I have an appointment with Mr./ Mrs. ...	**Ich bin mit Herrn/ Frau ... verabredet.**	ikh bin mit hehrn/frow ... fehrahpraydert
Can you give me an estimate of the cost?	**Können Sie mir einen Kostenvoranschlag machen?**	kurnern zee meer ighnern kosternfoarahnshlaak mahkhern
What's the rate of inflation?	**Wie hoch ist die Inflationsrate?**	vee hoakh ist dee inflahtsioansraater
Can you provide me with an interpreter/ a secretary?	**Können Sie mir einen Dolmetscher/eine Sekretärin besorgen?**	kurnern zee meer ighnern dolmehtsherr/ighner zaykraytairin berzoargern
Where can I make photocopies?	**Wo kann ich Foto- kopien machen?**	voa kahn ikh foato- kopeeern mahkhern

amount	**der Betrag**	derr bertraag
balance	**die Bilanz**	dee billahnts
capital	**das Kapital**	dahss kahpittaal
cheque book	**das Scheckbuch**	dahss shehkbookh
contract	**der Vertrag**	derr fehrtraag
expenses	**die Unkosten**	dee oonkostern
interest	**die Zinsen**	dee tsinzern
investment	**die Kapitalanlage**	dee kahpittaalahnlaager
invoice	**die Rechnung**	dee rehkhnung
loss	**der Verlust**	derr fehrlust
mortgage	**die Hypothek**	dee hippotayk
payment	**die Zahlung**	dee tsaalung
percentage	**der Prozentsatz**	derr protsehntzahts
profit	**der Gewinn**	derr gervin
purchase	**der Kauf**	derr kowf
sale	**der Verkauf**	derr fehrkowf
share	**die Aktie**	dee ahktsier
transfer	**die Überweisung**	dee ewberrvightzung
value	**der Wert**	derr vayrt

At the post office

The offices of Germany's *Bundespost* are open from 8 a.m. to 6 p.m. They close at noon on Saturdays. Swiss post offices are open from 7.30 a.m. to midday and from 1.30 to 6.30 p.m. (8 to 11 a.m. on Saturdays). In Austria, post offices are open from 8 a.m. to midday and from 2 to 5 p.m. (8 to 10 or noon on Saturdays). Letter boxes (mailboxes) are painted yellow in Germany and Switzerland and yellow or blue in Austria. In principal cities, some post offices are open outside the normal hours. Remember that for telephoning and cables you should go to the post office—there are no separate telephone or cable offices.

Where's the nearest post office?	**Wo ist das nächste Postamt?**	voa ist dahss **naikh**ster **post**ahmt
What time does the post office open/close?	**Wann öffnet/schließt das Postamt?**	vahn **urf**nert/**shleest** dahss **post**ahmt
A stamp for this letter/postcard, please.	**Eine Briefmarke für diesen Brief/diese Postkarte, bitte.**	**ighner breef**maarker fewr **dee**zern breef/**dee**zer **post**kaarter bitter
A ...-pfennig stamp, please.	**Eine Briefmarke zu ... Pfennig, bitte.**	**ighner breef**maarker tsoo ... **pfehn**nikh bitter
What's the postage for a letter to London?	**Was kostet ein Brief nach London?**	vahss **kost**ert ighn breef naakh london
What's the postage for a postcard to Los Angeles?	**Was kostet eine Postkarte nach Los Angeles?**	vahss **kost**ert **ighner post**kaarter naakh los **ehnd**zehrlerss
Where's the letter box (mailbox)?	**Wo ist der Briefkasten?**	voa ist derr **breef**kahstern
I want to send this by ...	**Ich möchte dies ... senden.**	ikh **murkh**ter deess ... **zehn**dern
airmail	**per Luftpost**	pehr **luft**post
express (special delivery)	**per Expreß**	pehr **ehks**prehss
registered mail	**per Einschreiben**	pehr **ighn**shrighbern

I want to send this parcel.	Ich möchte dieses Paket schicken.	ikh **murkh**ter **dee**zers pah**kayt shikk**ern
At which counter can I cash an international money order?	An welchem Schalter kann ich eine internationale Postanweisung einlösen?	ahn **vehl**kherm **shahl**terr kahn ikh **igh**ner interr**naht**sio**anaaler post**ahn**vighzung **ighn**lurzern
Where's the poste restante (general delivery)?	Wo ist der Schalter für postlagernde Sendungen?	voa ist derr **shahl**terr fewr **post**laagerrnder **zehn**dungern
Is there any mail for me? My name is ...	Ist Post für mich da? Ich heiße ...	ist post fewr mikh daa? ikh **highss**er

BRIEFMARKEN	STAMPS
PAKETE	PARCELS
POSTANWEISUNGEN	MONEY ORDERS

Telegrams *Telegramme*

For telegrams you should go to the post-office—there are no separate cable offices.

I want to send a telegram/telex. May I please have a form?	Ich möchte ein Telegramm/Telex aufgeben. Kann ich bitte ein Formular haben?	ikh **murkh**ter ighn tay**lay**grahm/**tay**lehks **owf**gaybern. kahn ikh **bitt**er ighn formu**laar haa**bern
How much is it per word?	Was kostet es pro Wort?	vahss **kost**ert ehss proa vort
How long will a cable to Chicago take?	Wie lange braucht ein Telegramm nach Chicago?	vee **lahn**ger browkht ighn tay**lay**grahm naakh tshik**kaa**go

Telephoning *Telefonieren*

The telephone networks of Germany, Austria and Switzerland are almost entirely automated. Coin-operated booths are to be found on the street, with instructions posted inside, often in English.

International calls can be made from almost all public telephones in Germany and in Switzerland. In Austria, only some are equipped for long-distance calls. If you need assistance in placing the call, go to the post office or ask at your hotel.

Phone numbers are given in pairs. Note that, in telephoning, *zwei* becomes *zwo* (tsvoa).

Where's the telephone?	**Wo ist das Telefon?**	voa ist dahss taylayfoan
Where's the nearest telephone booth?	**Wo ist die nächste Telefonzelle?**	voa ist dee naikhster taylayfoantsehler
May I use your phone?	**Darf ich Ihr Telefon benutzen?**	dahrf ikh eer taylayfoan bernutsern
Do you have a telephone directory for Bonn?	**Haben Sie ein Telefonbuch von Bonn?**	haabern zee ighn taylayfoanbukh fon bon
What's the dialling (area) code for ...?	**Wie ist die Vorwähl-nummer von ...?**	vee ist dee foarvail-nummerr fon
How do I get the international operator?	**Welche Nummer hat die (internationale) Vermittlung?**	vehlkher nummerr haht dee (interrnahtsionnaaler) fehrmitlung

Operator *Vermittlung*

Good morning, I want Hamburg 12 34 56.	**Guten Morgen. Ich möchte Hamburg 12 34 56.**	gootern morgern. ikh murkhter hahmboorg 12 34 56
Can you help me get this number?	**Können Sie mir helfen, diese Nummer zu bekommen?**	kurnern zee meer hehlfern deezer nummerr tsoo berkommern
I want to place a personal (person-to-person) call.	**Ich möchte ein Gespräch mit Voranmeldung.**	ikh murkhter ighn gershpraikh mit foarahnmehldung
I want to reverse the charges (call collect).	**Ich möchte ein R-Gespräch anmelden.**	ikh murkhter ighn ehr-gershpraikh ahnmehldern

NUMBERS, see page 147

Speaking *Am Apparat*

Hello. This is ... speaking.	**Hallo. Hier spricht ...**	hahloa. heer shprikht
I want to speak to ...	**Ich möchte ... sprechen.**	ikh murkhter ... shprehkhern
I want extension ...	**Ich möchte Nebenanschluß ...**	ikh murkhter naybern-ahnshluss
Speak louder/more slowly, please.	**Sprechen Sie bitte etwas lauter/lang-samer.**	shprehkhern zee bitter ehtvass lowterr/lahng-zaamerr

Bad luck *Pech gehabt*

Would you please try again later?	**Würden Sie es bitte später noch einmal versuchen?**	vewrdern zee ehss bitter shpaiterr nokh ighnmaal fehrzookhern
Operator, you gave me the wrong number.	**Fräulein, Sie haben mich falsch verbunden.**	froylighn zee haabern mikh fahlsh fehrbundern
We were cut off.	**Wir sind unter-brochen worden.**	veer zint unterrbrokhern vordern

Telephone alphabet *Buchstabiertabelle*

A	**Anton**	ahntoan	O	**Otto**	otto
Ä	**Ärger**	ehrgerr	Ö	**Ökonom**	urkonnoam
B	**Berta**	behrtah	P	**Paula**	powlah
C	**Caesar**	tsaizahr	Q	**Quelle**	kvehler
CH	**Charlotte**	shahrlotter	R	**Richard**	rikhahrt
D	**Dora**	doarah	S	**Samuel**	zaamuehl
E	**Emil**	aymeel	SCH	**Schule**	shooler
F	**Friedrich**	freedrikh	T	**Theodor**	tayoddoar
G	**Gustav**	gustahf	U	**Ulrich**	ulrikh
H	**Heinrich**	highnrikh	Ü	**Übel**	ewberl
I	**Ida**	eedah	V	**Viktor**	viktor
J	**Julius**	yooliuss	W	**Wilhelm**	vilhehlm
K	**Kaufmann**	kowfmahn	X	**Xanthippe**	ksahntipper
L	**Ludwig**	loodvikh	Y	**Ypsilon**	ewpseelon
M	**Martha**	mahrtah	Z	**Zacharias**	tsahkhahreeahss
N	**Nordpol**	nortpoal			

Not there *Nicht da*

When will he/she be back?	**Wann ist er/sie zurück?**	vahn ist ehr/zee tsoorewk
Will you tell him/her I called?	**Würden Sie ihm/ihr sagen, daß ich angerufen habe?**	vewrdern zee eem/eer zaagern dahss ikh ahngerroofern haaber?
My name's ...	**Mein Name ist ...**	mighn naamer ist
Would you ask him/her to call me?	**Würden Sie ihn/sie bitten, mich anzurufen?**	vewrdern zee een/zee bittern mikh ahntsooroofern
Would you please take a message?	**Würden Sie bitte etwas ausrichten?**	vewrdern zee bitter ehtvahss owsrikhtern

Charges *Gebühren*

| What was the cost of that call? | **Was hat das Gespräch gekostet?** | vahss haht dahss gershpraikh gerkostert |
| I want to pay for the call. | **Ich möchte das Gespräch bezahlen.** | ikh murkhter dahss gershpraikh bertsaalern |

Ein Anruf für Sie.	There's a telephone call for you.
Welche Nummer haben Sie gewählt?	What number are you calling?
Die Linie ist besetzt.	The line's engaged.
Es meldet sich niemand.	There's no answer.
Sie sind falsch verbunden.	You've got the wrong number.
Das Telefon funktioniert nicht.	The phone is out of order.
Einen Augenblick, bitte.	Just a moment.
Bitte bleiben Sie am Apparat.	Hold on, please.
Er/Sie ist im Augenblick nicht da.	He's/She's out at the moment.

Doctor

To be at ease, make sure your health insurance policy covers any illness or accident while on holiday. If not, ask your insurance representative, automobile association or travel agent for details of special health insurance.

General   *Allgemeines*

Can you get me a doctor?	**Können Sie einen Arzt holen?**	kurnern zee **igh**nern ahrtst **hoa**lern
Is there a doctor here?	**Gibt es hier einen Arzt?**	gipt ehss heer **igh**nern ahrtst
I need a doctor quickly.	**Ich brauche schnell einen Arzt.**	ikh **brow**kher shnehl **igh**nern ahrtst
Where's there a doctor who speaks English?	**Wo gibt es einen Arzt, der Englisch spricht?**	voa gipt ehss **igh**nern ahrtst derr **ehn**glish shprikht
Where's the surgery (doctor's office)?	**Wo ist die Arztpraxis?**	voa ist dee ahrtstprahksiss
What are the surgery (office) hours?	**Wann sind die Sprechstunden?**	vahn zint dee **shprekh**shtundern
Could the doctor come to see me here?	**Könnte der Arzt mich hier behandeln?**	**kurn**ter derr ahrtst mikh heer ber**hahn**derln
What time can the doctor come?	**Wann kann der Arzt kommen?**	vahn kahn derr ahrtst **kom**mern
Can you recommend a/an ...?	**Können Sie mir ... angeben?**	kurnern zee meer ... **ahn**gaybern
general practitioner	**einen praktischen Arzt**	**igh**nern **prahk**tishern ahrtst
children's doctor	**einen Kinderarzt**	**igh**nern **kinder**rahrtst
eye specialist	**einen Augenarzt**	**igh**nern **owger**nahrtst
gynaecologist	**einen Frauenarzt**	**igh**nern **frower**nahrtst
Can I have an appointment ...?	**Kann ich ... einen Termin haben?**	kahn ikh ... **igh**nern tehrmeen **haa**bern
tomorrow	**morgen**	**morger**n
as soon as possible	**so bald wie möglich**	zo bahlt vee **murg**likh

CHEMIST'S, see page 108

Parts of the body *Körperteile*

appendix	der Blinddarm	derr blintdahrm
arm	der Arm	derr ahrm
artery	die Arterie	dee ahrtayrier
back	der Rücken	derr rewkern
bladder	die Blase	dee blaazer
bone	der Knochen	derr knokhern
bowel	der Darm	derr dahrm
breast	die Brust	dee brust
chest	der Brustkorb	derr brustkorp
ear	das Ohr	dahss oar
eye	das Auge	dahss owger
face	das Gesicht	dahss gerzikht
finger	der Finger	derr fingerr
foot	der Fuß	derr fooss
gland	die Drüse	dee drewzer
hand	die Hand	dee hahnt
head	der Kopf	derr kopf
heart	das Herz	dahss hehrts
jaw	der Kiefer	derr keeferr
joint	das Gelenk	dahss gerlehnk
kidney	die Niere	dee neerer
knee	das Knie	dahss knee
leg	das Bein	dahss bighn
lip	die Lippe	dee lipper
liver	die Leber	dee layberr
lung	die Lunge	dee lunger
mouth	der Mund	derr munt
muscle	der Muskel	derr muskerl
neck	der Hals	derr hahls
nerve	der Nerv	derr nehrf
nervous system	das Nervensystem	dahss nehrfernzewstaym
nose	die Nase	dee naazer
rib	die Rippe	dee ripper
shoulder	die Schulter	dee shulterr
skin	die Haut	dee howt
spine	die Wirbelsäule	dee veerberlzoyler
stomach	der Magen	derr maagern
tendon	die Sehne	dee zayner
thigh	der Schenkel	derr shehnkerl
throat	der Hals	derr hahls
thumb	der Daumen	derr dowmern
toe	die Zehe	dee tsayer
tongue	die Zunge	dee tsunger
tonsils	die Mandeln	dee mahnderln
vein	die Vene	dee vayner

Accident—Injury *Unfall – Verletzung*

There has been an accident.	Es ist ein Unfall passiert.	ehss ist ighn unfahl pahsseert
My child has had a fall.	Mein Kind ist hingefallen.	mighn kint ist hingerfahlern
He/She has hurt his/her head.	Er/Sie ist am Kopf verletzt.	ehr/zee ist ahm kopf fehrlehtst
He's/She's unconscious.	Er/Sie ist bewußtlos.	ehr/zee ist bervustloass
He's/She's bleeding (heavily).	Er/Sie blutet (stark).	ehr/zee blootert (shtahrk)
He's/She's (seriously) injured.	Er/Sie ist (schwer) verletzt.	ehr/zee ist (shvayr) fehrlehtst
His/Her arm is broken.	Sein/Ihr Arm ist gebrochen.	zighn/eer ahrm ist gerbrokhern
His/Her ankle is swollen.	Sein/Ihr Knöchel ist geschwollen.	zighn/eer knurkherl ist gershvollern
I've been stung.	Ich bin gestochen worden.	ikh bin gershtokhern voardern
I've got something in my eye.	Ich habe etwas im Auge.	ikh haaber ehtvahss im owger
I've got a/an ...	Ich habe ...	ikh haaber
blister	eine Blase	ighner blaazer
boil	einen Furunkel	ighnern foorunkerl
bruise	eine Quetschung	ighner kvehtshung
burn	eine Brandwunde	ighner brahntvunder
cut	eine Schnittwunde	ighner shnitvunder
graze	eine Abschürfung	ighner ahpshewrfung
insect bite	einen Insektenstich	ighnern inzehkternshtikh
lump	eine Beule	ighner boyler
rash	einen Ausschlag	ighnern owsshlaag
sting	einen Stich	ighnern shtikh
strained muscle	eine Muskelzerrung	ighnern muskerltsehrrung
swelling	eine Schwellung	ighner shvehlung
wound	eine Wunde	ighner vunder
Could you have a look at it?	Sehen Sie es bitte mal an.	zayern zee ehss bitter maal ahn
I can't move my ... It hurts.	Ich kann den/die/das ... nicht bewegen. Es tut weh.	ikh kahn dayn/dee/dahss ... nikht bervaygern. ehss toot vay

Wo haben Sie Schmerzen?	Where does it hurt?
Was für Schmerzen haben Sie?	What kind of pain is it?
dumpfe/stechende	dull/sharp
pulsierende/anhaltende	throbbing/constant
unregelmäßig auftretende	on and off
Es ist ...	It's ...
gebrochen/verstaucht	broken/sprained
verrenkt/gerissen	dislocated/torn
Sie müssen geröntgt werden.	I want you to have an X-ray taken.
Sie bekommen einen Gipsverband.	You'll get a plaster.
Es ist infiziert.	It is infected.
Sind Sie gegen Wundstarrkrampf geimpft?	Have you been vaccinated against tetanus?
Ich gebe Ihnen ein Antiseptikum/Schmerzmittel.	I'll give you an antiseptic/ a painkiller.
In ... Tagen möchte ich Sie wiedersehen.	I'd like you to come back in ... days.

Illness *Krankheit*

I'm not feeling well.	**Ich fühle mich nicht wohl.**	ikh fewler mikh nikht voal
I'm ill.	**Ich bin krank.**	ikh bin krahnk
I feel dizzy/ sick.	**Mir ist schwindlig/ übel.**	meer ist shvindlikh/ ewberl
I've got a fever.	**Ich habe Fieber.**	ikh haaber feeberr
My temperature is 38 degrees.	**Ich habe 38° Fieber.**	ikh haaber 38 graat feeberr
I've been vomiting.	**Ich habe mich übergeben.**	ikh haaber mikh ewberrgaybern
I'm constipated.	**Ich habe Verstopfung.**	ikh haaber fehrshtopfung
I've got diarrhoea.	**Ich habe Durchfall.**	ikh haaber doorkhfahl
My ... hurts.	**Mein ... tut weh.**	mighn ... toot vay

I've got (a/an) ...	Ich habe ...	ikh **haaber**
asthma	**Asthma**	**ahst**mah
backache	**Rückenschmerzen**	**rew**kernshmehrtsern
cold	**eine Erkältung**	**ighner ehr**kehltung
cough	**Husten**	**hoo**stern
cramps	**Krämpfe**	**krehm**pfer
earache	**Ohrenschmerzen**	**oar**ernshmehrtsern
headache	**Kopfschmerzen**	**kopf**shmehrtsern
indigestion	**eine Magen-verstimmung**	**ighner maa**gern-fehrshtimmung
nosebleed	**Nasenbluten**	**naa**zernblooern
palpitations	**Herzklopfen**	**hehrts**klopfern
rheumatism	**Rheumatismus**	**roy**mahtismuss
sore throat	**Halsschmerzen**	**hahls**shmehrtsern
stiff neck	**einen steifen Nacken**	**ighnern shtigh**fern **nah**kern
stomach ache	**Magenschmerzen**	**maa**gernshmehrtsern
sunstroke	**einen Sonnenstich**	**ighnern zon**nernshtikh
I have difficulties breathing.	**Ich habe Atem-beschwerden.**	ikh **haaber aa**term-bershvayrdern
I have a pain in my chest.	**Ich habe Schmerzen in der Brust.**	ikh **haaber shmehrts**ern in derr brust
I had a heart attack ... years ago.	**Ich hatte vor ... Jahren einen Herz-anfall.**	ikh **hah**ter for ... **yaa**rern **igh**nern **hehrts-ahn**fahl
My blood pressure is too high/too low.	**Mein Blutdruck ist zu hoch/zu niedrig.**	mighn **bloot**druk ist tsu **hoakh**/tsu **nee**drikh
I'm allergic to ...	**Ich bin gegen ... allergisch.**	ikh bin **gay**gern ... ah**lehr**gish
I'm a diabetic.	**Ich bin Diabetiker.**	ikh bin diah**bay**tikkerr

Women's complaints *Frauenbeschwerden*

I have period pains.	**Ich habe Menstrua-tionsbeschwerden.**	ikh **haaber** mehnstruah-tsioansbershvayrdern
I have a vaginal infection.	**Ich habe eine Scheidenentzündung.**	ikh **haaber ighner shigh**dernehntsewndung
I'm on the pill.	**Ich nehme die Pille.**	ikh **nay**mer dee **pil**ler
I haven't had my period for 2 months.	**Ich habe seit zwei Monaten meine Periode nicht mehr gehabt.**	ikh **haaber** zight tsvigh **moa**nahtern **migh**ner pehrioader nikht mayr ger**hahpt**
I'm pregnant.	**Ich bin schwanger.**	ikh bin **shvahng**err

Wie lange fühlen Sie sich schon so?	How long have you been feeling like this?
Haben Sie das zum ersten Mal?	Is it the first time you've had this?
Ich werde Ihre Temperatur/ Ihren Blutdruck messen.	I'll take your temperature/ blood pressure.
Streifen Sie bitte den Ärmel hoch.	Roll up your sleeve, please.
Bitte machen Sie den Oberkörper frei.	Please undress down to the waist.
Legen Sie sich bitte hierhin.	Please lie down over here.
Machen Sie den Mund auf.	Open your mouth.
Tief atmen, bitte.	Breathe deeply.
Husten Sie bitte.	Cough, please.
Wo haben Sie Schmerzen?	Where do you feel the pain?
Sie haben ...	You've got (a/an) ...
Blasenentzündung	cystitis
Blinddarmentzündung	appendicitis
...entzündung	inflammation of ...
Gelbsucht	jaundice
eine Geschlechtskrankheit	venereal disease
Grippe	flu
Lebensmittelvergiftung	food poisoning
Lungenentzündung	pneumonia
Magenschleimhautentzündung	gastritis
Masern	measles
Ich gebe Ihnen eine Spritze.	I'll give you an injection.
Ich brauche eine Blutprobe/ Stuhlprobe/Urinprobe.	I want a specimen of your blood/stools/urine.
Sie müssen ... Tage im Bett bleiben.	You must stay in bed for ... days.
Sie sollten einen Spezialisten aufsuchen.	I want you to see a specialist.
Sie müssen zu einer General- untersuchung ins Krankenhaus.	I want you to go to the hospital for a general check-up.

Prescription—Treatment *Rezept – Behandlung*

This is my usual medicine.	**Gewöhnlich nehme ich dieses Medikament.**	gervurnlikh naymer ikh deezerss maydikahmehnt
Can you give me a prescription for this?	**Können Sie mir dafür ein Rezept geben?**	kurnern zee meer dahfewr ighn rehtsehpt gaybern
Can you prescribe some sleeping pills/an antidepressant?	**Können Sie mir Schlaftabletten/ein Mittel gegen Depressionen verschreiben?**	kurnern zee mir shlaaftahblehtern/ighn mitterl gaygern dayprehssioanern fehrshrighbern
I'm allergic to antibiotics/penicillin.	**Ich bin allergisch gegen Antibiotika/Penizillin.**	ikh bin ahlehrgish gaygern ahntibbioatikkah/pehnitsillin
I don't want anything too strong.	**Ich möchte kein zu starkes Mittel.**	ikh murkhter kighn tsu shtahrkers mitterl
How many times a day should I take it?	**Wie oft täglich soll ich es nehmen?**	vee oft taiglikh zol ikh ehss naymern
Must I swallow them whole?	**Muß ich sie ganz schlucken?**	muss ikh zee gahnts shlukkern

Wie werden Sie behandelt?	What treatment are you having?
Welches Medikament nehmen Sie?	What medicine are you taking?
Als Spritze oder Tabletten?	By injection or orally?
Nehmen Sie von dieser Medizin ... Teelöffel ...	Take ... teaspoons of this medicine ...
Nehmen Sie eine Tablette mit einem Glas Wasser ...	Take one pill with a glass of water ...
alle ... Stunden	every ... hours
... mal täglich	... times a day
vor/nach jeder Mahlzeit	before/after each meal
morgens/abends	in the morning/at night
wenn Sie Schmerzen haben	if there is any pain
während ... Tagen	for ... days

CHEMIST'S, see page 108

144

Fee *Honorar*

How much do I owe you?	**Wieviel bin ich Ihnen schuldig?**	veefeel bin ikh eenern shuldikh
May I have a receipt for my health insurance?	**Kann ich bitte eine Quittung für meine Krankenkasse haben?**	kahn ikh bitter ighner kvittung fewr mighner krahnkernkahsser haabern
Can I have a medical certificate?	**Können Sie mir ein ärztliches Zeugnis ausstellen?**	kurnern zee meer ighn ehrtstlikhers tsoygniss owsshtehlern
Would you fill in this health insurance form, please?	**Würden Sie bitte dieses Krankenkassen-Formular ausfüllen?**	vewrdern zee bitter deezers krahnkernkahssern-formullaar owsfewlern

Hospital *Krankenhaus*

Please notify my family.	**Benachrichtigen Sie bitte meine Familie.**	bernahkhrikhtiggern zee bitter mighner fahmeelier
What are the visiting hours?	**Wann ist Besuchs-zeit?**	vahn ist berzookhstsight
When can I get up?	**Wann darf ich auf-stehen?**	vahn dahrf ikh owf-shtayern
When will the doctor come?	**Wann kommt der Arzt?**	vahn komt derr ahrtst
I'm in pain.	**Ich habe Schmerzen.**	ikh haaber shmehrtsern
I can't eat/sleep.	**Ich kann nicht essen/schlafen.**	ikh kahn nikht ehssern/shlaafern
Where is the bell?	**Wo ist die Klingel?**	voa ist dee klingerl

nurse	**die Kranken-schwester**	dee krahnkernshvehsterr
patient	**der Patient/die Patientin**	derr pahtsiehnt/dee pahtsiehntin
anaesthesia	**die Narkose**	dee nahrkoazer
blood transfusion	**die Bluttransfusion**	dee bloottrahnsfuzioan
injection	**die Spritze**	dee shpritser
operation	**die Operation**	dee oppehrahtsioan
bed	**das Bett**	dahss beht
bedpan	**die Bettpfanne**	dee behtpfanner
thermometer	**das Thermometer**	dahss tehrmommayterr

Dentist   *Zahnarzt*

Can you recommend a good dentist?	**Können Sie mir einen guten Zahnarzt empfehlen?**	kurnern zee meer **igh**nern gootern tsaanahrtst ehmpfaylern
Can I make an (urgent) appointment to see Dr ...?	**Kann ich einen (dringenden) Termin bei Herrn/Frau Dr. ... haben?**	kahn ikh **igh**nern (**dring**erndern) tehr**meen** bigh hehrn/frow **dok**tor ... **haa**bern
Can't you possibly make it earlier than that?	**Geht es wirklich nicht eher?**	gayt ehss **virk**likh nikht ayer
I have toothache.	**Ich habe Zahnschmerzen.**	ikh **haa**ber **tsaan**shmehrtsern
Is it an abscess/ infection?	**Ist es ein Abszeß/ eine Infektion?**	ist ehss ighn ahpst**sehss**/ **igh**ner infehk**tsioan**
This tooth hurts.	**Dieser Zahn schmerzt.**	**dee**zerr tsaan shmehrtst
at the top	**oben**	**oa**bern
at the bottom	**unten**	**un**tern
in the front	**vorne**	**for**ner
at the back	**hinten**	**hin**tern
Can you fix it temporarily?	**Können Sie ihn provisorisch behandeln?**	kurnern zee een provvi**zoa**rish ber**hahn**derln
I don't want it extracted.	**Ich möchte ihn nicht ziehen lassen.**	ikh **murkh**ter een nikht **tseee**ern **lahs**sern
Could you give me an anaesthetic?	**Können Sie mir eine Spritze geben?**	kurnern zee meer **igh**ner **shprit**ser **gay**bern
I've lost a filling.	**Ich habe eine Plombe verloren.**	ikh **haa**ber **igh**ner **plom**ber fehr**loa**rern
The gum ...	**Das Zahnfleisch ...**	dahss **tsahn**flighsh
is very sore	**ist wund**	ist vunt
is bleeding	**blutet**	**bloo**tert
I've broken this denture.	**Mein Gebiß ist zerbrochen.**	mighn ger**biss** ist tsehr**brok**hern
Can you repair this denture?	**Können Sie das Gebiß reparieren?**	kurnern zee dahss ger**biss** rehpah**ree**rern
When will it be ready?	**Wann ist es fertig?**	vahn ist ehss **fehr**tikh

Reference section

Where do you come from? *Woher kommen Sie?*

I'm from ...	Ich komme aus ...	ikh kommer ows
Africa	**Afrika**	ahfrikkah
Asia	**Asien**	aaziern
Australia	**Australien**	owstraaliern
Europe	**Europa**	oyroapah
North America	**Nordamerika**	nortahmayrikkah
South America	**Südamerika**	zewdahmayrikkah
Austria	**Österreich**	ursterrighkh
Belgium	**Belgien**	behlgiern
Canada	**Kanada**	kahnahdah
Czechoslovakia	**der Tschechoslo-wakei**	derr chehkhoslovvahkigh
China	**China**	kheenah
Denmark	**Dänemark**	dainermahrk
England	**England**	ehnglahnt
Finland	**Finnland**	finlahnt
France	**Frankreich**	frahnkrighkh
Germany	**Deutschland**	doychlahnt
East Germany	**der DDR**	derr day day ehr
West Germany	**der Bundesrepublik**	derr bundersrehpublik
Great Britain	**Großbritannien**	groasbrittahniern
Greece	**Griechenland**	greekhernlahnt
Ireland	**Irland**	eerlahnt
Israel	**Israel**	izrahayl
Italy	**Italien**	itaaliern
Japan	**Japan**	yaapahn
Liechtenstein	**Liechtenstein**	likhternshtighn
Luxembourg	**Luxemburg**	luksermboorg
Netherlands	**den Niederlanden**	dayn neederrlahndern
Norway	**Norwegen**	norvaygern
Poland	**Polen**	poalern
Portugal	**Portugal**	portuggahl
Scotland	**Schottland**	shotlahnt
South Africa	**Südafrika**	zewdahfrikkah
Soviet Union	**der Sowjetunion**	derr zovyehtunnioan
Spain	**Spanien**	shpaaniern
Sweden	**Schweden**	shvaydern
Switzerland	**der Schweiz**	derr shvights
United States	**den Vereinigten Staaten**	dayn fehrighnigtern shtaatern
Wales	**Wales**	"Wales"

Numbers *Zahlen*

0	**null**	nul
1	**eins**	ighns
2	**zwei**	tsvigh
3	**drei**	drigh
4	**vier**	feer
5	**fünf**	fewnf
6	**sechs**	zehks
7	**sieben**	zeebern
8	**acht**	ahkht
9	**neun**	noyn
10	**zehn**	tsayn
11	**elf**	ehlf
12	**zwölf**	tsvurlf
13	**dreizehn**	drightsayn
14	**vierzehn**	feertsayn
15	**fünfzehn**	fewnftsayn
16	**sechzehn**	zehkhtsayn
17	**siebzehn**	zeeptsayn
18	**achtzehn**	ahkhtsayn
19	**neunzehn**	noyntsayn
20	**zwanzig**	tsvahntsikh
21	**einundzwanzig**	ighnunttsvahntsikh
22	**zweiundzwanzig**	tsvighunttsvahntsikh
23	**dreiundzwanzig**	drighunttsvahntsikh
24	**vierundzwanzig**	feerunttsvahntsikh
25	**fünfundzwanzig**	fewnfunttsvahntsikh
26	**sechsundzwandzig**	zehksunttsvahntsikh
27	**siebenundzwanzig**	zeebernunttsvahntsikh
28	**achtundzwanzig**	ahkhtunttsvahntsikh
29	**neunundzwanzig**	noynunttsvahntsikh
30	**dreißig**	drighssikh
31	**einunddreißig**	ighnuntdrighssikh
32	**zweiunddreißig**	tsvighuntdrighssikh
33	**dreiunddreißig**	drighuntdrighssikh
40	**vierzig**	feertsikh
50	**fünfzig**	fewnftsikh
60	**sechzig**	zehkhtsikh
70	**siebzig**	zeeptsikh
80	**achtzig**	ahkhtsikh
90	**neunzig**	noyntsikh
100	**(ein)hundert**	(ighn)hunderrt
101	**hunderteins**	hunderrtighnss
102	**hundertzwei**	hunderrttsvigh
110	**hundertzehn**	hunderrttsayn
120	**hundertzwanzig**	hunderrttsvahntsikh

200	**zweihundert**	**tsvigh**hunderrt
300	**dreihundert**	**drigh**hunderrt
400	**vierhundert**	**feer**hunderrt
500	**fünfhundert**	**fewnf**hunderrt
600	**sechshundert**	**zehks**hunderrt
700	**siebenhundert**	**zeebern**hunderrt
800	**achthundert**	**ahkht**hunderrt
900	**neunhundert**	**noyn**hunderrt
1000	**(ein)tausend**	**(ighn)tow**zernt
1100	**tausendeinhundert**	towzernt**tighn**hunderrt
1200	**tausendzweihundert**	towzernt**tsvigh**hunderrt
2000	**zweitausend**	**tsvigh**towzernt
10,000	**zehntausend**	**tsayn**towzernt
50,000	**fünfzigtausend**	**fewnftsikh**towzernt
100,000	**hunderttausend**	**hunderrt**towzernt
1,000,000	**eine Million**	**ighner** millioan
1,000,000,000	**eine Milliarde**	**ighner** milliahrder
first	**erste**	**ehr**ster
second	**zweite**	**tsvigh**ter
third	**dritte**	**dritt**er
fourth	**vierte**	**feer**ter
fifth	**fünfte**	**fewnf**ter
sixth	**sechste**	**zehks**ter
seventh	**siebte**	**zeeb**ter
eighth	**achte**	**ahkht**er
ninth	**neunte**	**noyn**ter
tenth	**zehnte**	**tsayn**ter
once	**einmal**	**ighn**maal
twice	**zweimal**	**tsvigh**maal
three times	**dreimal**	**drigh**maal
a half	**eine Hälfte**	**ighner** hehlfter
half a ...	**ein halber ...**	ighn **hahl**berr
half of ...	**die Hälfte von ...**	dee **hehl**fter fon
half (adj.)	**halb**	hahlp
a quarter	**ein Viertel**	ighn **feer**terl
one third	**ein Drittel**	ighn **dritt**erl
a pair of	**ein Paar**	ighn paar
a dozen	**ein Dutzend**	ighn **dutsernd**
3.4%	**3,4 Prozent**	drigh **kommah** feer pro**tsehnt**
1981	**neunzehnhundert-einundachtzig**	noyntsaynhunderrt-**ighn**untahkhtsikh
1992	**neunzehnhundert-zweiundneunzig**	noyntsaynhunderrt-**tsvigh**undnoyntsikh
2003	**zweitausenddrei**	tsvightowzernt**drigh**

Year and age *Jahre und Alter*

year	**das Jahr**	dahss yaar
leap year	**das Schaltjahr**	dahss shahltyaar
decade	**das Jahrzehnt**	dahss yaartsaynt
century	**das Jahrhundert**	dahss yaarhundert
this year	**dieses Jahr**	deezers yaar
last year	**letztes Jahr**	lehtsters yaar
next year	**nächstes Jahr**	naikhsters yaar
each year	**jedes Jahr**	yayders yaar
2 years ago	**vor 2 Jahren**	foar tsvigh yaarern
in one year	**in einem Jahr**	in ighnerm yaar
in the eighties	**in den achtziger Jahren**	in dayn ahkhtsiggerr yaarern
from the 19th century	**vom 19. Jahrhundert**	fom noyntsayntern yaarhunderrt
in the 20th century	**im 20. Jahrhundert**	im tsvahntsikhstern yaarhunderrt
old/young	**alt/jung**	ahlt/yung
old/new	**alt/neu**	ahlt/noy
How old are you?	**Wie alt sind Sie?**	vee ahlt zint zee
I'm 30 years old.	**Ich bin 30 Jahre alt.**	ikh bin drighssikh yaarer ahlt
He/She was born in 1960.	**Er/Sie ist 1960 geboren.**	ehr/zee ist noyntsaynhunderrtzehkhtsikh gerboarern
What is his/her age?	**Wie alt ist er/sie?**	vee ahlt ist ehr/zee
Children under 16 are not admitted.	**Kindern unter 16 Jahren ist der Zutritt verboten.**	kinderrn unterr zehkhtsayn yaarern ist derr tsutrit fehrboatern

Seasons *Jahreszeiten*

spring	**der Frühling**	derr frewling
summer	**der Sommer**	derr zommerr
autumn	**der Herbst**	derr hehrpst
winter	**der Winter**	derr vinterr
in spring	**im Frühling**	im frewling
during the summer	**während des Sommers**	vairernt dehss zommerrs
high season	**die Hauptsaison**	dee howptzehzong
low season (before/after season)	**die Vorsaison/ die Nachsaison**	dee foarzehzong/ dee nahkhzehzong

Months *Monate*

January	**Januar**	yahnuaar
February	**Februar**	faybruaar
March	**März**	mehrts
April	**April**	ahpril
May	**Mai**	migh
June	**Juni**	yooni
July	**Juli**	yooli
August	**August**	owgust
September	**September**	sehptehmberr
October	**Oktober**	oktoaberr
November	**November**	novvehmberr
December	**Dezember**	daytsehmberr
after June	**nach Juni**	nahkh yooni
before July	**vor Juli**	foar yooli
during the month of August	**während des Monats August**	vairernt dehss moanahts owgust
in September	**im September**	im zehptehmberr
until October	**bis Oktober**	biss oktoaberr
not until November	**nicht vor November**	nikht foar novehmberr
since December	**seit Dezember**	zight dehtsehmberr
last month	**im letzten Monat**	im lehtstern moanaht
next month	**im nächsten Monat**	im naikhstern moanaht
the month before	**der vorhergehende Monat**	derr foarhayrgayernder moanaht
the month after	**der folgende Monat**	derr folgernder moanaht
the beginning of January	**Anfang Januar**	ahnfahnk yahnuaar
the middle of February	**Mitte Februar**	miterr faybruaar
the end of March	**Ende März**	ehnder mehrts

Days and date *Tage – Datum*

What day is it today?	**Welchen Tag haben wir heute?**	vehlkhern taag haabern veer hoyter
Sunday	**Sonntag**	zontaag
Monday	**Montag**	moantaag
Tuesday	**Dienstag**	deenstaag
Wednesday	**Mittwoch**	mitvokh
Thursday	**Donnerstag**	donnerrstaag
Friday	**Freitag**	frightaag
Saturday	**Samstag/Sonnabend**	zahmstaag/zonnaabernt

What's the date today?	Den wievielten haben wir heute?	dayn veefeeltern haabern veer hoyter
It's ...	Es ist ...	ehss ist
July 1	der 1. Juli	derr ehrster yooli
March 10	der 10. März	derr tsaynter mehrts
When's your birthday?	Wann haben Sie Geburtstag?	vahn haabern zee gerburtstaag
August 2nd.	Am 2. August.	ahm tsvightern owgust
in the morning	am Morgen	ahm morgern
during the day	tagsüber	taagsewberr
in the afternoon	am Nachmittag	ahm nahkhmittaag
in the evening	am Abend	ahm aabernt
at night	nachts	nahkhts
the day before yesterday	vorgestern	foargehsterrn
yesterday	gestern	gehsterrn
today	heute	hoyter
tomorrow	morgen	morgern
the day after tomorrow	übermorgen	ewberrmorgern
the day before	der vorhergehende Tag	derr foarhayrgayernder taag
the next day	der Tag danach	derr taag dahnaakh
two days ago	vor zwei Tagen	foar tsvigh taagern
in three days' time	in drei Tagen	in drigh taagern
last week	letzte Woche	lehtster vokher
next week	nächste Woche	naikhster vokher
for a fortnight (two weeks)	zwei Wochen lang	tsvigh vokhern lahng
day off	der freie Tag	derr frigher taag
holiday	der Feiertag	derr figherrtaag
holidays (vacation)	die Ferien/der Urlaub	dee fayriern/derr oorlowp
week	die Woche	dee vokher
weekend	das Wochenende	dahss vokhernehnder
working day	der Werktag	derr vehrktaag

Greetings and wishes *Grüße und Wünsche*

| Merry Christmas! | Fröhliche Weihnachten! | frurlikher vighnahkhtern |
| Happy New Year! | Glückliches Neues Jahr! | glewklikhers noyers yaar |

Happy Easter!	**Frohe Ostern!**	froaer oasterrn
Happy birthday!	**Alles Gute zum Geburtstag!**	ahlerss gooter tsum gerburtstaag
Best wishes!	**Alles Gute!**	ahlers gooter
Congratulations!	**Herzlichen Glück-wunsch!**	hehrtslikhern glewkvunsh
Good luck/All the best!	**Viel Glück!**	feel glewk
Have a good trip!	**Gute Reise!**	gooter righzer
Have a good holiday!	**Schöne Ferien!**	shurner fayriern
Best regards from ...	**Herzliche Grüße von ...**	hehrtslikher grewsser fon
My regards to ...	**Beste Grüße an ...**	behster grewsser ahn

Public holidays *Feiertage*

Only national holidays in Germany (D), Austria (A) or Switzerland (CH) are cited below.

Jan. 1	**Neujahr**	New Year's Day	D A CH
Jan. 2			CH*
Jan. 6	**Dreikönigstag**	Epiphany	A
May 1	**Tag der Arbeit**	Labour Day	D A
June 17	**Tag der Deutschen Einheit**	National Unity Day	D
Aug. 1	**Nationalfeiertag**	National Day	CH*
Aug. 15	**Mariä Himmel-fahrt**	Assumption Day	A
Oct. 26	**Nationalfeiertag**	National Day	A
Nov. 1	**Allerheiligen**	All Saints' Day	A
Dec. 8	**Mariä Empfängnis**	Immaculate Conception	A
Dec. 25	**1. Weihnachtstag**	Christmas Day	D A CH
Dec. 26	**2. Weihnachtstag**	St. Stephen's Day	D A CH*
Movable dates:	**Karfreitag**	Good Friday	D CH*
	Ostermontag	Easter Monday	D A CH*
	Christi Himmelfahrt	Ascension	D A CH
	Pfingstmontag	Whit Monday	D A CH*
	Fronleichnam	Corpus Christi	A

*Most cantons

What time is it? *Wie spät ist es?*

Excuse me. Can you tell me the time?	**Verzeihung. Können Sie mir bitte sagen, wie spät es ist?**	fehrtsighung. kurnern zee meer bitter zaagern vee shpait ehss ist
It's ...	**Es ist ...**	ehss ist
five past one	**fünf nach eins***	fewnf nakh ighns
ten past two	**zehn nach zwei**	tsayn nakh tsvigh
a quarter past three	**viertel nach drei**	feerterl nahkh drigh
twenty past four	**zwanzig nach vier**	tsvahntsikh nahkh feer
twenty-five past five	**fünf vor halb sechs**	fewnf foar hahlp zehks
half past six	**halb sieben**	hahlp zeebern
twenty-five to seven	**fünf nach halb sieben**	fewnf nakh hahlp zeebern
twenty to eight	**zwanzig vor acht**	tsvahntsikh foar ahkht
a quarter to nine	**viertel vor neun**	feerterl foar noyn
ten to ten	**zehn vor zehn**	tsayn foar tsayn
five to eleven	**fünf vor elf**	fewnf foar ehlf
twelve o'clock (noon/midnight)	**zwölf Uhr (Mittag/Mitter-nacht)**	tsvurlf oor (mittaag/mitterrnahkht)
in the morning	**morgens**	morgerns
in the afternoon	**nachmittags**	nahkhmittaags
in the evening	**abends**	aabernds
The train leaves at ...	**Der Zug fährt um ...**	derr tsoog fairt um
13.04 (1.04 p.m.)	**dreizehn Uhr vier**	drightsayn oor feer
0.40 (0.40 a.m.)	**null Uhr vierzig**	nul oor feertsikh
in five minutes	**in fünf Minuten**	in fewnf minnootern
in a quarter of an hour	**in einer Viertelstunde**	in ighnerr feerterlshtunder
half an hour ago	**vor einer halben Stunde**	foar ighnerr hahlbern shtunder
about two hours	**ungefähr zwei Stunden**	ungerfair tsvigh shtundern
more than 10 minutes	**über 10 Minuten**	ewber tsayn minnootern
less than 30 seconds	**weniger als 30 Sekunden**	vayniggerr ahlss drighssikh zehkundern
The clock is fast/slow.	**Die Uhr geht vor/nach.**	dee oor gayt foar/nahkh

---

*In ordinary conversation, time is expressed as shown here. However, official time uses a 24-hour clock which means that after noon hours are counted from 13 to 24.

Common abbreviations   *Gebräuchliche Abkürzungen*

ACS	Automobil-Club der Schweiz	Automobile Association of Switzerland
ADAC	Allgemeiner Deutscher Automobil-Club	General Automobile Association of Germany
a.M.	am Main	on the river Main
a.Rh.	am Rhein	on the river Rhine
AvD	Automobil-Club von Deutschland	Automobile Club of Germany
Bhf	Bahnhof	railway station
BRD	Bundesrepublik Deutschland	Federal Republic of Germany (West Germany)
DB	Deutsche Bundesbahn	Federal German Railway
DDR	Deutsche Demokratische Republik	German Democratic Republic (East Germany)
d.h.	das heißt	i.e. (that is)
DIN	Deutsche Industrie-Norm	German Industrial Standard
Frl.	Fräulein	Miss
G.	Gasse	lane
Hbf.	Hauptbahnhof	main railway station
Hr.	Herr	Mr.
LKW	Lastkraftwagen	lorry/truck
MEZ	Mitteleuropäische Zeit	Central European Time
Mio.	Million	million
Mrd.	Milliarde	1000 millions (billion)
n.Chr.	nach Christus	A.D.
ÖAMTC	Österreichischer Automobil-Motorrad- und Touring-Club	Austrian Automobile, Motorcycle and Touring Association
ÖBB	Österreichische Bundesbahnen	Austrian Federal Railways
PKW	Personenkraftwagen	motor car
Pl.	Platz	square
PS	Pferdestärke	horsepower
PTT	Post, Telephon, Telegraph	Post, Telephone and Telegraph Office
SBB	Schweizerische Bundesbahnen	Swiss Federal Railways
St.	Stock	floor
Str.	Straße	street
TCS	Touring-Club der Schweiz	Swiss Touring Club
usw.	und so weiter	etc.
v.Chr.	vor Christus	B.C.
z.B.	zum Beispiel	e.g. (for example)
z.Z.	zur Zeit	at present

Signs and notices *Aufschriften und Hinweise*

Achtung	Caution
Aufzug	Lift (elevator)
Ausgang	Exit
Auskunft	Information
Außer Betrieb	Out of order
Ausverkauf	Sale
Ausverkauft	Sold out
Belegt	Full/No vacancies
Besetzt	Occupied
Bitte klingeln	Please ring
Bitte nicht stören	Do not disturb
Damen	Ladies
Drücken	Push
Eingang	Entrance
Eintreten ohne zu klopfen	Enter without knocking
Eintritt frei	No admission charge
Frei	Vacant
Frisch gestrichen	Wet paint
Für Unbefugte verboten	No trespassing
Gefahr	Danger
Geschlossen	Closed
Heiß	Hot
Herren	Men
Kalt	Cold
Kasse	Cash desk
Kein Zutritt	No entrance
Lebensgefahr	Danger of death
Lift	Lift (elevator)
Nicht berühren	Do not touch
Notausgang	Emergency exit
Notruf	Emergency
Nur für Anlieger	Residents only
Privatweg	Private road
Radweg	Cycle path
Rauchen verboten	No smoking
Reserviert	Reserved
Unbefugtes Betreten verboten	No trespassing
... verboten	... forbidden/prohibited
Vorsicht	Caution
Vorsicht, bissiger Hund	Beware of the dog
Ziehen	Pull
Zimmer frei	Vacancies
Zu verkaufen	For sale
Zu vermieten	To let (for hire)

Emergency *Notfall*

Call the police	**Rufen Sie die Polizei**	roofern zee dee pollitsigh
DANGER	**GEFAHR**	gerfaar
FIRE	**FEUER**	foyerr
Gas	**Gas**	gaass
Get a doctor	**Holen Sie einen Arzt**	hoalern zee ighnern ahrtst
Go away	**Gehen Sie weg**	gayern zee vehk
HELP	**HILFE**	hilfer
Get help	**Holen Sie Hilfe**	hoalern zee hilfer
I'm ill	**Ich bin krank**	ikh bin krahnk
I'm lost	**Ich habe mich verirrt**	ikh haaber mikh fehreert
LOOK OUT	**VORSICHT**	foarzikht
POLICE	**POLIZEI**	pollitsigh
Quick	**Schnell**	shnehl
STOP	**HALT**	hahlt
Stop that man/ woman	**Haltet den Mann/ die Frau**	hahltert dayn mahn/ dee frow
STOP THIEF	**HALTET DEN DIEB**	hahltert dayn deep

Emergency telephone numbers *Notrufnummern*

	Austria	Germany	Switzerland
Fire	122	112	118
Ambulance	144	112	144
Police	133	110	117

Lost property—Theft *Fundsachen – Diebstahl*

Where's the ...?	**Wo ist ...?**	voa ist
lost-property (lost and found) office	**das Fundbüro**	dahss funtbewroa
police station	**die Polizeiwache**	dee pollitsighvahkher
I want to report a theft.	**Ich möchte einen Diebstahl anzeigen.**	ikh murkhter ighnern deepshtaal ahntsighgern
My ... has been stolen.	**Mein(e) ... ist mir gestohlen worden.**	mighn(er) ... ist meer gershtoalern voardern
I've lost my wallet.	**Ich habe meine Brieftasche verloren.**	ikh haaber mighner breeftahsher fehrloarern

CAR ACCIDENTS, see page 78

Conversion tables

Centimetres and inches

To change centimetres into inches, multiply by .39.

To change inches into centimetres, multiply by 2.54.

	in.	feet	yards
1 mm.	0.039	0.003	0.001
1 cm.	0.39	0.03	0.01
1 dm.	3.94	0.32	0.10
1 m.	39.40	3.28	1.09

	mm.	cm.	m.
1 in.	25.4	2.54	0.025
1 ft.	304.8	30.48	0.305
1 yd.	914.4	91.44	0.914

(32 metres = 35 yards)

Temperature

To convert centigrade into degrees Fahrenheit, multiply centigrade by 1.8 and add 32.

To convert degrees Fahrenheit into centigrade, subtract 32 from Fahrenheit and divide by 1.8.

Kilometres into miles

1 kilometre (km.) = 0.62 miles

km.	10	20	30	40	50	60	70	80	90	100	110	120	130
miles	6	12	19	25	31	37	44	50	56	62	68	75	81

Miles into kilometres

1 mile = 1.609 kilometres (km.)

miles	10	20	30	40	50	60	70	80	90	100
km.	16	32	48	64	80	97	113	129	145	161

Fluid measures

1 litre (l.) = 0.88 imp. quart or 1.06 U.S. quart

1 imp. quart = 1.14 l.	1 U.S. quart = 0.95 l.
1 imp. gallon = 4.55 l.	1 U.S. gallon = 3.8 l.

litres	5	10	15	20	25	30	35	40	45	50
imp. gal.	1.1	2.2	3.3	4.4	5.5	6.6	7.7	8.8	9.9	11.0
U.S. gal.	1.3	2.6	3.9	5.2	6.5	7.8	9.1	10.4	11.7	13.0

Weights and measures

1 kilogram or kilo (kg.) = 1000 grams (g.)

100 g. = 3.5 oz.	½ kg. = 1.1 lb.
200 g. = 7.0 oz.	1 kg. = 2.2 lb.

1 oz. = 28.35 g.
1 lb. = 453.60 g.

CLOTHING SIZES, see page 115/YARDS AND INCHES, see page 112

Basic Grammar

Here is a brief outline of some essential features of German grammar.

Articles

All nouns in German are either masculine, feminine or neuter, and they are classified by the article which precedes them.

1. **Definite article** (the):   Plural:

masc. *der* **Mann**   the man   *die* **Männer**
fem. *die* **Frau**   the woman   *die* **Frauen**
neut. *das* **Kind**   the child   *die* **Kinder**

2. **Indefinite article** (a/an):

masc. *ein* **Zug**   a train
fem. *eine* **Reise**   a trip
neut. *ein* **Flugzeug**   a plane

Nouns and adjectives

1. All nouns are written with a capital letter. The rules for constructing the plural are very complex.

2. **Declension:** According to their use in the sentence, German articles, nouns and modifying adjectives undergo related changes. The tables below show the declension of all three parts of speech.

	masc. sing.	masc. plur.
subject	**der reiche Mann**	**die reichen Männer**
direct object	**den reichen Mann**	**die reichen Männer**
possessive	**des reichen Mannes**	**der reichen Männer**
indirect object	**dem reichen Mann**	**den reichen Männern**

	fem. sing.	fem. plur.
subject	die schöne Frau	die schönen Frauen
direct object	die schöne Frau	die schönen Frauen
possessive	der schönen Frau	der schönen Frauen
indirect object	der schönen Frau	den schönen Frauen

	neuter sing.	neuter plur.
subject	das kleine Kind	die kleinen Kinder
direct object	das kleine Kind	die kleinen Kinder
possessive	des kleinen Kindes	der kleinen Kinder
indirect object	dem kleinen Kind	den kleinen Kindern

The indefinite article is declined in a slightly different way, as is the modifying adjective.

	masc.	fem.
subject	ein reicher Mann	eine schöne Frau
direct object	einen reichen Mann	eine schöne Frau
possessive	eines reichen Mannes	einer schönen Frau
indirect object	einem reichen Mann	einer schönen Frau

	neuter	plur.
subject	ein kleines Kind	keine* großen Leute
direct object	ein kleines Kind	keine großen Leute
possessive	eines kleinen Kindes	keiner großen Leute
indirect object	einem kleinen Kind	keinen großen Leuten

If declined without an article the adjectives take the endings of the definite article, except in the possessive, which you'll hardly use: **guter Wein** (good wine), **kalte Milch** (cold milk), **warmes Wasser** (hot water).

3. **Demonstrative adjectives:** In spoken German "that" is usually expressed by the definite article, but contrary to the

---
* **ein** has no plural, but the negative **kein** (declined in singular like **ein**) does.

article, it is stressed. "This" **dieser, diese, dieses** and plural **diese** is declined like the definite article.

das Buch (that book)   **dieser Platz** (this seat)

4. **Possessive adjectives:** These agree in number and gender with the noun they modify, i.e., with the thing possessed and not the possessor. In singular they are declined like the indefinite article, and in plural like the definite. Note that **Ihr** meaning "your" in the polite form is capitalized.

	masc. or neut.	fem. or plur.
my	mein	meine
your	dein	deine
his/its	sein	seine
her	ihr	ihre
our	unser	unsere
your	euer	eure
their	ihr	ihre
your (pol.)	Ihr	Ihre

5. **Comparatives and superlatives:** These are formed by adding **-er (-r)** and **-est (-st)** respectively, very often together with an umlaut.

alt (old)   **kurz** (short)
älter (older)   **kürzer** (shorter)
ältest (oldest)   **kürzest** (shortest)

Adverbs

Many adjectives are used in their undeclined form as adverbs.

schnell   quick, quickly
gut   good, well

There are a few irregularities:

glücklich – glücklicherweise   happy—happily
anders   differently
besonders   especially
gleichfalls   as well, (the) same

Viel indicates quantity and **sehr** intensity:

Er arbeitet viel.	He works a lot.
Er ist sehr müde.	He's very tired.

Personal pronouns

	subject	direct object	indirect object
I	ich	mich	mir
you	du	dich	dir
he	er	ihn	ihm
she	sie	sie	ihr
it	es	es	ihm
we	wir	uns	uns
you	ihr	euch	euch
they	sie	sie	ihnen
you	Sie	Sie	Ihnen

Note: There are two forms for "you" in German: **du** and **Sie**; **du** (plur.: **ihr**) is used when talking to relatives, close friends and children (and between young people); **Sie** (both sing. and plur.) in all other cases. **Sie** is written with a capital **S**. The verb has the same form as that of the 3rd person plural.

Verbs

Here we are concerned only with the infinitive, the present tense, and the imperative.

Learn these two important **auxiliary verbs**:

sein (to be)	**haben** (to have)
ich bin (I am)	**ich habe** (I have)
du bist (you are)	**du hast** (you have)
er, sie, es ist (he, she, it is)	**er, sie, es hat** (he, she, it has)
wir sind (we are)	**wir haben** (we have)
ihr seid (you are)	**ihr habt** (you have)
sie sind (they are)	**sie haben** (they have)
Sie sind (you are)	**Sie haben** (you have)

The infinitive of practically all verbs ends in **-en.** Here are the endings for the present tense:

ich lieb*e*	I love
du lieb*st*	you love
er, sie, es lieb*t*	he, she, it loves
wir lieb*en*	we love
ihr lieb*t*	you love
sie, Sie lieb*en*	they, you love

Here are four useful irregular verbs in the present tense:

	können (to be able)	gehen (to go)	sehen (to see)	tun (to do)
ich	kann	gehe	sehe	tue
du	kannst	gehst	siehst	tust
er/sie/es	kann	geht	sieht	tut
wir	können	gehen	sehen	tun
ihr	könnt	geht	seht	tut
sie/Sie	können	gehen	sehen	tun

For both regular and irregular verbs, the **imperative** is formed by reversing the order of the verb and the personal pronoun.

Gehen wir!	Let's go!
Gehen Sie!	Go!

Negatives

Negatives are formed with **nicht.**

Er ist nicht hier.	He is not here.

Questions

These are formed by inverting the subject and the verb (putting the verb first, the subject second).

Sprechen Sie English?	Do you speak English?

Dictionary
and alphabetical index

English–German

f feminine	*m* masculine	*nt* neuter	*pl* plural

a ein(e) 159
abbey Abtei *f* 81
abbreviation Abkürzung *f* 154
able, to be können 163
about *(approximately)* ungefähr 78, 153
above oben 14
abscess Abszeß *m* 145
absorbent cotton Watte *f* 109
accept, to (an)nehmen 63, 102
accessories Zubehör *nt* 116, 125
accident Unfall *m* 78, 139
accommodation Unterkunft *f* 22
account Konto *nt* 130, 131
ache Schmerz *m* 141
acne cream Aknesalbe *f* 110
adaptor Zwischenstecker *m* 119
address Adresse *f* 21, 31, 76; Anschrift *f* 79, 102
adhesive selbstklebend 105
admission Eintritt *m* 82, 89, 155
Africa Afrika *(nt)* 146
after nach 14, 77
afternoon Nachmittag *m* 151, 153
after-shave lotion Rasierwasser *nt* 110
against gegen 140
age Alter *nt* 149
ago vor 149, 151
air conditioner Klimaanlage *f* 23, 28
airmail per Luftpost 132
airplane Flugzeug *nt* 65
airport Flughafen *m* 16, 21, 65
alarm clock Wecker *m* 121
alcohol Alkohol *m* 37
alcoholic alkoholisch 59

all alles 103
allergic allergisch 141, 143
alley Gasse *f* 81
almond Mandel *f* 53
alphabet Alphabet *nt* 15
also auch 15
alter, to ändern 116
amazing erstaunlich 84
amber Bernstein *m* 122
ambulance Krankenwagen *m* 79, 156
American Amerikaner(in) *m/f* 93
American amerikanisch 105, 126
American plan Vollpension *f* 24
amount Betrag *m* 63, 131
amplifier Verstärker *m* 19
amusement park Vergnügungspark *m* 81
anaesthesia Narkose *f* 144
analgesic Schmerzmittel *nt* 109
anchovy Sardelle *f* 41
and und 15
animal Tier *nt* 85
aniseed Anis *m* 51
ankle Knöchel *m* 139
anorak Anorak *m* 116
answer Antwort *f* 136
antibiotic Antibiotikum *nt* 143
antidepressant Mittel gegen Depressionen *nt* 143
antiques Antiquitäten *f/pl* 83
antique shop Antiquitätengeschäft *nt* 98
antiseptic Antiseptikum *nt* 140
any etwas, einige 14
anyone (irgend) jemand 11
anything (irgend) etwas 17, 25, 113

anywhere irgendwo
apartment (flat) Wohnung f 22
aperitif Aperitif m 59
appendicitis Blinddarmentzündung f 142
appendix Blinddarm m 138
appetizer Vorspeise f 41
apple Apfel m 53, 64, 120
apple juice Apfelsaft m 61
appliance Gerät nt 119
appointment Verabredung f 131; Termin m 137, 145
apricot Aprikose f 53
April April m 150
archaeology Archäologie f 83
architect Architekt m 83
area code Vorwählnummer f 134
arm Arm m 138, 139
arrangement (set price) Pauschale f 20
arrival Ankunft f 16, 65, 68
arrive, to ankommen 68, 130
art Kunst f 83
artery Arterie f 138
art gallery Kunstgalerie f 81, 98
artichoke Artischocke f 41
artificial künstlich 124
artist Künstler(in) m/f 83
ashtray Aschenbecher m 27, 36
Asia Asien (nt) 146
ask, to fragen 36, 76; bitten 136
asparagus Spargel m 41, 50
aspirin Aspirin m 109
asthma Asthma nt 141
at an, bei 14
at least mindestens 26
at once sofort 31
aubergine Aubergine f 49
August August m 150
aunt Tante f 93
Australia Australien (nt) 146
Austria Österreich (nt) 146
Austrian österreichisch 18
automatic automatisch 122, 124; mit Automatik 20
autumn Herbst m 149
avalanche Lawine f 79
awful scheußlich 84, 94

B
baby Baby nt 24; Säugling m 111
baby food Säuglingsnahrung f 111
babysitter Babysitter m 27
back Rücken m 138

backache Rückenschmerzen m/pl 141
bacon Speck m 38, 46
bad schlecht 14, 95
bag Tasche f 17, 18; Tragetasche f 103
baggage Gepäck nt 17, 18, 26, 31, 71
baggage cart Kofferkuli m 18, 71
baggage check Gepäckaufbewahrung f 67, 71
baggage locker Schließfach nt 18, 67, 71
baked gebacken 44, 47
baker's Bäckerei f 98
balance (account) Bilanz f 131
balcony Balkon m 23
ball (inflated) Ball m 128
ballet Ballett nt 88
ball-point pen Kugelschreiber m 104
banana Banane f 53, 64
bandage Verband m 109
Band-Aid Heftpflaster nt 109
bangle Armreif m 121
bank (finance) Bank f 98, 129, 130
bank card Kontokarte f 130
banknote Schein m 130
bar (chocolate) Tafel f 64
barber's Friseur m 30, 98
bass (fish) Barsch m 44
bath (hotel) Bad 23, 24, 27
bathing cap Badekappe f 116
bathing suit Badeanzug m 116
bathrobe Bademantel m 116
bathroom Bad nt 27
bath towel Badetuch nt 27
battery Batterie f 75, 78, 119, 121, 125
bay leaf Lorbeer m 50
be, to sein 10, 162
beach Strand m 90
bean Bohne f 49
beard Bart m 31
beautiful schön 13, 84
beauty salon Kosmetiksalon m 30, 98
be back, to zurück sein 21, 136
bed Bett nt 24, 142, 144
bed and breakfast Übernachtung mit Frühstück f 24
bedpan Bettpfanne f 144
beef Rindfleisch nt 45
beer Bier nt 56, 64
beer stein Bierkrug m 127
beet(root) rote Beete f 50
before vor 14
begin, to beginnen 80, 87, 88

building Gebäude *nt* 81, 82, 83
building blocks/bricks Baukasten *m* 128
bulb (Glüh)birne *f* 28, 75, 119
burn Brandwunde *f* 139
bus Bus *m* 18, 19, 65, 72, 73, 80
business Geschäft *nt* 131
business trip Geschäftsreise *f* 93
bus stop Bushaltestelle *f* 72, 73
busy beschäftigt 96
but aber 15
butane gas Butangas *nt* 32, 106
butcher's Fleischerei *f*, Metzgerei *f* 98
butter Butter *f* 36, 38, 64
button Knopf *m* 29, 117
buy, to kaufen 82, 100

C

cabbage Kohl *m* 50
cabin (ship) Kabine *f* 74
cable Telegramm *nt* 133
cable car Seilbahn *f* 74
café Café *nt* 33
cake Kuchen *m* 37, 54, 64
cake shop Konditorei *f* 33, 98
calculator Rechner *m* 105
calendar Kalender *m* 104
call (phone) (Telefon)gespräch *nt* 135, 136; Anruf *m* 136
call, to (give name) heißen 10; (summon) rufen 78, 79, 156; (phone) anrufen 136; (wake) wecken 71
call at, to (boat) anlegen 74
calm ruhig 90
camel-hair Kamelhaar *nt* 114
camera Fotoapparat *m* 124, 125
camera case Fototasche *f* 125
camera shop Fotogeschäft *nt* 98
camp, to zelten 32
campbed Feldbett *nt* 106
camping Camping *nt* 32
camping equipment Camping-ausrüstung *f* 106
camp site Campingplatz *m* 32
can (of peaches) Büchse *f* 120
can (to be able) können 11, 12, 163
Canada Kanada (nt) 146
Canadian Kanadier(in) *m/f* 93
cancel, to annullieren 65
candle Kerze *f* 106
candy Bonbon *m* 126
can opener Büchsenöffner *m* 106

cap Mütze *f* 116
caper Kaper *f* 51
capital (finance) Kapital *nt* 131
car Auto *nt*, Wagen *m* 19, 20, 26, 32, 75, 76, 78
carat Karat *nt* 121
caravan Wohnwagen *m* 32
caraway Kümmel *m* 51
carbon paper Durchschlagpapier *nt* 104
carbonated mit Kohlensäure 61
carburetor Vergaser *m* 78
card Karte *f* 93, 131
card game Kartenspiel *nt* 128
cardigan Wolljacke *f* 116
car hire Autoverleih *m* 19, 20
car number Kraftfahrzeugnummer *f* 25
car park Parkplatz *m* 77
car racing Autorennen *nt* 89
car radio Autoradio *nt* 119
car rental Autoverleih *m* 19, 20
carrot Karotte *f* 50
carry, to tragen 21
carton (of cigarettes) Stange (Zigaretten) *f* 17, 126
cartridge (camera) Kassette *f* 124
case (cigarettes, glasses) Etui *nt* 121, 123
cash, to einlösen 130, 133
cash desk Kasse *f* 103, 155
cassette Kassette *f* 119, 127, 128
castle Schloß *nt*, Burg *f* 85
catalogue Katalog *m* 82
cathedral Kathedrale *f*, Dom *m* 81
Catholic katholisch 84
cauliflower Blumenkohl *m* 49
caution Vorsicht *f* 79, 155; Achtung *f* 155
cave Höhle *f* 81
celery Sellerie *m* 50
cellophane tape Klebstreifen *m* 104
cemetery Friedhof *m* 81
centimetre Zentimeter *m* 112
centre Zentrum *m* 21, 76
century Jahrhundert *nt* 149
ceramics Keramik *f* 83
cereal Getreideflocken *f/pl* 38
certificate Zeugnis *nt* 144
chain (jewellery) Kette *f* 121
chair Stuhl *m* 106
chamber music Kammermusik *f* 128
champagne (German) Sekt *m* 59
change (money) Kleingeld *nt* 77, 130

change, to wechseln 18, 123, 130; *(train)* umsteigen 65, 68, 73; *(reservation)* umbuchen 65
chapel Kapelle *f* 81
charcoal Holzkohle *f* 106
charge Gebühr *f* 32, 136; Rechnung *f* 28
charge, to berechnen 24; *(commission)* erheben 130
cheap billig 14, 24, 25, 101
check Scheck *m* 130; *(restaurant)* Rechnung *f* 63
check, to kontrollieren 75, 123; prüfen 75; *(luggage)* aufgeben 71
check book Scheckbuch *nt* 131
check in, to *(airport)* einchecken 65
check out, to abreisen 31
checkup *(medical)* Untersuchung *f* 142
cheers! Prost! 60
cheese Käse *m* 37, 38, 52, 64
chef Küchenchef *m* 40
chemist's Apotheke *f* 98, 108
cheque Scheck *m* 130
cheque book Scheckbuch *nt* 131
cherry Kirsche *f* 53
chess Schach *nt* 93
chess set Schachspiel *nt* 128
chest Brust(korb) *m* 138, 141
chewing gum Kaugummi *m* 126
chicken Huhn *nt* 48
chicory Endivie *f*; *(Am.)* Chicorée *f* 49
child Kind *nt* 24, 62, 82, 93, 139, 149, 159
children's doctor Kinderarzt *m* 137
China China *(nt)* 146
chips Pommes frites *f/pl* 49; *(Am.)* Kartoffelchips *m/pl* 64
chives Schnittlauch *m* 51
chocolate Schokolade *f* 38, 61, 64, 120, 126, 127
choice Wahl *f* 40
chop Kotelett *nt* 46
Christmas Weihnachten *nt* 151
church Kirche *f* 81, 84
cider Apfelwein *m* 59
cigar Zigarre *f* 126
cigarette Zigarette *f* 17, 95, 126
cigarette lighter Feuerzeug *nt* 121
cine camera Filmkamera *f* 124
cinema Kino *nt* 86, 96
cinnamon Zimt *m* 51
circle *(theatre)* Rang *m* 87
city Stadt *f* 81, 92

clam Muschel *f* 44
classical klassisch 128
clean sauber 62
clean, to reinigen 29, 76
cleansing cream Reinigungscreme *f* 110
cloakroom Garderobe *f* 87
clock Uhr *f* 119, 121, 153
clock-radio Radiowecker *m* 119
close *(near)* nahe 78, 98
close, to schließen 10, 82, 108, 132, 155
closed geschlossen 155
cloth Stoff *m* 118
clothes Kleider *nt/pl* 29, 116
clothes peg Wäscheklammer *f* 106
clothing Bekleidung *f* 112
cloud Wolke *f* 94
clove Nelke *f* 50
coach *(bus)* Bus *m* 72
coat Mantel *m* 116
coconut Kokosnuß *f* 54
cod Kabeljau *m*, Dorsch *m* 44
coffee Kaffee *m* 38, 61, 64
cognac Kognak *m* 59
coin Münze *f* 83
cold kalt 13, 24, 38, 62, 155
cold *(illness)* Erkältung *f* 108, 141
cold cuts Aufschnitt *m* 64
collect call R-Gespräch *nt* 134
cologne Kölnischwasser *nt* 110
colour Farbe *f* 103, 112, 124, 125
colour chart Farbtabelle *f* 30
colour fast farbecht 112
colour film Farbfilm *m* 124
colour negative Farbnegativ *nt* 124
colour shampoo Tönungsshampoo *nt* 111
colour slide Farbdia *nt* 124
colour television *(set)* Farbfernseher *m* 119
comb Kamm *m* 111
come, to kommen 36, 59, 92, 95, 137, 144, 146
comedy Komödie *f* 86
commission Gebühr *f* 130
common *(frequent)* gebräuchlich 154
compact disc Compact Disc *f* 127
compartment Abteil *nt* 70
compass Kompaß *m* 106
complaint Reklamation *f* 62
concert Konzert *nt* 88
concert hall Konzerthalle *f* 81, 88
conductor *(orchestra)* Dirigent *m* 88

confirm, to bestätigen 65
confirmation Bestätigung f 23
congratulation Glückwunsch m 152
connection (train) Anschluß m 65, 68
constipation Verstopfung f 140
contact lens Kontaktlinse f 123
contain, to enthalten 37
contraceptive Verhütungsmittel nt 109
contract Vertrag m 131
control Kontrolle f 16
convent Kloster nt 81
convention hall Kongreßhalle f 81
conversion Umrechnung f 157
cookie Keks m 64
cool box Kühltasche f 106
copper Kupfer nt 122
corduroy Kordsamt m 114
cork Korken m 62
corkscrew Korkenzieher m 106
corn (Am.) Mais m 50; (foot) Hühnerauge nt 109
corner Ecke f 21, 36, 77
corn plaster Hühneraugenpflaster nt 109
cost Kosten pl 131
cost, to kosten 10, 20, 80, 133
cotton Baumwolle f 114
cotton wool Watte f 109
cough Husten m 108, 141
cough, to husten 142
cough drops Hustenpastillen f/pl 109
counter Schalter m 133
country Land nt 93
countryside Landschaft f, Land nt 85
court house Gericht(sgebäude) nt 81
cousin Cousin(e) m/f 93
cramp Krampf m 141
cranberry Preiselbeere f 53
crayfish (river) Krebs m 41, 44
crayon Buntstift m 104
cream Sahne f 54, 61; (toiletry) Creme f 110
credit Kredit m 130
credit card Kreditkarte f 20, 31, 63, 102, 130
cress Kresse f 51
crisps Kartoffelchips m/pl 64
crockery Geschirr nt 106, 107
croissant Hörnchen nt 38
cross Kreuz nt 121
cross-country skiing Langlauf m 91
crossing (by sea) Überfahrt f 74
crossroads Kreuzung f 77

cruise Kreuzfahrt f 74
crystal Kristall m 122
cuckoo clock Kuckucksuhr f 121, 127
cucumber Gurke f 50
cuff link Manschettenknopf m 121
cuisine Küche f 35
cup Tasse f 36, 61, 107
curler Lockenwickler m 111
currency Währung f 129
currency exchange office Wechselstube f 18, 67, 129
current Strömung f 90
curtain Vorhang m 28
customs Zoll m 16, 102
cut (wound) Schnittwunde f 139
cut, to schneiden 30
cut off, to (phone) unterbrechen 135
cut glass geschliffenes Glas nt 122
cutlery Besteck nt 106, 107; Tafelbesteck nt 121
cutlet Kotelett nt 45
cycling Radfahren nt 89
cystitis Blasenentzündung f 142
Czechoslovakia Tschechoslowakei f 146

D

dairy Milchhandlung f 98
dance, to tanzen 88, 96
danger Gefahr f 155, 156
dangerous gefährlich 90
dark dunkel 24, 56, 101, 112, 113
date (day) Datum nt 25, 150; (appointment) Verabredung f 95; (fruit) Dattel f 53
daughter Tochter f 93
day Tag m 16, 20, 26, 32, 80, 150, 151
daylight Tageslicht nt 124
day off freier Tag m 151
decade Jahrzehnt nt 149
decaffeinated koffeinfrei 38, 61
December Dezember m 150
decision Entscheidung f 24, 102
deck (ship) Deck nt 74
deck-chair Liegestuhl m 91, 106
declare, to (customs) verzollen 17
deep tief 142
delay Verspätung f 69
delicatessen Delikatessengeschäft nt 98
deliver, to liefern 102
delivery Lieferung f 102
Denmark Dänemark (nt) 146

dentist Zahnarzt m 98, 145
denture Gebiß nt 145
deodorant Deodorant nt 110
department Abteilung f 83, 100
department store Warenhaus nt 98
departure Abflug m 65; Abfahrt f 69
depilatory cream Haarentfernungs-
  mittel nt 110
deposit, to *(bank)* einzahlen 130,
  131; *(car hire)* hinterlegen 20
dessert Nachtisch m, Nachspeise f,
  Süßspeise f 37, 40, 54
detour *(traffic)* Umleitung f 79
develop, to entwickeln 124
diabetic Diabetiker(in) m/f 37, 41
dialling code Vorwählnummer f 134
diamond Diamant m 122
diaper Windel f 111
diarrhoea Durchfall m 140
dictionary Wörterbuch nt 104
diesel Diesel(öl) nt 75
diet Diät f 37
difficult schwierig 13
difficulty Schwierigkeit f 28, 102, 141
digital Digital- 122
dill Dill m 51
dining-car Speisewagen m 66, 68, 71
dining-room Speisesaal m 27
dinner Abendessen nt 34, 94
direct direkt 65
direct to, to den Weg zeigen 12
direction Richtung f 76
director *(film)* Regisseur m 86
directory *(phone)* Telefonbuch nt 134
disabled Behinderte m/f 82
discotheque Diskothek f 88, 96
disease Krankheit f 142
dish Gericht nt 36, 37, 40
dishwashing detergent Spülmittel nt
  106
disinfectant Desinfektionsmittel nt
  109
dislocate, to verrenken 140
display case Vitrine f 100
dissatisfied unzufrieden 103
district *(town)* Viertel nt 81
disturb, to stören 155
diversion *(traffic)* Umleitung f 79
dizzy schwindlig 140
do, to tun 163
doctor Arzt m, Ärztin f 79, 98, 137;
  Herr(Frau) Doktor m/f 145
doctor's office Arztpraxis f 137
dog Hund m 155

doll Puppe f 128
dollar Dollar m 18, 102, 130
door Tür(e) f 28
double bed Doppelbett nt 23
double cabin Zweierkabine f 74
double room Doppelzimmer nt 19,
  23
down hinunter 15
downhill skiing Abfahrtslauf m 91
downstairs unten 69
downtown Innenstadt f 81
dozen Dutzend nt 120, 149
draught beer Bier vom Faß nt 56
drawing paper Zeichenpapier nt 104
drawing pin Reißzwecke f 104
dress Kleid nt 116
dress shop Modengeschäft nt 99
dressing gown Morgenrock m 116
drink Getränk nt 40, 59, 61, 62
drink, to trinken 35, 36
drinking water Trinkwasser nt 32
drip, to *(tap)* tropfen 28
drive, to fahren 21, 76
driving licence Führerschein m 20,
  79
drop *(liquid)* Tropfen m 109
drugstore Apotheke f 98, 108
dry trocken 30, 59, 110, 111
dry cleaner's chemische Reinigung f
  29, 98
dry shampoo Trockenshampoo nt 111
duck Ente f 48
dummy Schnuller m 111
during während 14, 150
duty *(customs)* Zoll m 17
duty-free shop Duty-free-Shop m 19
dye, to färben 30

E

each jede(r/s) 125, 143, 149
ear Ohr nt 138
earache Ohrenschmerzen m/pl 141
early früh 14, 31
earring Ohrring m 121
east Ost(en) m 77
Easter Ostern nt 152
East Germany DDR f 146
easy leicht 14
eat, to essen 36, 37, 144
eel Aal m 41, 43
egg Ei nt 38, 40, 64
eggplant Aubergine f 49
eight acht 147

eighteen achtzehn 147
eighth achte 148
eighty achtzig 147
elastic elastisch 109
elastic bandage elastische Binde f 109
Elastoplast Heftpflaster nt 109
electric(al) elektrisch 119
electrician Elektriker m 98
electricity (facilities) Stromanschluß m 32
electronic elektronisch 125, 128
elevator Fahrstuhl m 27, 100; Aufzug m 155
eleven elf 147
embarkation point Anlegeplatz m 74
embroidery Stickerei f 127
emerald Smaragd m 122
emergency Notfall m 156; (phone) Notruf m 155, 156
emergency exit Notausgang m 27, 99, 155
emery board Sandpapierfeile f 110
empty leer 13
enamel Email nt 122
end Ende m 69, 150
endive Chicorée f; (Am.) Endivie f 49
engaged (phone) besetzt 136
engagement ring Verlobungsring m 122
engine (car) Motor m 78
England England (nt) 146
English englisch 104, 126
English Englisch m 11, 16, 84, 137
English Engländer(in) m/f 93
enjoyable angenehm 31
enjoy oneself, to sich gut unterhalten 96
enlarge, to vergrößern 125
enough genug 14
enquiry Auskunft f 68
entrance Eingang m 67, 99; Zutritt m 155
entrance fee Eintritt m 82
envelope Briefumschlag m 27, 104
equipment Ausrüstung f 91, 106
eraser Radiergummi m 105
escalator Rolltreppe f 100
especially besonders 161
estimate (cost) Kostenvoranschlag m 131
Europe Europa (nt) 146
evening Abend m 9, 87, 95, 96, 151, 153

evening dress Abendgarderobe f 88; (woman) Abendkleid nt 116
everything alles 31
exchange, to umtauschen 103
exchange rate Wechselkurs m 18, 130
excursion Ausflug m 80
excuse me Entschuldigung 26, 78; Verzeihung 70, 153
exercise book Schreibheft nt 104
exhaust pipe Auspuff m 78
exhibition Ausstellung f 81
exit Ausgang m 67, 99, 155; (motorway) Ausfahrt f 79
expect, to erwarten 130
expenses Unkosten pl 131
expensive teuer 13, 19, 24, 101
exposure (photography) Aufnahme f 124
express per Expreß 132
expression Ausdruck m 9; Redewendung f 100
expressway Autobahn f 76
extension (phone) Nebenanschluß m 135
extension cord/lead Verlängerungsschnur f 119
extra zusätzlich 24
extract, to (tooth) ziehen 145
eye Auge nt 123, 138, 139
eye drops Augentropfen m/pl 109
eye liner Lidstift m 110
eye pencil Augenbrauenstift m 110
eye shadow Lidschatten m 110
eye specialist Augenarzt m 137

F
fabric Stoff m 113
face Gesicht nt 138
face-pack Gesichtsmaske f 30
face powder Gesichtspuder m 110
factory Fabrik f 81
fair Messe f 81
fall (autumn) Herbst m 149
family Familie f 93, 144
fan Ventilator m 28
fan belt Keilriemen m 75
far weit 14, 21, 100
fare Fahrpreis m 21, 68, 73
farm Bauernhof m 85
fat Fett m 37
father Vater m 93
faucet Wasserhahn m 28
February Februar m 150

fee *(doctor)* Honorar nt 144
feeding bottle Saugflasche f 111
feel, to *(physical state)* sich fühlen 140, 142
felt Filz m 114
felt-tip pen Filzstift m 105
fennel Fenchel m 50
ferry Fähre f 74
fever Fieber nt 140
few wenige 14; *(a)* einige 14
field Feld nt 85
fifteen fünfzehn 147
fifth fünfte 148
fifty fünfzig 147
fig Feige f 53
file *(tool)* Feile f 110
fill in, to ausfüllen 26, 144
filling *(tooth)* Plombe f 145
filling station Tankstelle f 75
film Film m 86, 124, 125
film winder Filmtransport m 125
filter Filter m 125, 126
filter-tipped mit Filter 126
find, to finden 10, 11, 84, 100
fine *(OK)* gut 24
fine arts bildende Künste f/pl 83
fine grain *(film)* Feinkorn 124
finger Finger m 138
fire Feuer nt 156
first erste 68, 72, 148
first-aid kit Verbandkasten m 106
first class erste Klasse f 69
first name Vorname m 25
fish Fisch m 43
fish, to angeln 90
fishing permit Angelschein m 90
fishing tackle Angelzeug nt 106
fishmonger's Fischhandlung f 98
fit, to passen 115
fitting room Umkleidekabine f 115
five fünf 147
fix, to flicken 75, 145
fizzy *(mineral water)* mit Kohlensäure 61
flannel Flanell m 114
flash *(photography)* Blitzlicht nt 125
flash attachment Blitzgerät nt 125
flashlight Taschenlampe f 106
flat flach 118
flat *(apartment)* Wohnung f 22
flat tyre Reifenpanne f 75; Platter m 78
flea market Flohmarkt m 81
flight Flug m 65

flight number Flugnummer f 65
floor Etage f 27; Stock m 154
florist's Blumengeschäft nt 98
flounder Flunder f 44
flour Mehl nt 37
flower Blume f 85
flu Grippe f 142
fluid Flüssigkeit f 75
fog Nebel m 94
folding chair Klappstuhl m 106
folding table Klapptisch m 107
folk music Volksmusik f 128
food Essen nt 37, 62; Nahrung f 111
food box Proviantbehälter m 106
food poisoning Lebensmittelvergiftung f 142
foot Fuß m 138
football Fußball m 89
foot cream Fußcreme f 110
footpath Fußweg m 85
foot powder Fußpuder m 110
for für 14; während 143
forbid, to verbieten 155
forest Wald m 85
fork Gabel f 36, 62, 107
form *(document)* Formular nt 133; Schein m 25, 26
fortnight zwei Wochen f/pl 151
fortress Festung f 81
forty vierzig 147
forwarding address Nachsendeadresse f 31
fountain Brunnen m, Springbrunnen m 81
fountain pen Füllfederhalter m 105
four vier 147
fourteen vierzehn 147
fourth vierte 148
fowl Geflügel nt 48
frame *(glasses)* Gestell nt 123
France Frankreich *(nt)* 146
free frei 13, 70, 82, 95, 155
french fries Pommes frites f/pl 49
fresh frisch 53, 62
Friday Freitag m 150
fried gebraten 44, 47
fried egg Spiegelei nt 38
friend Freund(in) m/f 93, 95
fringe Ponyfransen f/pl 30
frock Kleid nt 116
frog Frosch m 41
from von 14
front vorne, Vorder- 75
frost Frost m 94

fruit Obst *nt* 37, 53
fruit cocktail Obstsalat *m* 53, 54
fruit juice Fruchtsaft *m* 37, 61
frying-pan Bratpfanne *f* 106
full voll 13; belegt 155
full board Vollpension *f* 24
full insurance Vollkaskoversicherung *f* 20
fur coat Pelzmantel *m* 116
furniture Möbel *nt/pl* 83
furrier's Pelzgeschäft *nt* 98

G

gallery Galerie *f* 81
game Spiel *nt* 128; *(food)* Wild *nt* 40
garage *(parking)* Garage *f* 26; *(repairs)* Reparaturwerkstatt *f* 78
garden Garten *m* 85
gardens Grünanlage *f* 81
garlic Knoblauch *m* 51
gas Gas *nt* 156
gasoline Benzin *nt* 75, 78
gastritis Magenschleimhautentzündung *f* 142
gauze Verbandmull *m* 109
gem Edelstein *m* 121
general allgemein 26, 100
general delivery postlagernd 133
general practitioner praktischer Arzt *m* 137
gentleman Herr *m* 155
genuine echt 118
geology Geologie *f* 83
German deutsch 114
German Deutsch *nt* 11, 95
Germany Deutschland *(nt)* 146
get, to *(find)* finden 19, 21; *(obtain)* bekommen 10, 32, 90, 108, 134; *(taxi)* bestellen 31; *(fetch)* holen 137, 156
get back, to zurück sein 80
get off, to aussteigen 73
get to, to kommen nach/zu 19, 100; ankommen in 70
get up, to aufstehen 144
gherkin Essiggurke *f* 50, 64
gift *(present)* Geschenk *nt* 17
ginger Ingwer *m* 51
girdle Hüfthalter *m* 116
girl Mädchen *nt* 112, 128
girlfriend Freundin *f* 93, 95
give, to geben 12, 13, 123, 126
give way *(traffic)* Vorfahrt gewähren 79

glad *(to know you)* sehr erfreut 92
gland Drüse *f* 138
glass Glas *nt* 36, 56, 59, 60, 62, 143
glasses Brille *f* 123
glassware Glaswaren *f/pl* 127
gloomy düster 84
glove Handschuh *m* 116
glue Leim *m* 105
go, to gehen 96, 163
go away, to weggehen 156
go out, to ausgehen 96
gold Gold *nt* 121, 122
golden golden 113
gold-plated vergoldet 122
golf Golf *nt* 89
golf course Golfplatz *m* 89
good gut 13, 101
good-bye auf Wiedersehen 9
Good Friday Karfreitag *m* 152
goods Waren *f/pl* 16
goose Gans *f* 48
gooseberry Stachelbeere *f* 53
gram Gramm *nt* 120
grammar book Grammatik *f* 105
grape (Wein)traube *f* 53, 64
grape juice Traubensaft *m* 61
grapefruit Grapefruit *f*, Pampelmuse *f* 53
grapefruit juice Grapefruitsaft *m* 38
gravy Soße *f* 48
gray grau 113
graze Abschürfung *f* 139
greasy fettig 30, 110, 111
great *(excellent)* prima 95
Great Britain Großbritannien *(nt)* 146
Greece Griechenland *(nt)* 146
green grün 113
green bean grüne Bohne *f* 49
greengrocer's Gemüsehandlung *f* 98
green salad grüner Salat *m* 50
greeting Begrüßung *f* 9; Gruß *m* 151
grey grau 113
grilled gegrillt 44, 47; vom Rost 40
grocery Lebensmittelgeschäft *nt* 98, 120
groundsheet Zeltboden *m* 106
group Gruppe *f* 82
guide Fremdenführer(in) *m/f* 80
guidebook (Reise)führer *m* 82, 104, 105
gum *(teeth)* Zahnfleisch *nt* 145
gynaecologist Frauenarzt *m* 137

H

habit Gewohnheit f 34
haddock Schellfisch m 44
hair Haar nt 30, 111
hairbrush Haarbürste f 111
haircut Haarschnitt m 30
hairdresser's Friseur m 27, 30, 99
hair dryer Haartrockner m 119
hair dye Haarfärbemittel nt 111
hairgrip Haarklemme f 111
hair lotion Haarwasser nt 111
half Hälfte f 148
half a dozen halbes Dutzend nt 120
half an hour halbe Stunde f 153
half board Halbpension f 24
half price (ticket) zum halben Preis 69
halibut Heilbutt m 44
hall (large room) Halle f 81, 88
ham Schinken m 38, 41, 46, 64
hammer Hammer m 106
hand Hand f 138
handbag Handtasche f 116
hand cream Handcreme f 110
handicrafts Kunsthandwerk nt 83
handkerchief Taschentuch nt 116
handmade Handarbeit f 113
hanger Kleiderbügel m 27
hangover Kater m 108
happy glücklich, froh 151, 152
harbour Hafen m 74, 81
hard hart 52, 123
hard-boiled (egg) hartgekocht 38
hardware shop Eisenwarenhandlung f 98
hare Hase m 48
hat Hut m 116, 127
have, to haben 162
hay fever Heufieber nt 108
hazelnut Haselnuß f 53
he er 162
head Kopf m 138, 139
headache Kopfschmerzen m/pl 141
headphones Kopfhörer m 119
head waiter Oberkellner m 62
health food shop Reformhaus nt 98
health insurance Krankenkasse f 144
health insurance form Kranken-
kassenformular nt 144
heart Herz nt 138
heart attack Herzanfall m 141
heat, to heizen 90
heating Heizung f 28
heavy schwer 13, 101
heel Absatz m 118

helicopter Hubschrauber m 74
hello! (phone) Hallo! 135
help Hilfe f 156
help, to helfen 12, 21, 71, 100,
134; (oneself) sich bedienen 120
her ihr 161
herb Kraut nt 51
herb tea Kräutertee m 60
here hier 15
herring Hering m 41, 44
high hoch 85, 141
high season Hauptsaison f 149
high-speed (photo) hochempfindlich
124
high tide Flut f 90
hike, to wandern 74
hill Hügel m 85
hire Verleih m 74
hire, to mieten 19, 20, 74, 89, 91;
vermieten 155
his sein 161
history Geschichte f 83
hitchhike, to trampen 74
hole Loch nt 29
holiday Feiertag m 151
holidays Ferien pl, Urlaub m 151
home address Wohnort m 25; Wohn-
adresse f 31
home-made hausgemacht 40
homeopathic homöopathisch 109
honey Honig m 38
horse racing Pferderennen nt 89
horseback riding Reiten nt 89
horseradish Meerrettich m 51
hospital Krankenhaus nt 142, 144
hot heiß 14, 24, 38, 61, 155
hotel Hotel nt 19, 21, 22, 80
hotel guide Hotelverzeichnis nt 19,
22
hotel reservation Hotelreservierung f
20
hot water warmes Wasser nt 23, 28
hot-water bottle Wärmflasche f 27
hour Stunde f 153
house Haus nt 83, 85
how wie 10
how far wie weit 10, 76, 85
how long wie lange 10, 24
how many wie viele 10
how much wieviel 10, 24
hundred (ein)hundert 147
hungry hungrig 35; (to be) Hunger
haben 12, 35
hurry (to be in a) es eilig haben 21, 31

hurt, to weh tun 139; schmerzen 145; *(oneself)* sich verletzen 139
husband Mann *m* 93
hydrofoil Tragflächenboot *nt* 74

I

I ich 162
ice Eis *nt* 94
ice-cream Eis *nt* 54, 64
ice cube Eiswürfel *m* 27
iced tea Eistee *m* 61
ice pack Kühlbeutel *m* 106
ill krank 140, 156
illness Krankheit *f* 140
important wichtig 12
imported importiert 113
impressive eindrucksvoll 84
in in 14
included inbegriffen 20, 24, 31, 32, 40, 63, 80
indigestion Magenverstimmung *f* 141
inexpensive preiswert 35; billig 124
infect, to infizieren 140
infection Infektion *f* 145
inflammation Entzündung *f* 142
inflation Inflation *f* 131
inflation rate Inflationsrate *f* 131
influenza Grippe *f* 142
information Auskunft *f* 67, 155
injection Spritze *f* 142, 144, 145
injure, to verletzen 139
injured verletzt 79, 139
injury Verletzung *f* 139
ink Tinte *f* 105
inn Gasthaus *nt*, Gasthof *m* 22, 33
inquiry Auskunft *f* 68
inside drinnen 15
instead statt 37
insurance Versicherung *f* 20, 79
insurance company Versicherungsgesellschaft *f* 79
interest *(on investment)* Zinsen *m/pl* 131
interested, to be sich interessieren 83, 96
interesting interessant 84
international international 133, 134
interpreter Dolmetscher *m* 131
intersection Kreuzung *f* 77
introduce, to vorstellen 92

introduction *(social)* Vorstellung *f* 92; *(letter)* Empfehlungsbrief *m* 130
investment Kapitalanlage *f* 131
invitation Einladung *f* 94
invite, to einladen 94
invoice Rechnung *f* 131
iodine Jod *nt* 109
Ireland Irland *(nt)* 146
Irish Ire (Irin) *m/f* 93
iron *(laundry)* Bügeleisen *nt* 119
iron, to bügeln 29
ironmonger's Eisenwarenhandlung *f* 99
Italy Italien *(nt)* 146
its sein 161
ivory Elfenbein *nt* 122

J

jacket Jackett *nt*, Jacke *f* 116
jade Jade *nt* 122
jam Marmelade *f* 38, 120
jam, to klemmen 28, 125
January Januar *m* 150
Japan Japan *(nt)* 146
jar Glas *nt* 120
jaundice Gelbsucht *f* 142
jaw Kiefer *m* 138
jeans Jeans *pl* 116
jersey Strickjacke *f* 116
jewel Edelstein *m* 121
jeweller's Juwelier *m* 99, 121
joint Gelenk *nt* 138
journey Fahrt *f* 72
juice Saft *m* 38, 61
July Juli *m* 150
jumper *(sweater)* Pullover *m* 116
June Juni *m* 150
juniper Wacholder *m* 51
just *(only)* nur 16, 37, 100

K

kerosene Petroleum *nt* 106
ketchup Tomatenketchup *nt* 51
key Schlüssel *m* 26
kidney Niere *f* 138
kilogram Kilo(gramm) *nt* 120
kilometre Kilometer *m* 20
kind nett, freundlich 95
king-size extra lang 126
knee Knie *nt* 138
knife Messer *nt* 36, 61, 107
knock, to klopfen 155
know, to wissen 16, 26; kennen 96, 114

L

label Etikett nt 105
lace Spitze f 114
lady Dame f 155
lake See m 23, 81, 85, 90
lamb Lamm(fleisch) nt 45
lamp Lampe f 29, 106, 119
landmark Wahrzeichen nt 85
landscape Landschaft f 92
lane (in town) Gasse f 154
lantern Laterne f 106
large groß 20, 101, 118, 130
last letzte 13, 68, 72, 149, 150, 151
last name (Familien)name m 25
late spät 13
later später 135
laugh, to lachen 95
launderette Waschsalon m 99
laundry (place) Wäscherei f 29, 99; (clothes) Wäsche f 29
laundry service Wäschedienst m 23
laxative Abführmittel nt 109
lead (theatre) Hauptrolle f 86
lead-free bleifrei 75
leap year Schaltjahr nt 149
leather Leder nt 114, 118
leather goods Lederwaren f/pl 127
leather trousers Lederhose f 116
leave, to lassen 26, 96, 156; (go away) abreisen 31; abfahren 68, 74
leek Lauch m 50
left linke 13; links 21, 30, 63, 69, 77, 79
left-luggage office Gepäck-aufbewahrung f 67, 71
leg Bein nt 138
lemon Zitrone f 37, 38, 53, 54, 60
lemonade Limonade f 61
lens (glasses) Glas nt 123; (camera) Objektiv nt 125
lentil Linse f 43
less weniger 14
let, to (hire out) vermieten 155
letter Brief m 132
letter box Briefkasten m 132
letter of credit Kreditbrief m 130
lettuce Lattich m 50
library Bibliothek f 81, 99
licence (for driving) Führerschein m 20, 79
lie down, to sich hinlegen 142
life belt Rettungsring m 74
life boat Rettungsboot nt 74
lifeguard Rettungsdienst m 90

lift Fahrstuhl m 27, 100; Aufzug m 155
light leicht 13, 54, 59, 101; (colour) hell 101, 112, 113, 126
light Licht nt 28, 124; (cigarette) Feuer nt 95
lighter Feuerzeug nt 126
lighter fluid Benzin fürs Feuerzeug nt 126
lighter gas Gas fürs Feuerzeug nt 126
light meter Belichtungsmesser m 125
light music Unterhaltungsmusik f 128
lightning Blitz m 94
like, to (want) gerne haben 12, 23; mögen 20, 38; (take pleasure) gefallen 24, 92, 102, 112
line Linie f 73
linen (cloth) Leinen nt 114
lip Lippe f 138
lipsalve Lippenpomade f 110
lipstick Lippenstift m 110
liqueur Likör m 59, 60
liquid Flüssigkeit f 123
listen, to hören 127
litre Liter m 75, 120
little (a) ein wenig 14
live, to leben 83; (reside) wohnen 83
liver Leber f 46, 138
lobster Hummer m 41, 44
local hiesig 36, 60
local train Nahverkehrszug m 66, 69
long lang 26, 62, 76, 77, 78, 116
long-sighted weitsichtig 123
look, to sehen 123; sich umsehen 100
look for, to suchen 12
look out! Vorsicht! 156
loose (clothes) weit 116
lose, to verlieren 123, 156; (one's way) sich verirren 12, 156
loss Verlust m 131
lost and found office Fundbüro nt 67, 156
lost property office Fundbüro nt 67, 156
lot (a) eine Menge 14; viel 162
lotion Lotion f 110
loud (voice) laut 135
love, to lieben 163
lovely (wunder)schön 84; herrlich 94
low niedrig 141
lower untere 69, 70

low season Vorsaison *f*, Nachsaison *f* 149
low tide Ebbe *f* 90
luck Glück *nt* 152
luggage Gepäck *nt* 18, 26, 31, 71
luggage locker Schließfach *nt* 18, 67, 71
luggage trolley Kofferkuli *m* 18, 71
lump *(bump)* Beule *f* 139
lunch Mittagessen *nt* 34, 80, 94
lung Lunge *f* 138
Luxembourg Luxemburg *(nt)* 146

M

machine Maschine *f* 114
mackerel Makrele *f* 41, 44
magazine Illustrierte *f* 105
magnificent großartig 84
maid Zimmermädchen *nt* 26
mail, to aufgeben 28
mail Post *f* 28, 133
mailbox Briefkasten *m* 132
main Haupt- 40, 67, 80
make, to machen 131
make a mistake, to *(bill)* sich verrechnen 31, 63, 102
make up, to machen 28, 71, 108
man Herr *m* 115, 155; Mann *m* 159
manager Direktor *m* 26
manicure Maniküre *f* 30
many viele 14
map Karte *f* 76, 105; Plan *m* 105
March März *m* 150
marinated mariniert 44
marjoram Majoran *m* 51
market Markt *m* 81, 99
marmalade Apfelsinenmarmelade *f* 38
married verheiratet 93
mass *(church)* Messe *f* 84
match Streichholz *nt* 106, 126; *(sport)* Wettkampf *m* 89
match, to *(colour)* passen 112
material *(fabric)* Stoff *m* 113
matinée Nachmittagsvorstellung *f* 87
mattress Matratze *f* 106
May Mai *m* 150
may *(can)* können 11, 12, 163
meadow Wiese *f* 85
meal Mahlzeit *f* 24, 143; Essen *nt* 34, 63
mean, to bedeuten 10, 25
means Mittel *nt* 74
measles Masern *f/pl* 142

measure, to Maß nehmen 114
meat Fleisch *nt* 40, 45, 46, 62
mechanic Mechaniker *m* 78
medical ärztlich 144
medical certificate ärztliches Zeugnis *nt* 144
medicine Medizin *f* 83; *(drug)* Medikament *nt* 143
medium *(meat)* mittel 47
medium-sized mittlere 20
meet, to treffen 96
melon Melone *f* 53
memorial Denkmal *nt* 81
mend, to flicken 75; *(clothes)* ausbessern 29
menu Gedeck *nt* 36, 39; Menü *nt* 39; *(printed)* Speisekarte *f* 36, 39, 40
merry fröhlich 151
message Nachricht *f* 28, 136
metre Meter *m* 112
middle Mitte *f* 69, 87, 150
midnight Mitternacht *f* 153
mild mild 52, 126
mileage Kilometergeld *nt* 20
milk Milch *f* 38, 61, 64
milkshake Milchmixgetränk *nt* 61
million Million *f* 148
mineral water Mineralwasser *nt* 61
minister *(religion)* Pfarrer *m* 84
mint Pfefferminz(e) *f* 51
minute Minute *f* 21, 153
mirror Spiegel *m* 115, 123
miscellaneous verschieden 127
Miss Fräulein *nt* 9
miss, to fehlen 18, 29, 62
mistake Irrtum *m* 62
mixed gemischt 50
modified American plan Halbpension *f* 24
moment Augenblick *m* 11, 136
monastery Kloster *nt* 81
Monday Montag *m* 150
money Geld *nt* 129, 130
money order Postanweisung *f* 133
month Monat *m* 16, 150
monument Denkmal *nt* 81
moon Mond *m* 94
moped Moped *nt* 74
more mehr 14
morning Morgen *m* 151, 153
mortgage Hypothek *f* 131
mosque Moschee *f* 84
mother Mutter *f* 93
motorbike Motorrad *nt* 74

DICTIONARY

motorboat Motorboot nt 91
motorway Autobahn f 76
mountain Berg m 23, 85
mountaineering Bergsteigen nt 89
moustache Schnurrbart m 31
mouth Mund m 138
mouthwash Mundwasser nt 109
move, to bewegen 139
movie Film m 86
movie camera Filmkamera f 124
movies Kino nt 86, 96
Mr. Herr m 9, 131
Mrs. Frau f 9, 131
much viel 14
mug Becher m 107; (beer) Maß f 56
muscle Muskel m 138
museum Museum nt 81
mushroom Pilz m 41, 50
music Musik f 83, 128
musical Musical nt 86
music box Spieldose f 121, 127
mussel Muschel f 41, 44
must, to müssen 23, 31, 95, 101
mustard Senf m 37, 51, 64
mutton Hammelfleisch nt 45
my mein 161
myself selbst 120

N

nail (human) Nagel m 110
nail brush Nagelbürste f 110
nail clippers Nagelzange f 110
nail file Nagelfeile f 110
nail polish Nagellack m 110
nail polish remover Nagellack-
    entferner m 110
nail scissors Nagelschere f 110
name Name m 23, 25, 79, 136
napkin Serviette f 36, 105, 106
nappy Windel f 111
narrow eng 118
nationality Nationalität f 25
natural history Naturkunde f 83
near nah 13
nearby in der Nähe 77, 84
nearest nächste 78, 98
neat (drink) pur 59
necessary nötig 88
neck Hals m 138; (nape) Nacken m
    30
necklace Halskette f 121
need, to brauchen 29, 118, 163
needle Nadel f 27
negative Negativ nt 125

nephew Neffe m 93
nerve Nerv m 138
nervous system Nervensystem nt
    138
Netherlands Niederlande pl 146
never nie 15
new neu 13
newsagent's Zeitungshändler m 99
newspaper Zeitung f 104, 105
newsstand Zeitungsstand m 19, 67,
    99, 104
New Year Neujahr nt 151
New Zealand Neuseeland (nt) 146
next nächste 13, 65, 68, 73, 76,
    149, 150
next time nächstes Mal 95
next to neben 14
nice (beautiful) schön 94, 152
niece Nichte f 93
night Nacht f 9, 24, 151
nightclub Nachtlokal nt 88
night cream Nachtcreme f 110
nightdress Nachthemd nt 116
nine neun 147
nineteen neunzehn 147
ninety neunzig 147
ninth neunte 148
no nein 9
noisy laut 24
nonalcoholic alkoholfrei 61
none kein 15
nonsmoker Nichtraucher m 70
non-smoking Nichtraucher- 36
noodle Nudel f 49
noon Mittag m 153
normal normal 30, 110
north Nord(en) m 77
North America Nordamerika (nt) 146
Norway Norwegen (nt) 146
nose Nase f 138
nosebleed Nasenbluten nt 141
nose drops Nasentropfen m/pl 109
not nicht 15, 163
note (banknote) Schein m 130
notebook Notizheft nt 105
note paper Briefpapier nt 105
nothing nichts 15, 17
notice (sign) Tafel f, Hinweis m 155
notify, to benachrichtigen 144
November November m 150
now jetzt 15
number Nummer f 25, 65, 134,
    136; Zahl f 124, 147
nurse Krankenschwester f 144

Wörterverzeichnis

O

occupation *(job)* Beruf m 93
occupied besetzt 13, 70, 155
October Oktober m 150
office Büro nt 22, 80
oil Öl nt 51, 75, 111
oily *(greasy)* fettig 30, 111
old alt 13
old town Altstadt f 82
omelet Omelett nt 64
on an, auf 14
once einmal 148
one eins 147
one-way *(ticket)* einfach 69
on foot zu Fuß 76
onion Zwiebel f 50
only nur 15
on time pünktlich 68
onyx Onyx m 122
open offen 13, 82
open, to öffnen 10, 17, 82, 108, 132; *(account)* eröffnen 130
opening hours Öffnungszeiten f/pl 82
opera Oper f 88
opera house Opernhaus nt 82, 88
operation Operation f 144
operator Vermittlung f 134
operetta Operette f 88
opposite gegenüber 77
optician Optiker m 99, 123
or oder 15
orange 113
orange Orange f 53, 64; Apfelsine f 53
orange juice Orangensaft m 38, 61
orangeade Orangeade f 61
orchestra Orchester nt 88; *(seats)* Parkett nt 87
orchestral music Orchestermusik f 128
order *(goods, meal)* Bestellung f 40, 102
order, to *(goods, meal)* bestellen 36, 62, 102, 103
ornithology Vogelkunde f 83
other andere 59
our unser 161
out of order außer Betrieb 155
out of stock nicht vorrätig 103
outlet *(electric)* Steckdose f 27
outside draußen 15, 36
oval oval 101
over über 14

over there dort drüben 69
overalls Overall m 116
overdone zu stark gebraten 62
overheat, to *(engine)* heißlaufen 78
overnight *(stay)* eine Nacht 26
overwhelming überwältigend 84
owe, to schulden 144
oyster Auster f 41, 43

P

pacifier Schnuller m 111
packet Packung f 120; Schachtel f 126
page *(hotel)* Page m 26
pail Eimer m 106, 128
pain Schmerz m 140, 141, 144
painkiller Schmerzmittel nt 109
paint Farbe f 155
paint, to malen 83
paintbox Malkasten m 105
painter Maler m 83
painting Malerei f 83
pair Paar nt 116, 118, 149
pajamas Schlafanzug m 117
palace Palast m, Schloß nt 81
palpitation Herzklopfen nt 141
panties Schlüpfer m 116
pants *(trousers)* Hose f 116
panty girdle Strumpfhalterhöschen nt 116
panty hose Strumpfhose f 116
paper Papier nt 105
paperback Taschenbuch nt 105
paperclip Büroklammer f 105
paper napkin Papierserviette f 105
paraffin *(fuel)* Petroleum nt 106
parcel Paket nt 133
pardon? Wie bitte? 10
parents Eltern pl 93
park Park m 82
park, to parken 26, 77
parking Parken nt 77, 79
parking disc Parkscheibe f 77
parking meter Parkuhr f 77
parliament Parlament nt 82
parsley Petersilie f 51
part Teil m 138
parting *(part)* Scheitel m 30
partridge Rebhuhn nt 48
party *(social gathering)* Party f 95
pass *(rail, bus)* Mehrfahrkarte f 72
pass *(mountain)* Paß m 85
passport Paß m 16, 17, 25, 26
passport photo Paßbild nt 124

pass through, to auf der Durchreise sein 16
pasta Teigwaren f/pl 49
paste (glue) Klebstoff m 105
pastry Gebäck nt 54
pastry shop Konditorei f 99
patch, to (clothes) flicken 29
path Weg m 85
patient Patient(in) m/f 144
pay, to (be)zahlen 31, 63, 68, 102, 136
payment Zahlung f 131
pea Erbse f 50
peach Pfirsich m 53
peak Bergspitze f 85
peanut Erdnuß f 53
pear Birne f 53
pearl Perle f 122
pedestrian Fußgänger m 79
peg (tent) Hering m 107
pen Feder f 105
pencil Bleistift m 105
pencil sharpener Bleistiftspitzer m 105
pendant Anhänger m 121
penicillin Penizillin nt 143
penknife Taschenmesser nt 106
pensioner Rentner(in) m/f 82
people Leute pl 93
pepper Pfeffer m 37, 51, 64
per cent Prozent nt 148
percentage Prozentsatz m 131
perch Barsch m 43
per day pro Tag 20, 32, 89
performance (session) Vorstellung f 87
perfume Parfüm nt 110
perhaps vielleicht 15
per hour pro Stunde 77, 89
period (monthly) Periode f 141
period pains Menstruations-beschwerden f/pl 141
permanent wave Dauerwelle f 30
per night pro Nacht 24
per person pro Person 32
person Person f 32, 36
personal persönlich 17
personal call Gespräch mit Vor-anmeldung nt 134
per week pro Woche 20, 24
petrol Benzin nt 75, 78
pewter Zinn nt 122
pheasant Fasan m 48
phone Telefon nt 28, 78, 79, 134

phone, to telefonieren 134
phone booth Telefonzelle f 134
phone call (Telefon)gespräch nt 135, 136; Anruf m 136
phone number Telefonnummer f 96, 134, 135
photo Foto nt 124, 125
photocopy Fotokopie f 131
photograph, to fotografieren 82
photographer Fotograf m 99
photography Fotografie f 124
phrase Ausdruck m 11
pick up, to (person) abholen 80, 96
picnic Picknick nt 63
picture Bild nt 82; (photo) Foto nt 82
piece Stück nt 29, 52, 64, 120
pigeon Taube f 48
pill Pille f 141; Tablette f 143
pillow Kopfkissen nt 27
pin Nadel f 110; (brooch) Ansteck-nadel f 121
pineapple Ananas f 53
pink rosa 113
pipe Pfeife f 126, 127
pipe cleaner Pfeifenreiniger m 126
pipe tobacco Pfeifentabak m 126
place Ort m 25, 76
place of birth Geburtsort m 25
plaice Scholle f 44
plane Flugzeug nt 65, 159
plaster (cast) Gipsverband m 140
plastic Plastik nt 107
plastic bag Plastikbeutel m 106
plate Teller m 36, 62, 107
platform (station) Bahnsteig m 67, 68, 69, 70
platinum Platin nt 122
play (theatre) Stück nt 86
play, to spielen 86, 88, 89, 93
playground Spielplatz m 32
playing card Spielkarte f 105
please bitte 9
plimsolls Turnschuhe m/pl 118
plug (electric) Stecker m 29, 119
plum Pflaume f 53
pneumonia Lungenentzündung f 142
pocket Tasche f 117
pocket calculator Taschenrechner m 105
pocket dictionary Taschenwörter-buch nt 104
pocket watch Taschenuhr f 121
point, to (show) zeigen 11
poison Gift nt 109

poisoning Vergiftung *f* 142
Poland Polen *(nt)* 146
police Polizei *f* 78, 156
police station Polizeiwache *f* 99, 156
pond Teich *m* 85
pop music Popmusik *f* 128
poplin Popeline *m* 114
porcelain Porzellan *nt* 127
pork Schweinefleisch *nt* 45
port Hafen *m* 74; *(wine)* Portwein *m* 59
portable tragbar, Koffer- 119
porter Gepäckträger *m* 18, 71; *(hotel)* Hausdiener *m* 26
portion Portion *f* 37, 54, 62
possible möglich 137
post *(letters)* Post *f* 28, 133
post, to aufgeben 28
postage Porto *nt* 132
postage stamp Briefmarke *f* 28, 126, 132
postcard Postkarte *f* 105, 126, 132
poste restante postlagernd 133
post office Postamt *nt* 99, 132
potato Kartoffel *f* 48, 49
pottery Töpferei *f* 83
poultry Geflügel *nt* 48
pound *(money)* Pfund *nt* 18, 102, 130; *(weight)* Pfund *nt* 120
powder Puder *m* 110
powder compact Puderdose *f* 122
prawn Garnele *f* 44
pregnant schwanger 141
premium *(gasoline)* Super *nt* 75
prescribe, to verschreiben 143
prescription Rezept *nt* 108, 143
present *(gift)* Geschenk *nt* 17, 121
press, to *(iron)* dampfbügeln 29
press stud Druckknopf *m* 117
pressure Druck *m* 75
pretty hübsch 84
price Preis *m* 40, 69
priest Priester *m* 84
print *(photo)* Abzug *m* 125
private privat 91, 155
private toilet eigene Toilette *f* 23
processing *(photo)* Entwickeln *nt* 124
profession Beruf *m* 25
profit Gewinn *m* 131
programme Programm *nt* 87
prohibit, to verbieten 155
pronunciation Aussprache *f* 6

Protestant protestantisch, evangelisch 84
provide, to besorgen 131
prune Backpflaume *f* 53
public holiday Feiertag *m* 152
pull, to ziehen 155
pullover Pullover *m* 117
pumpkin Kürbis *m* 50
puncture Reifenpanne *f* 75
purchase Kauf *m* 131
pure rein 114
purple violett 113
push, to *(button)* drücken 155
put, to stellen 24
put through, to verbinden 28
pyjamas Schlafanzug *m* 117

Q

quality Qualität *f* 103, 113
quantity Menge *f* 14, 103
quarter Viertel *nt* 148
quarter of an hour Viertelstunde *f* 153
quartz Quarz *m* 122
question Frage *f* 10
quick schnell 13, 156
quickly schnell 79, 137
quiet ruhig 23, 25

R

rabbi Rabbiner *m* 84
rabbit Kaninchen *nt* 48
race course/track (Pferde)rennbahn *f* 90
racket *(sport)* Schläger *m* 89
radiator *(car)* Kühler *m* 78
radio *(set)* Radio *nt* 23, 28, 119
radish Radieschen *nt* 50
railway station Bahnhof *m* 19, 21, 67
rain Regen *m* 94
rain, to regnen 94
rain boot Gummistiefel *m* 118
raincoat Regenmantel *m* 117
raisin Rosine *f* 53
rare *(meat)* blutig 47
rash Ausschlag *m* 139
raspberry Himbeere *f* 53
rate Tarif *m* 20; *(exchange)* Kurs *m* 18, 130; *(inflation)* Rate *f* 131
rayon Kunstseide *f* 114
razor Rasierapparat *m* 110
razor blade Rasierklinge *f* 110
ready fertig 29, 118, 123, 125, 145
real echt 121
rear hinten, Hinter- 75

DICTIONARY

Wörterverzeichnis

same selbe 40; gleiche 118
sand Sand m 90
sandal Sandale f 118
sandwich Sandwich nt 64; (open) belegtes Brot 64
sanitary towel/napkin Damenbinde f 109
sapphire Saphir m 122
sardine Sardine f 41
satin Satin m 114
Saturday Samstag m, Sonnabend m 150
sauce Soße f 48
saucepan Kochtopf m 107
saucer Untertasse f 107
sauerkraut Sauerkraut nt 50
sausage Wurst f 47, 64
scallop Jakobsmuschel f 44
scarf Halstuch nt 117
scenic route landschaftlich schöne Straße f 85
school Schule f 79
scissors Schere f 107, 110
scooter Motorroller m 74
Scotland Schottland (nt) 146
scrambled egg Rührei nt 38
screwdriver Schraubenzieher m 107
sculptor Bildhauer m 83
sculpture Bildhauerei f 83
sea Meer nt 85, 90
sea bass Seebarsch m 44
seafood Meeresfrüchte f/pl 43
season Jahreszeit f 149; Saison f 149
seasoning Würze f 37, 51
seat Platz m 69, 70, 87
seat belt Sicherheitsgurt m 75
second zweite 148
second Sekunde f 153
second class zweite Klasse f 69
second hand Sekundenzeiger m 122
second-hand (books) antiquarisch 104
second-hand shop Gebrauchtwaren-laden m 99
secretary Sekretär(in) m/f 27, 131
see, to sehen 163; (check) nach-schauen
sell, to verkaufen 100
send, to schicken 78, 132; senden 102, 103, 132
send up, to hinaufschicken 26
sentence Satz m 11
separately getrennt 63
September September m 150

service Bedienung f 24, 40, 63, 100; (religion) Gottesdienst m 84
serviette Serviette f 36
set, to (hair) legen 30
set menu Tagesgedeck m 36, 40
setting lotion Haarfestiger m 30, 111
seven sieben 147
seventeen siebzehn 147
seventh siebte 148
seventy siebzig 147
sew, to nähen 29
shampoo Haarwaschmittel nt 30, 111
shape Form f 103
shape, to (hair) legen 30
share (finance) Aktie f 131
sharp scharf 52; (pain) stechend 140
shave, to rasieren 30
shaver Rasierapparat m 27, 119
shaving brush Rasierpinsel m 111
shaving cream Rasiercreme f 111
she sie 162
shelf Regal nt 120
ship Schiff nt 74
shirt Hemd nt 117
shoe Schuh m 118
shoelace Schnürsenkel m 118
shoemaker's Schuhmacher m 99
shoe polish Schuhcreme f 118
shoe shop Schuhgeschäft nt 99
shop Geschäft nt, Laden m 98
shopping Einkaufen m 98
shopping area Geschäftsviertel nt 81, 100
shopping centre Einkaufszentrum nt 99
shop window Schaufenster nt 100, 112, 124
short kurz 30, 116, 117
shorts Shorts pl 117
short-sighted kurzsichtig 123
shoulder Schulter f 138
shovel Schaufel f 128
show (theatre) Vorstellung f 86, 87
show, to zeigen 11, 12, 76, 100, 101, 103, 119, 124
shower Dusche f 23, 32
shrimp Garnele f 44
shrink, to einlaufen 114
shut geschlossen 13
shutter (window) Fensterladen m 29; (camera) Verschluß m 125
sick (ill) krank 140, 156
sickness (illness) Krankheit f 140
side Seite f 30

sideboards/burns Koteletten *f/pl* 31
sightseeing Besichtigung *f* 80
sightseeing tour Stadtrundfahrt *f* 80
sign *(notice)* Schild *nt*, Aufschrift *f* 155
sign, to unterschreiben 26, 130
signature Unterschrift *f* 25
signet ring Siegelring *m* 122
silk Seide *f* 114
silver silbern 113
silver Silber *nt* 121, 122
silver plated versilbert 122
silverware Tafelsilber *nt* 122
simple einfach 124
since seit 14, 150
sing, to singen 88
single *(not married)* ledig 93; *(ticket)* einfach 69
single cabin Einzelkabine *f* 74
single room Einzelzimmer *nt* 19, 23
sinister unheimlich 84
sister Schwester *f* 93
six sechs 147
sixteen sechzehn 147
sixth sechste 148
sixty sechzig 147
size Format *nt* 124; *(clothes)* Größe *f* 114, 115; *(shoes)* Nummer *f* 118
skate Schlittschuh *m* 91
skating rink Eisbahn *f* 91
ski Ski *m* 91
ski, to skifahren 91
skiboot Skischuh *m* 91
skiing Skifahren *nt* 89, 91
ski lift Skilift *m* 91
skin Haut *f* 110, 138
skin-diving Tauchen *nt* 91
ski pole Skistock *m* 91
skirt Rock *m* 117
ski run Skipiste *f* 91
sky Himmel *m* 94
sleep, to schlafen 144
sleeping bag Schlafsack *m* 107
sleeping-car Schlafwagen *m* 66, 68, 69, 70
sleeping pill Schlaftablette *f* 109, 143
sleeve Ärmel *m* 117
slice Scheibe *f* 120
slide *(photo)* Dia *nt* 124
slip Unterrock *m* 117
slipper Hausschuh *m* 118
slow langsam 13
slow down, to langsam fahren 79
slowly langsam 11, 21, 135

small klein 13, 20, 24, 37, 62, 101, 118, 130
smoke, to rauchen 95
smoked geräuchert 44
smoker Raucher *m* 70
snack Imbiß *m* 63
snack bar Schnellimbiß *m* 34, 63, 67
snail Schnecke *f* 41
snap fastener Druckknopf *m* 117
sneakers Turnschuhe *m/pl* 118
snow Schnee *m* 94
snow, to schneien 94
soap Seife *f* 27, 111
soccer Fußball *m* 89
sock Socke *f* 117
socket *(outlet)* Steckdose *f* 27
soft weich 52, 123
soft-boiled *(egg)* weich(gekocht) 38
soft drink alkoholfreies Getränk *nt* 64
sold out ausverkauft 87
sole Sohle *f* 118; *(fish)* Seezunge *f* 44
soloist Solist *m* 88
some etwas, einige 14
someone jemand 95
something etwas 36, 54, 108, 112, 113, 125, 139
son Sohn *m* 93
song Lied *nt* 128
soon bald 15, 137
sore throat Halsschmerzen *m/pl* 141
sorry *(I'm)* Entschuldigung, Verzeihung 10; es tut mir leid 16
sort *(kind)* Sorte *f* 52, 120
soufflé Auflauf *m* 54
soup Suppe *f* 42
sour sauer 62
south Süd(en) *m* 77
South Africa Südafrika *(nt)* 146
South America Südamerika *(nt)* 146
souvenir Andenken *nt* 127
souvenir shop Andenkenladen *m* 99
Soviet Union Sowjetunion *f* 146
spade Schaufel *f* 128
spare tyre Ersatzreifen *m* 75
sparking plug Zündkerze *f* 75
sparkling *(wine)* Schaum- 59
spark plug Zündkerze *f* 75
speak, to sprechen 11, 135, 163
speaker *(loudspeaker)* Lautsprecher *m* 119
special Sonder- 20; Spezial- 37
special delivery per Expreß 132
specialist Spezialist(in) *m/f* 142
speciality Spezialität *f* 40, 60

specimen *(medical)* Probe f 142
spectacle case Brillenetui nt 123
spell, to buchstabieren 11
spend, to ausgeben 101
spice Gewürz nt 51
spinach Spinat m 50
spine Wirbelsäule f 138
spiny lobster Languste f 41, 44
sponge Schwamm m 111
spoon Löffel m 36, 62, 107
sport Sport m 89
sporting goods shop Sportgeschäft nt 99
sprain, to verstauchen 140
spring *(season)* Frühling m 149; *(water)* Quelle f 85
square viereckig 101
square Platz m 82
stadium Stadion nt 82
staff Personal nt 26
stain Fleck m 29
stainless steel rostfreier Stahl m 107, 122
stalls *(theatre)* Parkett nt 87
stamp *(postage)* Briefmarke f 28, 126, 132, 133
staple Heftklammer f 105
star Stern m 94
start, to beginnen 80, 87, 88; *(car)* anspringen 78
starter *(appetizer)* Vorspeise f 41
station *(railway)* Bahnhof m 19, 21, 67; *(underground, subway)* Station f 73
stationer's Schreibwarengeschäft nt 99
statue Statue f 82
stay Aufenthalt m 31
stay, to bleiben 16, 26; *(reside)* wohnen 93
steak Steak nt 46
steal, to stehlen 156
steamed gedämpft 44
stew Eintopfgericht nt 42
stewed gedämpft 47, 51
stew pot Schmortopf m 107
stiff neck steifer Nacken m 141
sting Stich m 139
sting, to stechen 139
stitch, to nähen 29, 118
stock *(supply)* Vorrat m 103
stock exchange Börse f 82
stocking Strumpf m 117
stomach Magen m 138

stomach ache Magenschmerzen m/pl 141
stools Stuhl(gang) m 142
stop *(bus)* Haltestelle f 72, 73
stop! Halt! 156
stop, to halten 21, 68, 70, 72
stop thief! Haltet den Dieb! 156
store *(shop)* Laden m, Geschäft nt 98
straight *(drink)* pur 59
straight ahead geradeaus 21, 77
strange seltsam 84
strawberry Erdbeere f 53
street Straße f 25, 82
streetcar Straßenbahn f 72
street map Stadtplan m 19, 105
string Bindfaden m, Schnur f 105
strong stark 126, 143
stuck *(to be)* klemmen 28
student Student(in) m/f 82, 93
study, to studieren 93
stuffed gefüllt 47
sturdy robust 101
subway *(railway)* U-Bahn f 73
suede Wildleder nt 114, 118
sugar Zucker m 37, 51, 64
suit *(man)* Anzug m 117; *(woman)* Kostüm nt 117
suitcase Koffer m 18
summer Sommer m 149
sun Sonne f 94
sunburn Sonnenbrand m 108
Sunday Sonntag m 150
sunglasses Sonnenbrille f 123
sunshade *(beach)* Sonnenschirm m 91
sun-tan cream Sonnencreme f 111
super *(petrol)* Super nt 75
superb prächtig 84
supermarket Supermarkt m 99
suppository Zäpfchen nt 109
surcharge Zuschlag m 68
surfboard Surfbrett nt 91
surgery *(consulting room)* Arztpraxis f 137
surname (Familien)name m 25
suspenders *(Am.)* Hosenträger m/pl 117
swallow, to schlucken 143
sweater Pullover m 117
sweatshirt Sweatshirt nt 117
Sweden Schweden (nt) 146
sweet süß 59, 62
sweet *(candy)* Bonbon nt 126
sweet corn Mais m 50

DICTIONARY

Wörterverzeichnis

sweetener Süßstoff m 37, 51
swell, to schwellen 139
swelling Schwellung f 139
swim, to schwimmen, baden 90
swimming pool Schwimmbad nt 32, 90; *(open-air)* Freibad nt 9; *(indoor)* Hallenbad nt 90
swimsuit Badeanzug m 117
Swiss schweizerisch, Schweizer
Swiss army knife Schweizer Armeemesser nt 127
switch Schalter m 29
switchboard operator Telefonist(in) m/f 26
Switzerland Schweiz f 146
swollen geschwollen 139
synagogue Synagoge f 84
synthetic synthetisch 114
system System nt 138

T

table Tisch m 36, 107; *(list)* Tabelle f 157
tablet Tablette f 109
tailor's Schneider m 99
take, to nehmen 18, 24, 72, 77; *(time)* dauern 62, 72, 76, 102; *(bring)* bringen 18, 21, 96
take away, to *(carry)* mitnehmen 63, 102
talcum powder Körperpuder m 111
tampon Tampon m 109
tangerine Mandarine f 53
tap *(water)* Wasserhahn m 28
tape recorder Kassettenrecorder m 119
tax Taxe f 32; Steuer f 24, 40, 102
taxi Taxi nt 18, 19, 21, 31, 67
taxi rank Taxistand m 21
tea Tee m 38, 61, 64
team Mannschaft f 89
tear, to reißen 140
teaspoon Teelöffel m 107, 143
telegram Telegramm nt 133
telegraph office Telegrafenamt nt 99
telephone Telefon nt 28, 78, 79, 134
telephone, to telefonieren 133
telephone booth Telefonzelle f 134
telephone call (Telefon)gespräch nt 135, 136; Anruf m 136
telephone directory Telefonbuch nt 134
telephone number Telefonnummer f 96, 135, 136

telephoto lens Teleobjektiv nt 125
television *(set)* Fernseher m 23, 28, 119
television room Fernsehraum m 27
telex Telex nt 133
telex, to ein Telex schicken 130
tell, to sagen 12, 73, 76, 136, 153
temperature Temperatur f 90, 142; *(fever)* Fieber nt 140
temporary provisorisch 145
ten zehn 147
tendon Sehne f 138
tennis Tennis nt 89
tennis court Tennisplatz m 89
tennis racket Tennisschläger m 89
tent Zelt nt 32, 107
tenth zehnte 148
tent peg Hering m 107
tent pole Zeltstange f 107
term Ausdruck m 131
terminus Endstation f 72
terrace Terrasse f 36
terrible schrecklich 84
tetanus Wundstarrkrampf m 140
than als 14
thank you danke 9
that der, die das 10, 160
the der, die das 159
theatre Theater nt 82, 86
theft Diebstahl m 156
their ihr 161
then dann 15
there dort 13, 15
thermometer Thermometer nt 109, 144
these diese 160
they sie 162
thief Dieb m 156
thigh Schenkel m 138
thin dünn 113
think, to *(believe)* glauben 31, 63, 94
third dritte 148
third Drittel nt 148
thirsty, to be Durst haben 12, 35
thirteen dreizehn 147
thirty dreißig 147
this diese(r/s) 160
those die 160
thousand tausend 148
thread Faden m 27
three drei 147
throat Hals m 138, 141
throat lozenge Halspastille f 109
through durch 14

through train durchgehender Zug *m* 68, 69
thumb Daumen *m* 138
thumbtack Reißzwecke *f* 105
thunder Donner *m* 94
thunderstorm Gewitter *nt* 94
Thursday Donnerstag *m* 150
thyme Thymian *m* 51
ticket Karte *f* 87, 89; *(plane)* Flugticket *nt* 65; *(train)* Fahrkarte *f* 69; *(bus)* Fahrschein *m* 72
ticket office Fahrkartenschalter *m* 67
tide *(high)* Flut *f* 90; *(low)* Ebbe *f* 90
tie Krawatte *f* 117
tie pin Krawattennadel *f* 122
tight *(clothes)* eng 116
tights Strumpfhose *f* 117
time Zeit *f* 80, 153; *(occasion)* -mal 148
timetable Fahrplan *m* 68
tin *(can)* Büchse *f* 120
tinfoil Aluminiumfolie *f* 107
tin opener Büchsenöffner *m* 107
tint Tönungsmittel *nt* 111
tinted getönt 123
tire Reifen *m* 75, 76
tired müde 12
tissue *(handkerchief)* Papiertuch *nt* 111
tissue paper Seidenpapier *nt* 105
to zu 14
toast Toast *m* 38
tobacco Tabak *m* 126
tobacconist's Tabakladen *m* 99, 126
today heute 29, 150, 151
toe Zehe *f* 138
toilet paper Toilettenpapier *nt* 111
toiletry Toilettenartikel *m/pl* 110
toilets Toilette *f* 27, 32, 37, 67
toilet water Toilettenwasser *nt* 111
tomato Tomate *f* 50
tomato juice Tomatensaft *m* 61
tomb Grab *nt* 82
tomorrow morgen 29, 151
tongs Zange *f* 107
tongue Zunge *f* 46, 138
tonic water Tonic *nt* 61
tonight heute abend 29, 86, 87, 88, 96
tonsil Mandel *f* 138
too zu 14; *(also)* auch 15
tooth Zahn *m* 145
toothache Zahnschmerzen *m/pl* 145
toothbrush Zahnbürste *f* 111, 119

toothpaste Zahnpasta *f* 111
torch *(flashlight)* Taschenlampe *f* 107
touch, to berühren 155
tough *(meat)* zäh 62
tour Rundfahrt *f* 80
tourist office Fremdenverkehrsbüro *nt* 22, 80
tourist tax Kurtaxe *f* 32
towards gegen 14
towel Handtuch *nt* 111
tower Turm *m* 82
town Stadt *f* 19, 76, 105
town hall Rathaus *nt* 82
tow truck Abschleppwagen *m* 78
toy Spielzeug *nt* 128
toy shop Spielwarengeschäft *nt* 99
track *(station)* Gleis *nt* 67, 68, 69
tracksuit Trainingsanzug *m* 117
traffic *(cars)* Verkehr *m* 79
traffic jam Stau *m* 79
traffic light Ampel *f* 77
trailer Wohnwagen *m* 32
train Zug *m* 66, 68, 69, 70, 73, 159
tram Straßenbahn *f* 72
tranquillizer Beruhigungsmittel *nt* 109
transfer *(bank)* Überweisung *f* 131
transformer Transformator *m* 119
translate, to übersetzen 11
transport Transport *m* 74
travel, to reisen 93
travel agency Reisebüro *nt* 99
traveller's cheque Reisescheck *m* 18, 63, 102, 130
travelling bag Reisetasche *f* 18
travel sickness Reisekrankheit *f* 108
treatment Behandlung *f* 143
tree Baum *m* 85
tremendous außerordentlich 84
trim, to *(beard)* stutzen 31
trip Reise *f* 93, 152, 159; Fahrt *f* 72
trousers Hose *f* 117
trout Forelle *f* 44
try, to versuchen 135; *(sample)* probieren 60; *(clothes)* anprobieren 115
T-shirt T-Shirt *nt* 117
tube Tube *f* 120
Tuesday Dienstag *m* 150
tumbler Wasserglas *nt* 107
tunny *(tuna)* Thunfisch *m* 41
turbot Steinbutt *m* 44
turkey Truthahn *m* 48
turn, to *(change direction)* abbiegen 21, 77

wash and wear bügelfrei 114
wash-basin Waschbecken *nt* 28
washing powder Waschpulver *nt* 107
washing-up liquid Spülmittel *nt* 107
watch Uhr *f* 121, 122, 127
watchmaker's Uhrmacher *m* 99, 121
watchstrap Uhrarmband *nt* 122
water Wasser *nt* 23, 28, 32, 38, 75, 90
water carrier Wasserkanister *m* 107
waterfall Wasserfall *m* 85
water flask Feldflasche *f* 107
watermelon Wassermelone *f* 53
waterproof wasserdicht 122
water-ski Wasserski *m* 91
wave Welle *f* 90
way Weg *m* 76
we wir 162
weather Wetter *nt* 94
weather forecast Wetterbericht *m* 94
wedding ring Ehering *m* 122
Wednesday Mittwoch *m* 150
week Woche *f* 20, 26, 80, 151
weekend Wochenende *nt* 20, 151
well gut 9, 115; *(healthy)* wohl 140
well Brunnen *m* 85
well-done *(meat)* gut durchgebraten 47
west West(en) *m* 77
West Germany Bundesrepublik *f* 146
what was 10
wheel Rad *nt* 78
when wann 10
where wo 10
which welche(r/s) 10
whipped cream Schlagsahne *f* 54
whisky Whisky *m* 59
white weiß 49, 59, 113
Whit Monday Pfingstmontag *m* 152
who wer 10
why warum 10
wide weit 118
wide-angle lens Weitwinkelobjektiv *nt* 125
wife Frau *f* 93
wig Perücke *f* 111
wild boar Wildschwein *nt* 48
wind Wind *m* 94
window Fenster *nt* 28, 36, 69; *(shop)* Schaufenster *m* 100, 112, 124
windscreen/shield Windschutzscheibe *f* 76
wine Wein *m* 57, 58, 59, 62

wine list Weinkarte *f* 59
wine merchant's Weinhandlung *f* 99
winter Winter *m* 149
winter sports Wintersport *m* 91
wiper Scheibenwischer *m* 76
wish Wunsch *m* 151
with mit 14
withdraw, to *(bank)* abheben 130
without ohne 14
woman Dame *f* 115; Frau *f* 159
wonderful wunderbar 96
wood *(material)* Holz *nt* 127; *(forest)* Wald *m* 85
wood alcohol Brennspiritus *m* 107
wood carving Holzschnitzarbeit *f* 127
woodcock Schnepfe *f* 48
wool Wolle *f* 114
word Wort *nt* 10, 14, 133
work, to *(function)* funktionieren 28, 119
working day Werktag *m* 151
worse schlechter 13
wound Wunde *f* 139
wrinkle resistant knitterfrei 114
wristwatch Armbanduhr *f* 122
write, to schreiben 11, 101
writing pad Schreibblock *m* 105
writing-paper Schreibpapier *nt* 27
wrong falsch 13, 77, 135

X

X-ray, to röntgen 140

Y

year Jahr *nt* 149
yellow gelb 113
yes ja 9
yesterday gestern 151
yet noch 15
yield, to *(traffic)* Vorfahrt gewähren 79
yoghurt Joghurt *m* 64
you du, Sie 162
young jung 13
your dein; Ihr 161
youth hostel Jugendherberge *f* 22, 32

Z

zero null 147
zip(per) Reißverschluß *m* 117
zoo Zoo *m* 82
zoology Zoologie *f* 83

Inhaltsverzeichnis